FEDERAL INCOME TAXATION

FEDERAL INCOME TAXATION

MODEL PROBLEMS AND OUTSTANDING ANSWERS

Camilla E. Watson

Stephen M. Sheppard
SERIES EDITOR, MODEL PROBLEMS AND OUTSTANDING ANSWERS

Oxford University Press, Inc., publishes works that further Oxford University's objective of excellence in research, scholarship, and education.

Oxford New York
Auckland Cape Town Dar es Salaam Hong Kong Karachi Kuala Lumpur Madrid Melbourne
Mexico City Nairobi New Delhi Shanghai Taipei Toronto

With offices in
Argentina Austria Brazil Chile Czech Republic France Greece Guatemala Hungary Italy
Japan Poland Portugal Singapore South Korea Switzerland Thailand Turkey Ukraine
Vietnam

Published by Oxford University Press, Inc.
198 Madison Avenue, New York, New York 10016

Library of Congress Cataloging-in-Publication Data

Watson, Camilla E.
Federal income taxation : model problems and outstanding answers / Camilla E. Watson.
p. cm.
Includes bibliographical references and index.
ISBN 978-0-19-539016-2 ((pbk.) : alk. paper)
1. Income tax—Law and legislation—United States. 2. Tax shelters—United States.
3. Tax administration and procedure—United States. I. Title.
KF6369.W38 2011
343.7305'2—dc22 2011012771

---

1 2 3 4 5 6 7 8 9

Printed in the United States of America on acid-free paper

Note to Readers
This publication is designed to provide accurate and authoritative information in regard to the subject matter covered. It is based upon sources believed to be accurate and reliable and is intended to be current as of the time it was written. It is sold with the understanding that the publisher is not engaged in rendering legal, accounting, or other professional services. If legal advice or other expert assistance is required, the services of a competent professional person should be sought. Also, to confirm that the information has not been affected or changed by recent developments, traditional legal research techniques should be used, including checking primary sources where appropriate.

(Based on the Declaration of Principles jointly adopted by a Committee of the American Bar Association and a Committee of Publishers and Associations.)

TABLE OF CONTENTS

INTRODUCTION

If you know the position a person takes on taxes, you can tell their whole philosophy. The tax code, once you get to know it, embodies all the essence of life: greed, politics, goodness, charity. Everything's in there. That's why it's so hard to get a simplified tax code. Life just isn't simple.
—Sheldon Cohen, *Former IRS Commissioner*

Federal income tax is a voluminous and complex area of law that covers nearly every aspect of life—birth, death, marriage, divorce, illness, accident, buying a house, starting a business. The power to tax all of these aspects derives from Article I, § 8, of the U.S. Constitution, which grants Congress the power to "lay and collect taxes" and "to make all laws which shall be necessary and proper" for executing this power. This seemingly broad power was cast into doubt by Article I, § 9, clause 4, which provides that "direct taxes shall be apportioned among the several states" according to population. This led to questions that linger today about what constitutes a direct tax. It also led to difficulties in enforcing an income tax since that tax is not apportioned among the states, according to population. The ratification of the Sixteenth Amendment in 1913, however, paved the way for the permanent imposition of a tax on income "from whatever source derived" without regard to the population of each State. At that time, less than one percent of the population was subject to the income tax.

When the United States entered into World War I, the immediate need for revenue was met under the 1916 Revenue Act, which raised the rates on individual income and imposed a tax on estates and excess business profits. Although the income tax rates have fluctuated greatly over the years, they reached an all-time high of 94 percent during World War II. At that time, the scope of the tax was expanded to include most Americans. Almost since its inception, the income tax has been this country's principal source of revenue.

The internal revenue laws had been codified in 1873 and were recodified several times over the next 66 years, but they remained scattered in the statutes at large. In 1939, all the internal revenue laws were consolidated and codified as the Internal Revenue Code under Title 26 of the U.S. Code. In 1954, there was a complete revision of the 1939 Code, which then became known as the 1954 Code. This Code was amended many times over the years, for various reasons, until it was replaced in 1986 by another wholesale revision, this time with the general goal of simplicity, fairness, and revenue neutrality. The 1986 Code, with many amendments, remains operative today.

While the income tax law is based on the tax Code, it also requires a consideration and understanding of Treasury regulations, IRS rulings, and cases: all of which explain, expand, or clarify the Code provisions. An introductory income tax course may employ a "survey" approach, hitting the highlights of many different Code sections and issues, or it may adopt a more focused pedagogical approach.

In either case, most introductory income tax courses begin with the concept of gross income and build upon that concept.

The following is a schematic that outlines the basic steps in computing income tax for individual taxpayers. It corresponds, in general, to the Form 1040, the U.S. Individual Income Tax Return. (Note that corporate tax does not use the concept of above-the-line and below-the-line deductions, standard deductions, or personal exemptions). Although the basic law school tax course does not focus specifically on tax forms and computation of tax liability, the schematic provides the "big picture" of most introductory federal income tax courses.

Gross Income
less § 62 Deductions (above the line)
Adjusted Gross Income
less Standard Deduction or § 63 Itemized Deductions (below the line)
less Personal Exemptions
Taxable Income
times Applicable tax rate
Tentative Tax Liability
less Credits
Tax Due

The concept of gross income includes terms that may be familiar to you in common parlance but which may have different meanings in the context of federal income tax. These include basic concepts of realization; recognition; timing (when the item of gross income is included on a tax return); exclusions (what items of economic benefit are not considered gross income); and gain, with its related concepts of basis and characterization. These general concepts are discussed in Problems I through III, although specific issues expanding upon these concepts are found throughout the problems. General timing principals are discussed in Problems XIX, XXII, and XXIV through XXVIII. Characterization of gain and loss is discussed generally in Problems XXI and XXIII.

Deductions are allowable items that reduce taxable income and thus reduce the ultimate tax liability. For individual taxpayers, there are two general types of deductions: (1) above-the-line deductions, allowed under § 62, are the more favorable type and are available to all individual taxpayers, whether or not they take the standard deduction; and (2) itemized deductions, authorized under § 63, which may be taken in lieu of the standard deduction. These concepts are discussed, in general, in Problems XXXIII and XXXIV, although various specific deductions are discussed in Problems XII through XVIII.

The standard deduction and personal exemptions are discussed in Problem XXXIV. A full discussion of all available tax credits is beyond the scope of this book, but educational credits, along with other tax incentives for education, are discussed in Problem XI; and tax credits, in general, are discussed in Problem XXXIV.

The discussion of tax credits finishes the above schematic and the computation of an individual's tax liability, but a couple of other issues that may be of concern to individual taxpayers—as well as students—are tax shelters, discussed in Problem XXXV; and tax procedure, discussed in Problem XXXVI.

FEDERAL INCOME TAXATION

1

THE CONCEPT OF GROSS INCOME

REALIZATION AND RECOGNITION

1. OPENING REMARKS

The starting point in the calculation of income tax is gross income. Section 61 of the tax Code is deceptively simple, defining gross income as "all income from whatever source derived, including (but not limited to) the following items. . . ." The provision then lists 15 specific items, but the "including (but not limited to)" language broadens the provision to include any economic benefit that is realized during the taxable year and is not excluded by specific statutory provision or administrative action, and is not a return of capital or accompanied by an obligation to repay.

Under the general rule, an item of income that is realized is also recognized unless there is specific authority to exclude it. This rule raises the concepts of realization and recognition. Realization is a difficult concept that does not always follow the economist's definition of an increase in net worth during the applicable accounting period. For instance, if a taxpayer holds stock that appreciates in value, she has an economic increase in net worth. But for tax purposes, there is no realization of this increase in net worth until the taxpayer sells or disposes of the stock.

The seminal cases addressing the concept of realization of income are two older U.S. Supreme Court cases. In *Eisner v. Macomber*, 252 U.S. 189, 40 S.Ct. 189, 64 L.Ed. 521 (1920), the Court addressed the phrase "income from whatever source derived" and concluded that a shareholder had not realized income upon receiving a dividend of common stock from a corporation whose capital shares consisted solely of one class of common stock. The taxpayer simply had exchanged her old shares for new shares, but her proportionate interest in the company remained the same. In *Commissioner v. Glenshaw Glass Co.*, 348 U.S. 426, 75 S.Ct. 473, 99 L.Ed. 483, *rehearing denied*, 349 U.S. 925, 75 S.Ct. 657, 99 L.Ed. 1256 (1955), a company received damages for fraud and antitrust violations. The Court held that the damages constituted "instances of undeniable accessions to wealth, clearly realized, and over which the taxpayers have complete dominion." 348 U.S. at 432.

Recognition is a simpler concept. It means that an item of realized income is subject to tax and therefore must be included on a tax return. There is a presumption that realized income is recognized, but this may not always be the case. For instance, in a nontaxable exchange of property, income may be realized but not recognized because there is a specific statutory provision that authorizes its exclusion. The burden is on the taxpayer to overcome the presumption of recognition by proving that Congress intended the item to be excluded from income.

2. HYPOTHETICAL

Andy and Angela Anderson are married, calendar year taxpayers who file a joint tax return. The Andersons have a two-year-old daughter named Annie. Andy is a doctor who practices with a group of doctors in a local hospital. Angela is a receptionist for an accounting firm in town. Last year, Andy received a salary of $250,000 and a year-end bonus of $20,000. Angela received a salary of $20,000.

Prior to his marriage, Andy had purchased and lived in a small duplex. After he married Angela, however, they needed a bigger residence, so they bought a house. Andy kept the duplex because he thought it was not an opportune time to sell, and eventually he rented it for $800 per month. Last year, the tenant called to say that the roof was leaking and needed to be repaired. Since the tenant was a carpenter, he offered to repair the roof in exchange for two months' rent, and Andy agreed.

Last year, Angela purchased a small desk at a garage sale for $350 and discovered that it had a "secret drawer." Inside the drawer was a diamond and sapphire ring valued at $3500. She tried to return the ring, but she was told that the people from whom she had purchased the desk had moved out of state, leaving no forwarding address. Angela sent a picture and a description of the desk to an antique appraiser and discovered that the desk was worth $5,000. She was thrilled and decided to have the desk redone and to give it a prominent place in their home.

What is the total amount of the Anderson's gross income for last year? Discuss fully.

3. LIST OF READINGS

Internal Revenue Code of 1986: §§ 61; 109; 6013; 6072
Regulations: §§ 1.61–1; 1.61–8; 1.61–14; 20.2031–1(b)
Cases: Commissioner v. Glenshaw Glass Co., 348 U.S. 426, 75 S.Ct. 473, 99 L.Ed. 483 (1955); Cesarini v. United States, 296 F. Supp. 3, *aff'd per curiam*, 428 F.2d 812 (6th Cir. 1970)

4. SAMPLE ESSAY

Most individual taxpayers are calendar year taxpayers, which means that all items of gross income realized during the calendar year (January 1 through December 31) must be included on their income tax return for that period. Individual income tax returns of calendar year taxpayers are due by April 15 of the year following the taxable year for which the return is being filed. See § 6072. So the return that is filed in the current year will be the return for the previous taxable (calendar) year.

Since Andy and Angela are married, they are entitled to file a joint income tax return. See § 6013. Section 61(a)(1) of the Code specifically requires compensation to be included in gross income, regardless of how and in what form the compensation is derived. Andy's salary, plus any bonuses that he earns from his medical practice, as well as the salary that Angela earns as a receptionist, is included under this provision. Thus, their total compensation income is $290,000.

Rental income is included under the specific language of § 61(a)(5), so the $800 per month that Andy receives from his tenant must be included in the couple's gross income. When the tenant/carpenter repaired the roof, he and Andy had agreed that the value of this repair would be in lieu of two months' rent.

Gross income is not confined to cash payments but also may be in the form of property (tangible or intangible) or services. Reg. § 1.61–1(a). Gross income is an accession to wealth, clearly realized, over which the taxpayer has control. See *Glenshaw Glass*. Since the roof repair is intended to be in lieu of rent, the value of the repair also must be included as rental income under § 61(a)(5). If it was not intended as rent, it may be excluded under § 109 but since this repair was intended as rent, the question is: what is the value of the repair? Is it the amount Andy would have paid an independent third party to make the repair? Or is it the increase in value of the property after the repair? Gross income is measured by the fair market value of the benefit received, not the cost of what is given up. Since Andy and his tenant presumably are dealing with each other at arm's length, with neither having a particular advantage over the other, the agreement between the parties, if it is reasonable, will control as to the value of the repair. Thus, Andy must include the $1600 repair in income as rent. Reg. § 1.61–8(c). This brings the total rental income for the year to $9600.

When Angela purchased the desk, she received a windfall, not only from the great deal that she made in purchasing the desk but also from the ring she found in it. These two windfall items are treated differently for tax purposes, though. The "bargain purchase" of the desk does not result in an income inclusion because there is no realization, provided the purchase was at arm's length (i.e., neither buyer nor seller was under a compulsion to buy or to sell, and both had knowledge of all relevant facts and circumstances). In that case, Angela got a great deal when she purchased the desk and therefore will not be required to recognize income until she sells it.

The ring that Angela found in the desk is a different story. Here, there will be an income inclusion equal to the value of the ring when Angela reduces the ring to "undisputed possession." At that time, she has received a windfall, the value of which is required to be included in income under the general language of § 61 and the specific authority of *Cesarini* and the regulations. See Reg. § 1.61–14(a). The first question is: when does Angela reduce the ring to undisputed possession? In *Cesarini*, the taxpayer argued that old currency found in a piano was reduced to undisputed possession when the piano was purchased, even though the buyer did not know the currency was there. The court held that the currency could not be reduced to undisputed possession until it had been found and until efforts had been made to locate the true owner, or it was clear that such efforts were useless. Possession and ownership of property are determined under state law, but under the common law rule, undisputed possession occurs when Angela is able to exert a claim over the ring that is superior to that of anyone else. See *Cesarini*. This would depend upon the length of time that the state law would give the true owner to claim the ring. Thus, the timing of the inclusion in this problem is not clear.

Once the timing issue has been resolved, the next question is: what amount is included in income? This depends upon the value of the ring at the time it is reduced to undisputed possession. The valuation must be determined by an independent appraisal, and the fair market value of the ring must be included in income when Angela is able to reduce it to undisputed possession. Fair market value is defined as "the price at which the property would change hands between a willing buyer and a willing seller, neither being under any compulsion to buy or to sell and both having reasonable knowledge of relevant facts." Reg. § 20.2031–1(b). If the ring is valued at $3500 at the time that Angela reduces it to undisputed possession, then that amount will be included in the Anderson's gross income in that year, presumably the year that Angela discovers it.

This brings the Anderson's total gross income for last year to $303,100, provided the value of the ring is included in that taxable year.

5. TOOLS FOR SELF-ASSESSMENT

[1] In working through a problem involving various items of gross income, different items may be treated differently, so it is important to determine initially what type of income is at issue. In some instances, there may be more than one way to characterize an item, depending on the facts, and the tax consequences of the characterizations may vary significantly. Therefore, the facts in that instance are particularly important.

[2] As a practical matter, an employee's salary is an easy item to determine because generally it will be listed on the Form W-2 that the employer will send to the employee at the end of the taxable year. But compensation includes items of economic benefit derived because of the employment relationship, and it does not have to be a cash benefit. It can be in property, either tangible or intangible, or a reciprocal performance of services. Thus, as far as inclusion, there is no difference between the receipt of cash and the receipt of any other benefit received as compensation. If the benefit is not in cash, though, some appropriate method of valuation must be determined.

[3] Section 109 is a short provision that excludes from the lessor's gross income the value of improvements made by a tenant. But the provision requires careful reading to reach the correct result in this case, because the parenthetical exempts improvements made in lieu of rent. So, if the parties intend for the improvement(s) to constitute rent, it is taxable under § 61(a)(5). If the parties do not intend for the improvements to constitute rent, then § 109 applies to exclude the value of the improvements from the lessor's gross income. Thus, if the tenant in this hypothetical had made an improvement to the property without having first made an agreement with Andy that the improvement would be in lieu of rent, the value of the improvement would not constitute rent. This would permit Andy to exclude that amount from income under § 109, even though he might have received an economic benefit from the improvement. Can you guess the policy rationale behind § 109?

[4] The inclusion of the repair as rental income is an easier concept to grasp if one thinks in terms of the overall tax consequences. If the value of the roof repair is not included in Andy's gross income as a taxable benefit, Andy could avoid paying taxes by structuring the rental transaction to receive all rental payments in a form other than cash. One can look at it this way: the overall transaction is the same as if the tenant had paid $1600 for the two months' rent, and Andy had hired an independent third party to repair the roof for $1600. A mere change in the form of the transaction without a change in the ultimate benefit should not change the tax consequences.

[5] In an arrangement between a lessor and a lessee in which the lessee makes improvements to the rental property, it is important to determine the specific understanding between the parties. In addition to rent, the

improvements also might constitute a repayment of a loan or a payment for other property or services that the lessee may have obtained from the lessor. Thus, the characterization of the understanding will greatly affect the tax consequences.

[6] One issue that might occur to students is whether the repair is deductible because repairs made to rental property generally are. As the schematic in the introduction to this book shows, gross income is determined before deductions are taken. Thus, the deductibility of the repair is a separate issue that is not relevant to the problem at this point.

[7] The purchase of the desk and discovery of the ring squarely present the issue of realization versus recognition, and the concept is often a difficult one for most beginning tax students to comprehend. Angela purchased the desk, not the ring. Hence, the desk was the basis of her bargain, similar to purchasing an item on sale that would have cost much more if it had been purchased at full price. There is no income inclusion upon the purchase of the desk because this was the bargain that the parties made. If Angela were taxed on the difference between the value of the desk ($5000) and the amount that she paid ($350), she would have to pay a tax liability on $4650. Thus, she might have to sell the desk to raise the money to pay the tax. This would mean that the government would be able to negate the arm's length deal that Angela had made, and she might regard that as unfair. Since the government relies on taxpayers to voluntarily file their returns and pay their tax liability, a policy such as this would seriously undermine the voluntary compliance system of federal taxation. Thus, it is an inopportune time for the government to require Angela to sell the desk since that is what she wanted and bargained for. Instead, the appropriate time to tax her is when she sells or exchanges the desk. Then there will be a realization event.

[8] The ring, on the other hand, is not the basis of the bargain that Angela made. On the contrary, she had not realized that the ring was in the desk; so it is a windfall to her, similar to something that "fell off a truck." If she is required to sell the ring to pay the tax liability, there is not the same sense of unfairness that there would have been if she had been required to sell the desk to pay the tax liability. In the latter case, the government would be stepping between the parties to a contract, while in the former case there was no contract to purchase the ring.

6. VARIATIONS ON THE THEME

How, if at all, would the Anderson's tax consequences differ if the tenant wanted to add a deck to the duplex, and Andy said that he did not mind but would not consider that in lieu of rent, so the tenant paid rent and built the deck at a cost of $1200, which added $600 to the value of the duplex?

7. OPTIONAL READINGS

Cases: Cottage Savings Association v. Commissioner, 499 U.S. 554, 111 S.Ct. 1503, 113 L.Ed.2d 589 (1991)

2 THE CONCEPT OF GROSS INCOME

EXCLUSIONS

1. OPENING REMARKS

Under the general rule, realized income is recognized, so the presumption is that any realized income will be taxable. There are several exceptions to this general rule, however. First, some items of income, such as gifts, may be excluded specifically by statute. Second, items that constitute a "return of capital" are not taxable. An example of this concept is a lender who lends $100 to a borrower and ultimately is repaid $105 at the agreed upon time of repayment. The additional $5 represents interest income for the use of the lender's $100, and this amount constitutes income to the lender. The return of the $100 is simply a return of the original amount that the lender lent to the borrower, so there is no economic benefit with respect to that amount. Third, the borrower also does not have income upon borrowing the $100 from the lender because the economic benefit of the use of the $100 is offset by the borrower's corresponding obligation to repay this amount. Finally, there are some narrow exceptions to the general rule of income inclusion in which the government does not require the inclusion of certain economic benefits because of the administrative inconvenience of determining the proper amount to include and the burden of collecting these amounts.

2. HYPOTHETICAL

Barry and Betty Barclay are a married couple who file a joint income tax return and live in middle America. They have two children, Barry Jr. and Barbara Ann, ages 8 and 5. Barry is an associate attorney for a law firm and earns $90,000 per year. Betty is a stay-at-home mom. She has always been an avid gardener, as well as an exceptional cook. After receiving many compliments on her homemade strawberry jam, she started selling the jam in the local supermarket and to her surprise, earned $8,000. Encouraged by her success, she entered a recipe in a magazine cook-off contest and won first prize: $1500 in cash plus an all-expenses paid trip to Atlanta, Georgia (a distance of about 800 miles) to compete in another contest.

Betty's favorite aunt died last year after a long illness. Betty had traveled several times during the year to stay with her aunt and to help her through her illness. In her will, the aunt left Betty $50,000 "in appreciation for all that you have done for me."

Two years ago, Betty was injured when a drunk driver struck her car. She fractured her wrist and dislocated her hip. The hip injury had required an operation and while the visible wounds have healed, her hip continues to bother her occasionally, and it was nearly a year before she was able to regain the self-confidence to get behind the wheel of a car again. Her medical expenses amounted to $98,000. They included $4000 for therapy from a psychiatrist for emotional distress. Betty's private insurance policy paid $50,000 of her expenses. She brought suit against the drunk driver, and toward the end of last year, she received $120,000 to cover her remaining medical expenses and to compensate for her pain and suffering. In addition, she recovered another $50,000 in punitive damages. The other driver's insurance company asked Betty whether she preferred a lump sum payment of the $170,000 or an annuity payable over a 10-year period at 7 percent interest. She opted for the annuity.

Ida May Greene lives next door to Barry and Betty, and she occasionally babysits for them. She is an elderly woman who lives alone on a fixed income. Ida May asked Barry if he would draft a will for her, and he readily agreed. When she inquired about the price, Barry, who normally would charge $650 for the will, told her "not to worry about it." But Ida May protested, so Barry suggested that she give them some free babysitting time. Ida May was delighted with the arrangement. When Barry finished preparing Ida May's will, he prepared one for himself and Betty as well.

Assume that all of these items and transactions occur in a single taxable year. What is the total amount of the Barclay's gross income? Discuss fully.

3. LIST OF READINGS

Internal Revenue Code: §§ 61; 72(a)-(c); 74; 102(a); 104(a); 213(a)
Regulations: §§ 1.61–1; 20.2031–1(b)
Rulings: Rev. Rul. 79–24, 1979–1 C.B. 60; Rev. Rul. 75–374, 1975–2 C.B. 261
Cases: Commissioner v. Duberstein, 363 U.S. 278, 80 S.Ct. 1190, 4 L.Ed.2d 1218 (1960); Commissioner v. Glenshaw Glass Co., 348 U.S. 426, 75 S.Ct. 473, *rehearing denied*, 349 U.S. 925, 75 S.Ct. 657 (1955); Wolder v. Commissioner, 493 F.2d 608 (2d Cir. 1974)
Articles: Donald B. Marsh, *The Taxation of Imputed Income*, 58 Pol. Sci. Q. 514–521 (1943)

4. SAMPLE ESSAY

The $90,000 that Barry earns will be included in his gross income as compensation income under § 61(a)(1). The $8000 that Betty earns from selling her jam is included under § 61(a)(2) as business income.

Section 74(a) of the Code includes the value of prizes and awards unless otherwise excluded. In order to exclude the value of the prize, the recipient must meet the four requirements of § 74(b): (1) the prize must be given in recognition of religious, charitable, scientific, educational, artistic, literary, or civic achievement; (2) the recipient must be selected without any action on her part to enter the contest; (3) there must be no substantial future services required of the recipient; and (4) the recipient must transfer the prize to a governmental unit or charitable organization.

Exclusionary provisions are matters of legislative grace and are strictly construed. Thus, the prize is excluded only if each of the requirements is strictly met. Betty may argue that her achievement was artistic, but this argument is unlikely to prevail. Moreover, she voluntarily entered the contest and has not transferred the prize to a designated entity. Therefore, the value of her prize is included in her gross income under § 74(a). Although prizes and awards are not specifically delineated under § 61, the inclusion falls under the general language of § 61, which includes "all income from whatever source derived. . . ."

The final issue is the amount of the inclusion. Clearly, the $1500 cash must be included in income as "an accession to wealth, clearly realized" under *Glenshaw Glass*. But gross income includes realized accessions to wealth, whether realized in cash, property, or services. Reg. § 1.61–1(a). In this case, the fair market value of the trip also must be included in income. Fair market value can be a very difficult issue in practice because it is a subjective determination, and reasonable minds can differ. It is defined generally as "the price a willing seller would pay a willing buyer, both having knowledge of all relevant facts and circumstances and neither being under a compulsion to buy or to sell." Reg. § 20.2031–1(b). The value of the trip will include the air fare, hotel accommodations, meals, etc., that are provided to Betty free of charge. (Note that if the trip occurs in a different taxable year, the value of the trip will be included in income for that taxable year.) As a practical matter, the company awarding the prize usually will send the recipient a Form 1099 at the end of the taxable year that states the amount of the prize that was reported to the IRS.

Betty also receives an economic benefit from the $50,000 that she inherits from her aunt. She has an "accession to wealth, clearly realized, over which she has dominion." See *Glenshaw Glass*. Thus, she realizes a benefit of $50,000. However, § 102 excludes from income the value of gifts, bequests, and devises. If this amount falls under § 102, it is excluded, and the Barclays do not have to report it. The question, however, is whether it truly falls under § 102. Since the tax Code contains no definition of a gift, the U.S. Supreme Court supplied one in the *Duberstein* case. Under *Duberstein*, whether a transfer constitutes a gift is determined under the facts and circumstances of each case, but the most important factor is the transferor's objective intent. If the transferor's dominant motive was "love, respect, affection, charity or like impulses," with no expectation of something in return, the transfer constitutes a gift. If, however, there is any quid pro quo involved (i.e., where the donor is paying for services rendered or expects to receive some benefit in the future) the transfer is not a gift. Under *Wolder*, if the dominant motive of the aunt was to compensate her niece for her services, then there is no miraculous transformation of the taxable compensation into a nontaxable bequest upon receiving this amount under the will. Instead, it will constitute compensation for services, regardless of how Betty is paid. If, however, the aunt's dominant motive was love, affection, and respect, the $50,000 constitutes an excludable bequest under § 102. In a situation such as this, i.e., the death of a close family member to whom the beneficiary has devoted time and attention with no expectation of compensation, the IRS generally considers the bequest an excludable gift.

The accident presents several issues. First, the payment of Betty's expenses by her insurance company normally does not result in gross income because § 104(a)(3) excludes amounts received from accident or health insurance policies paid for by the taxpayer. However, if Betty and Barry paid any of these expenses themselves and deducted them as medical expenses in a prior taxable year, the payment by the insurance company would be includable (see § 213(a)). This effectively restores the taxpayer to the position she otherwise was in and is tantamount to a "wash." In other words, the taxpayer had a tax benefit earlier (the deduction); later when there is a recovery of that amount, the recovery must be included in income, so it cancels the earlier tax benefit. This is an example of what is known as "the tax benefit doctrine." Second, when Betty receives the $100,000 in compensatory damages from the lawsuit, the entire amount will be excluded from income under § 104(a)(2) because her injuries were entirely physical. (Unless the tax benefit rule applies to include any of this amount). Emotional distress is not considered a physical injury, even though it may produce physical symptoms and ailments. In Betty's case, however, the emotional stress is caused by her physical injuries. Thus, the entire recovery, even the amount attributable to emotional distress, is excludable under § 104(a)(2). Third, the $50,000 of punitive damages is includable in income. Punitive damages are exempted from the exclusionary language of § 104(a)(2), even though they relate solely to a physical injury.

When Betty receives payments under the annuity, the entire amount of the principal is excluded because it is attributable to an excludable amount. The amount that constitutes interest, however, is included because that amount does not fall under § 104 and is specifically included in income under § 61(a)(4). See also § 72(a), (b), and (c).

The will preparation for Ida May raises a difficult issue of characterization. On the one hand, this looks like a typical barter transaction, in which there is an exchange of services for services (or property for property, or property for services). In a barter transaction, no cash changes hands. The government often refers to barter transactions as "the underground economy," because it is very difficult to trace these transactions since there usually is no discernible paper trail to follow, as there generally is with other transactions. If this is a barter transaction, then each party, Barry and Ida May, must include the value of the benefit he or she receives. Again, unless there are facts to indicate otherwise (and there do not appear to be here), it is assumed that the transaction is an arm's length transaction so that the benefit that each party receives is equal to the benefit that the other receives. On the other hand, this may be a reciprocal gift in which the dominant motive of each party is to bestow a gift on the other because of "respect, affection, charity, or like impulse." See *Duberstein*. If that is the case, then neither party will have to include the value of the benefit they receive. It will be excludable under § 102 as a gift. The determining factor will be the dominant motive of each party. Did they intend to bestow a gift on the other, or did they intend this to be a barter transaction? Given the facts of the hypothetical, it looks more like a barter transaction since Ida May indicates that she wants to pay and Barry suggests a noncash alternative. Thus, it looks like a quid pro quo and not donative intent. In that case, Ida May would include the value of the will preparation, $650, when Barry prepares her will and delivers it to her, and Barry will include the value of the babysitting services, presumably $650, as the services are rendered.

When Barry prepares a will for himself, this is known as "imputed income," defined as "a flow of satisfactions from durable goods owned and used by the taxpayer, or from goods and services arising out of the personal exertions of the taxpayer on his own behalf." See *Marsh, supra*. Such a benefit is not included in income. There is no specific exclusionary provision for this type of benefit, but the fact that Congress has not specifically included it, combined with the practice of the government not to tax this income, results in an exclusion. While there is an economic benefit from performing services for oneself instead of paying someone else to perform them, taxing such a benefit would be an administrative nightmare for the IRS. Moreover, it would impose an onerous burden on taxpayers to keep records of such services and activities and would likely lead to an undermining of the tax system.

5. TOOLS FOR SELF-ASSESSMENT

[1] In approaching any tax problem, it is helpful to keep in mind the policy rationale underlying the Code provision in question, particularly when confronting the provision for the first time. This provides a better understanding of how the provision works and why it is drafted the way it is. It also makes it easier to comprehend changes in the law, which occur frequently in the federal tax area.

[2] Also, in answering any tax question on an examination, it usually is best to begin with the applicable Code provision and then state the general rule of the provision. Finally, apply the rule to the facts of the problem, and state your conclusion. This results in a cleaner, clearer, more precise, and better organized answer.

[3] The advantage of including Betty's business income under § 61(a)(2) is that any deductible expenses incurred in deriving this income may be taken directly against it. Thus, the net amount is included in income. In this problem, since no such expenses are given, we can assume (illogically) that there are none, so the entire $8000 will be included.

[4] It is important to keep in mind the general rule that any realized economic benefit is taxable unless there is a specific provision authorizing its exclusion. In contrast, there does not have to be a specific inclusionary provision because of the general catch-all language of § 61. Despite the natural inclination of most students to classify prizes in the nature of gifts that should be excluded from income, § 74(a) is a general inclusionary provision for prizes and awards. Thus, the Nobel prize is includable in income, as is the value of the prize that Betty won. Betty's prize consists of cash and the trip. The cash presents the easier issue because it does not raise valuation issues. It is important to remember that income is not confined to cash but also includes both tangible and intangible property, as well as the value of services received in some cases. These noncash benefits raise valuation issues.

[5] Generally, it is easier to tackle a tax problem by considering the transactions chronologically as the income inclusions occur. Transactions do not always fit neatly into a single taxable year and when they do not, that raises issues of timing—when is the item of income included? The natural tendency is to assume that Betty took the trip in the year in which she won it, but that may not be the case. If Betty receives the prize in year one and does not take the trip until year two, she could be taxed in year one if she receives a benefit, such as an airline ticket. If, though, she receives merely the promise of a free trip in the following year, this would be taxed in the year in which she takes the trip. Of course, Betty may not actually take the trip. A recipient may refuse a prize without tax consequences (see Rev. Rul. 75–374), but if she directs any control over the prize (such as giving any portion of it to a friend

or relative), that amount must be included in income. Thus, Betty could be taxed on the value of the prize or a portion of it, even though she does not take the trip. Note that exerting control over a benefit, such as directing who or what entity shall receive it constitutes a taxable benefit, as a general rule. Section 74(b) allows a recipient to direct the prize or award to an entity under certain circumstances without incurring tax consequences as a result.

[6] Finally, note that § 74(a) is the specific authorizing provision that tells the taxpayer how to treat the item of income. It classifies this item as an includable prize. Section 61 is the general inclusionary provision. This means that § 74(a) determines the amount and timing of the inclusion, while § 61 is the general inclusionary provision for items of gross income.

[7] The dominant motive of a donor depends on the facts and circumstances. The first factor that the IRS generally will look to is the relationship of the parties. If the parties are family members, there is an initial presumption of excludability. If the parties are business associates, the presumption is that the benefit is includable. There may be exceptions in either case, but they tend to be narrow. For instance, if there was a written agreement between Betty and her aunt that Betty would render services in expectation of a bequest, this looks like a taxable quid pro quo. A difficult case is where a family member is also a business associate or employee. Then the important factor will be the dominant context in which the transfer occurs.

[8] It is important to determine in lieu of what is the recovery awarded. If the recovery relates to a physical injury, it is excluded, with the exception of punitive damages (except for the narrow exception of § 104(c), which does not apply in this hypothetical). If it relates to a nonphysical injury, it is included in income, except that awards for emotional distress are excluded to the extent of actual medical expenses incurred (provided they have not been deducted previously). Punitive damages are includable under *Glenshaw Glass*, which dealt specifically with punitive damages, but § 104(a)(2) specifically includes punitive damages, so that settles the issue without *Glenshaw Glass*. This is a good time to remember the general rule: "no double dipping." This means that a taxpayer cannot take both an exclusion and a deduction for the same item. So, Betty cannot obtain a deduction for her medical expenses and then exclude a recovery with respect to those same expenses.

[9] The form of the recovery does not alter the tax consequences. The annuity has two components: the excludable portion attributable to the recovery for Betty's physical injury and a taxable interest portion. These portions are treated very differently for tax purposes, even though they may be paid with a single check each month or year.

[10] Characterization issues occur frequently in the tax area, and they are very important because they often determine the tax consequences, as we see in the case of Ida May. Resist the temptation to assume that the more favorable outcome should apply automatically. In approaching a hypothetical, it is important to engage in an analysis of each transaction

before reaching your conclusion. Ask yourself what is really happening in this transaction. Because this transaction occurs between friends and neighbors, there is a natural tendency to assume that it is nontaxable. Note that the characterization by the parties of whether the benefit is taxable or nontaxable is not controlling. The important factor is the overall intent of each party and whether the service rendered was intended as a gift within the *Duberstein* definition or whether a quid pro quo was intended. But if it looks like a duck and walks like a duck, the IRS will assume that it is a duck!

[11] Imputed income is a very narrow exception to the general rule that there must be a specific statutory provision authorizing an exclusion. Other examples of imputed income include the rental value of your own home (while you are living there), food that you grow or produce for your own benefit, and any services that you perform for your own benefit.

6. VARIATIONS ON THE THEME

Would your answer change in any way if Betty's lawsuit was against her former employer for gender-based discrimination, and the recovery was attributable to lost wages and emotional distress as a result of the discrimination?

PROPERTY TRANSACTIONS

3

THE CONCEPT OF BASIS AND CAPITAL RECOVERY

1. OPENING REMARKS

Section 61(a)(3) includes in gross income gains derived from dealings in property. Section 1001(a) provides that the gain from a sale or other disposition of property is the excess of the amount realized over the adjusted basis. Section 1001(b) defines the amount realized as the sum of money plus the fair market value of any property received on the sale or other disposition of property. Section 1001(a) defines a loss as the excess of the adjusted basis over the amount realized.

Basis is a simple concept that can have difficult applications. The general basis provisions of the Code are found at §§ 1011 through 1019, but there also are some specialized provisions found in other Code sections. In general, basis is a mechanism to prevent double taxation on the one hand or a double tax benefit on the other. Basis measures not only the taxpayer's economic investment in property, but it also tracks the tax consequences of the property. So if a transaction generates a tax benefit, such as depreciation deductions, the basis may be reduced to reflect the benefit. If a transaction generates a tax liability, such as in a taxable exchange, the basis in the new property may be increased to reflect the tax liability of the transaction. Similarly, capital improvements to property result in a basis increase while income generated by the property generally does not affect the basis. Different transactions may affect basis in different ways, so it is very important to determine the character of the underlying transaction.

2. HYPOTHETICAL

Charles Carter is a young computer specialist and budding entrepreneur. Four years ago, his father gave him a gift of 50 acres of undeveloped land that he had purchased 10 years earlier for $40,000 and which had been appraised at $120,000 at the time of the gift. Charles's father paid $45,000 in gift taxes on the transfer. Two years later, Charles purchased the adjacent 50 acres for a price of $100,000. In this transaction, Charles paid $10,000 in cash from his own funds, and he financed the remaining $90,000 of the purchase price through a nonrecourse mortgage on which he had no personal liability. Last year, he built a rental residence on the property (the second 50 acres) for $185,000. This time he paid $50,000 in cash from his own funds, and he financed the remainder of the $135,000 cost through another nonrecourse mortgage. During the time that Charles has held the property, he has paid property taxes of $1000 in the first two years, $1800 in the third year, and $2500 in the fourth year. This year, the property will be subject to property taxes of $3000.

Charles recently has received an offer to buy the house and the entire 100 acres for $500,000. The purchaser, an unrelated third party, has proposed a transaction in which she will give Charles $75,000 in cash and $200,000 in stock of the

XYZ Company, a publicly traded company in which the purchaser has a basis of $65,000. In addition, the purchaser would take the property subject to the non-recourse mortgages, the principal amounts of which have been undiminished and are presently $90,000 and $135,000, for a total of $225,000. To "sweeten" the deal, the buyer also agrees to assume the property tax liability for the entire year.

If the sale takes place at the midpoint of the year, what will be the tax consequences to Charles and to the buyer? (Ignore any issues of depreciation on the rental house).

3. LIST OF READINGS

Internal Revenue Code of 1986: §§ 102; 164, 1001; 1011; 1012; 1015; 1016; 1031(a)

Regulations: § 1.1015–4

Cases: Crane v. Commissioner, 331 U.S. 1, 67 S.Ct. 1047, 91 L.Ed. 1301 (1947); Old Colony Trust Co. v. Commissioner, 279 U.S. 716, 49 S.Ct. 499, 73 L.Ed. 918 (1929); Estate of Franklin v. Commissioner, 544 F.2d 1045 (9th Cir. 1976); Philadelphia Park Amusement Co. v. U.S., 130 Ct. Cl. 166, 126 F.Supp. 184 (Ct.Cl. 1954)

4. SAMPLE ESSAY

When property is transferred by gift, there are several tax consequences to be considered. First, the donor may be subject to a gift tax on the transfer. In this case, Charles's father had to pay a $45,000 gift tax on the transfer of the property to Charles. The donee, Charles, realizes an economic benefit to the extent of the fair market value of the property that he receives ($120,000), but he does not recognize that benefit because § 102 excludes the value of gifts. Charles's basis in the 50 acres of land acquired from his father is determined under § 1015. The general basis rule for gifts is found at § 1015(a), which provides that the donee's basis in property acquired by gift is the donor's basis. This is also known as a "carryover" basis. Section 1015(d)(6) provides an adjustment for gift taxes paid after December 31, 1976. This adjustment is made through a ratio, the numerator of which is the net appreciation of the gift, and the denominator is the amount of the gift. The net appreciation is defined under § 1015(d)(6)(B) as the excess of the fair market of the gift over the donor's adjusted basis immediately before the gift. The amount of the gift tax paid on the transfer is multiplied by this ratio, and the product is the amount by which the § 1015(a) basis is adjusted.

Applying § 1015(d)(6) to this transfer, Charles's father was required to pay a gift tax of $45,000 on the transfer of the 50 acres to Charles. The net appreciation of this 50 acres is $80,000 ($120,000 fair market value at the time of the transfer less $40,000 donor's adjusted basis). The amount of the gift is the $120,000 value of the 50 acres at the time of the transfer. Thus, the § 1015(d)(6) ratio is $80,000/$120,000 or two-thirds. Since two-thirds of $45,000, the gift tax paid on the transfer, is $30,000, Charles's basis is increased under § 1015(d)(6) by $30,000. So Charles's basis in the 50 acres that he acquires from his father is the § 1015(a) carryover basis of $40,000 plus the § 1015(d)(6) gift tax adjustment of $30,000, for a total § 1015 basis of $70,000.

In the second transaction, Charles acquires the adjacent 50 acres through a straight purchase. Thus, his basis, determined under § 1012, is the cost of the property. Even though Charles pays for 90 percent of the property with a nonrecourse loan on which he has no personal liability, for tax purposes he is given credit for the full amount that he pays. See *Crane v. Commissioner*; *Estate of Franklin*. Thus, his basis under § 1012 is the full cost of the property, $100,000.

The third transaction is the construction of the rental residence at a cost of $185,000. Charles's basis in the house is a straight § 1012 cost basis of $185,000. The nonrecourse mortgage does not appear to be a sham, and therefore it will be a part of the basis in this property. See *Crane* and *Estate of Franklin*. The construction of the rental property is considered a capital improvement to the second 50 acres, so Charles's total basis in this property immediately after the construction of the rental residence is $285,000 under § 1016(a)(1).

The fourth transaction is the proposed exchange of the real property for cash, stock, and the relief of the mortgage indebtedness. This will be a taxable exchange because § 1031(a)(2)(A) excludes stock from nonrecognition treatment. Section 1001(b) provides that "the amount realized from the sale or other disposition of property shall be the sum of any money received plus the fair market value of the property (other than money) received." In the exchange, Charles will realize $75,000 in cash, $200,000 in stock, and a $225,000 benefit from the relief of the nonrecourse indebtedness under the principals of *Crane*. Section 1001(b)(2) further provides that "in determining the amount realized—there shall be taken into account amounts representing real property taxes which are treated under section 164(d) as imposed on the taxpayer if such taxes are to be paid by the purchaser." Since the property is subject to real property taxes of $3000 for the year, and the sale occurs in the midpoint of it, Charles is liable for half of the taxes or $1500. If this amount is paid by the purchaser, it will be included in Charles's amount realized on the sale. See also *Old Colony Trust Co.* Charles's total amount realized will be $501,500 ($75,000 cash, $200,000 stock, $225,000 mortgage relief and $1500—his share of the property taxes paid by the purchaser). His total basis in the property is $355,000 ($70,000 § 1015 basis on the first 50 acres; $100,000 § 1012 basis on the second 50 acres; and $185,000 § 1012 basis on the rental property). This will produce a realized gain of $146,500 ($501,500 amount realized less a basis of $355,000) under § 1001(a).

After the exchange, Charles will be holding the XYZ Co. stock. His basis in this stock will be a cost basis determined under § 1012, which applies to sales and taxable exchanges of property. In this case, though, cost means the value of the property received. See *Philadelphia Park*. Thus, Charles's § 1012 basis in the stock is $200,000 because that is the fair market value of the stock that he receives in the exchange. It is also the value of the stock on which he is taxed.

Ordinarily, unless there is a reason to think otherwise, an exchange (whether taxable or nontaxable) is presumed to be at arm's length so that the consideration given up in the exchange equals the property received. Thus, each side of the transaction is deemed to be equal to the other. In this problem, though, the purchaser indicated that she was willing to pay slightly more to "sweeten the deal." On the exchange, she receives property worth $500,000, so that is her amount realized on this transaction. The purchaser "pays" for the property with cash ($75,000), stock ($200,000), mortgage relief ($225,000), and property tax assumption ($1500). Since the cash, mortgage relief, and property tax assumption have no basis, they offset the amount realized dollar for dollar. The stock is treated differently than the other items because it has a basis of $65,000 and a value of $200,000. Thus, only the basis will offset the remaining amount realized, which will produce a realized gain of $135,000. This gain will be offset further by the amount of Charles's tax liability paid by the buyer, so the buyer's recognized gain under § 61(a)(3) will be $133,500.

The purchaser's basis in the real property will be $500,000 under § 1012, as interpreted by *Philadelphia Park*. This basis is equal to the fair market value of the property she receives. This also is consistent with what she paid (i.e., $75,000 cash plus $200,000 stock plus $225,000 mortgage liability). The $1500 property tax assumption attributable to Charles will be deductible by Charles under § 164(a) and the $1,500 of her own property tax on acquisition of the property will be deductible by her. Thus, these payments will not affect the basis of the property.

5. TOOLS FOR SELF-ASSESSMENT

[1] Problems of this type often are overwhelming for students initially because of the multiple transactions involved. In approaching a multiple transaction problem, it is important to separate the various transactions and to address them chronologically. It is also important to clarify the type of transaction in question because there are different basis provisions for different types of transactions. As we see in this problem, one transaction may have an effect on another transaction.

[2] In this problem, there are four transactions to consider: (1) the gift of the 50 acres of land, (2) the purchase of the second 50 acres, (3) the construction of the rental residence, and (4) the exchange of the properties.

[3] The first event/transaction is the gift of the 50 acres of land to Charles from his father. Since this is a donative transfer, Charles's basis in this property is determined under § 1015, the gift basis provision. Students often are inclined initially to think that the entire amount of gift tax paid should be applied to increase the donee's basis, and this is how the adjustment was made prior to December 31, 1976. Congress changed this rule in 1976, however, in an effort to raise revenue. The rationale for the change was that the basis should be adjusted only for the portion of the property that will be subject to both a gift tax and an income tax. This portion is the appreciation in the property at the time of the gift.

[4] When Charles purchases the second 50 acres, he does not realize an economic benefit on receipt of the property, even though he has no personal liability under the mortgage, because of his corresponding obligation to repay the debt in order to retain the property. On the other hand, he does obtain a tax advantage from this mortgage because it will become part of his basis in the property under *Crane* since it is a bona fide indebtedness that is used to purchase the property (see also *Estate of Franklin*). This also applies to the construction of the rental residence on this property.

[5] The property tax is irrelevant because state and local property taxes generally have no effect on the basis of the property. See § 1016(a)(1)(A). They may be deducted under § 164(a)(1); but otherwise they have no effect on the transactions in this problem, with the limited exception of the property taxes in the year of the sale, which will go into Charles's amount realized

under § 1001(b)(2) because the buyer is assuming Charles's portion of the taxes. This also is consistent with the principles of *Old Colony Trust Co.*

[6] In an exchange, whether taxable or nontaxable, the tricky part is keeping the various legs of the transaction separate. The first leg involves the determination of the gain or loss on the exchange. The amount realized on the exchange is offset by the basis in the property exchanged (i.e., the old basis). This basis is determined according to the transaction in which the taxpayer acquired the property. For instance, if the taxpayer acquired the property by cash purchase, the basis is a straight § 1012 cost basis. In Charles's case, his basis in the rental residence and the 100 acres is a blended §1015/§1012 basis. When the properties are exchanged, the amount realized is determined under the general rule of § 1001(b). Thus, the amount of money and the fair market value of any property received constitute the amount realized. Here, though, it is important to remember the rule of *Crane*: that the "property" received under § 1001(b) includes the relief of nonrecourse indebtedness.

[7] Students sometimes have problems with the terminology of § 1001. Note the distinction between amount realized and gain realized. The second leg of the transaction involves the determination of the basis in the new property after the exchange. Here, the general principles already discussed apply. Since the exchange in this problem is taxable, it is treated as a sale, and the basis in the new property, the XYZ shares, will be determined under § 1012 and *Philadelphia Park Amusement Co.* Thus, the "cost" for purposes of § 1012 will be the fair market value of what is received, not the value of what is given up in the transaction. It is important to note that *Philadelphia Park* applies only to the second leg of the transaction. Thus, it determines the basis in the new property that each party holds after the exchange.

[8] If one thinks about the tax consequences of the exchange, the rules equalize a cash transaction and a taxable exchange. If Charles had received $501,500 in cash, he would have had a realized gain of $146,500, the same gain that he realized in the exchange. He would have had to pay off the mortgage of $225,000 before he transferred the property, as well as his $1500 share of the property taxes, so he would walk away with $275,000 of cash. In the problem, he walks away with $75,000 of cash and $200,000 of stock, so the values are the same. Thus, there is no difference in economic result or tax result between a cash transaction and a taxable exchange of property. This makes sense because a mere change in form of the transaction should not change the result.

[9] In a taxable exchange, each party goes through the same gain/loss calculation under § 1001. The purchaser realizes $500,000 because that is the value of the property that she receives. Her basis in the stock is $65,000, but the other assets do not have a basis, so they offset the amount realized dollar for dollar. Thus, her taxable gain will be $133,500, attributable to the appreciation in the stock that she transferred to Charles. Section 1012 and *Philadelphia Park* also apply to the purchaser to determine the basis of the real property that she holds after the exchange. The total value of the real property that she receives is $500,000, so her new § 1012 basis, as defined by *Philadelphia Park* will be $500,000. (Note that for purposes of depreciation,

which we are asked to ignore in this problem, the basis will have to be apportioned between the land and the building.)

6. VARIATION ON THE THEME

Assume the same facts except for the following: (1) the first 50 acres are subject to a nonrecourse mortgage of $10,000 at the time of the gift, and Charles takes this property subject to the mortgage; and (2) the fair market value of the second 50-acre tract was $50,000 at the time of the sale, but the purchaser agreed to take this property subject to the $90,000 nonrecourse mortgage (all other consideration remains the same). How, if at all, will these changes affect your answer to this problem?

7. OPTIONAL READINGS

Cases: Tufts v. Commissioner, 461 U.S. 300, 103 S.Ct. 1826, 75 L.Ed.2d 863 (1983)

Articles: Jensen, *The Unanswered Question in Tufts: What Was the Purchaser's Basis?*, 10 Va. Tax Rev. 455 (1991); Andrews, *On Beyond Tufts*, 61 Taxes 949 (1983)

4

PURCHASE AND SALE OF A PRINCIPAL RESIDENCE

1. OPENING REMARKS

Historically, the real estate industry has been a powerful lobbying force in Congress, and as a result, there are several very favorable provisions in the tax Code to encourage investment in real estate. One of these provisions pertains to home ownership. In order to encourage the stability of the family, and in recognition of the fact that many people sell their homes and move because of a job relocation or to downsize in later years, the tax Code contains a special provision to prevent recognition of a gain upon the sale of a principal residence, provided certain requirements are met.

Section 121, which has been in effect since 1997, authorizes these benefits. Prior to that time, gain on the sale of a principal residence was governed by former § 1034, which had several defects leading to unintended tax consequences, so Congress repealed it and enacted new § 121. But many residences were sold and purchased under the old provisions, and since those provisions had an effect on the basis of newly purchased property, old §§ 1034 and 121 should be discussed because they may have an effect on the amount of gain realized on the sale of a current residence. This, in turn, may affect the application of current § 121.

Former § 1034 provided a rollover of gain realized on the sale or exchange of a principal residence, provided the taxpayer purchased a replacement residence within certain specified time limits and provided the purchase price of the replacement property exceeded the adjusted sales price of the old residence. Any realized gain on the old residence that was unrecognized reduced the basis in the new property.

There were several problems with this aspect of former § 1034. First, it forced taxpayers to purchase more expensive houses than they otherwise might have needed, simply to avoid the tax liability on the sale of their old residence. This was perceived as an inefficient use of financial resources. Second, § 1034 obviously was detrimental to the elderly, who were hit with an unexpected tax liability upon selling their residences in order to downsize. For this reason, former § 121 provided a one-time exclusion of up to $125,000 of gain on the sale of a principal residence by a taxpayer who was at least 55 years of age. The problem with this provision, though, was that it was perceived as too restrictive because it constrained the mobility of the elderly. Another problem with this provision was that if a taxpayer married or remarried later in life, and his/her spouse had previously used former § 121, the new spouse was tainted and as a result, neither could obtain the benefit of § 121. Fourth, the basis reduction of former § 1034 was complicated because if a taxpayer had multiple sales of principal residences, each sale could affect the basis of the next residence. If the taxpayer failed to properly reduce the basis, she could be subjected to an unanticipated tax liability later when the residence was sold or in the alternative, the government could be whipsawed. Finally, the basis reduction provision required taxpayers to keep records of the sales of all former residences for many years. For these reasons, Congress repealed former § 1034 in 1997 and enacted current § 121, which avoids the pitfalls of the former provisions.

Under current § 121, the age of the taxpayer does not matter, and neither does the cost of the new residence. The exclusion applies to gains of $500,000 and below for joint returns, and $250,000 and below for singe filers. Taxpayers may avail themselves of the benefits of § 121 only if they have not previously obtained a benefit under § 121 within a two-year period of the date of the sale. There are ownership and use requirements under new § 121, as there were under previous § 1034.

2. HYPOTHETICAL

Daniel Davis graduated from law school in 1992 and purchased a small house for $100,000. In 1996, he met Donna Williams, and they married in June 1998. Donna had a house of her own that she had purchased for $150,000 10 years before the marriage. Shortly before the wedding, both Daniel and Donna put their houses on the market, and both sold within a short period of time. Daniel's house sold for $300,000, and Donna's house sold for $500,000. In November 1998, Daniel and Donna purchased a house together for $650,000. The Davises file a joint income tax return and are calendar year taxpayers.

In February 1999, Daniel was offered a partnership by his law firm. A short time later, Donna became pregnant, and in November she had a baby boy named David. As time passed, Daniel and Donna decided that it would be nice to live further from the city, so they put their house on the market in February 2007, and in August, it sold for $1 million. They purchased a new residence in the country for $800,000 in September 2007. A year later, Daniel was transferred by his employer to a new location 400 miles away. The couple once again put their house on the market, and in March 2009, it sold for $1.2 million. Daniel and Donna then purchased another residence in their new location for $1 million in April 2009.

In January 2010, Daniel died suddenly of a heart attack, and Donna decided to sell the house and look for a smaller residence closer to her parents. She put the house on the market, and with great luck, she sold it in April 2010 for $1.2 million. She purchased a new residence in June 2010 for $600,000, and she and David moved in shortly afterward.

Discuss the tax consequences of the purchases and sales of these properties.

3. LIST OF READINGS

Internal Revenue Code of 1986: §§ 121; 6013(a); 7703(a)
Regulations: §§ 1.121–1 through 1.121–4

4. SAMPLE ESSAY

When Daniel purchased his first house for $100,000, his basis in this residence was $100,000 under § 1012, and assuming he had not made any capital improvements to the property, it remained $100,000 until he sold the house. Donna's basis in her house was $150,000, her cost of the property under § 1012, and again assuming that she made no capital improvements to her property, that was her basis at the time of her sale. When Daniel sold his residence in 1998, he realized a gain of $200,000, while Donna realized a gain of $350,000 on her sale. Since they were married at the time of the sales, together they realized a gain of $550,000.

Since the parties sold their respective properties in 1998, the former rules of § 1034 and old § 121 do not apply. Instead, the sales are governed by current § 121. Section 121 provides an exclusion of up to $500,000 of gain on the sale of a principal residence, provided several requirements are met. First, the couple must file a joint return. Second, they must meet the ownership and use requirements. Under these requirements, the property must have been owned and used as a principal residence for at least two years, in the aggregate, during the five years preceding the sale. If the property is jointly owned, either spouse may meet the ownership requirement, so both are not required to own the property but both must meet the use requirement. Third, the taxpayers may not have obtained a benefit under § 121(a) within the two-year period preceding the sale. A taxpayer may elect not to apply § 121 to a sale or exchange of property. See Reg. § 1.121–4(g). The following answer assumes that the parties do not make this election.

Marital status, for federal income tax purposes, is determined by the taxpayers' status on the last day of the taxable year. See § 7703(a)(1). Since the Davises married in 1998, they are considered married for the full 1998 taxable year and are entitled to file a joint federal income tax return for that taxable year. Both Daniel and Donna appear to meet the ownership and use tests for their own respective residences, but neither meets the ownership or use test for the other's residence. Since they are married at the end of the taxable year of the sales, they are eligible to file a joint return. Since each meets the ownership and use tests of their respective residences, they each may exclude up to $250,000 of their realized gain. Thus, Daniel may exclude his entire $200,000 realized gain. However, Donna may exclude only $250,000 of her $350,000 realized gain. She may not use the remainder of Daniel's limitation to exclude any of her gain. Reg. § 1.121–2(a). Thus, on their joint return, the couple will have to recognize a $100,000 gain attributable to the sale of Donna's house.

When the couple purchased their new residence in November 1998, their basis in this residence was $650,000. When they sold this residence in August 2007 for $1 million, they realized a gain of $350,000. Since their previous sale was more than two years prior to this time, they may use § 121 to exclude the entire amount of their gain. When they purchased their new residence for $800,000, their basis in this property was $800,000 under § 1012.

When Daniel is transferred the following year, neither he nor Donna meet the ownership and use requirements because they have owned the residence less than two years and used it as a principal residence only for about a year. However, the Code anticipates that taxpayers on occasion may not be able to meet these requirements because of circumstances beyond their control. Section 121(c) allows a portion of the gain to be excluded if the sale occurs as a result of a change in employment. The regulations provide that the change in employment must occur during the period that the taxpayer owns and uses the property as a principal residence. The Davises meet this requirement. The regulations also provide a distance requirement for a change in employment. Under this requirement, the new place of employment must be at least 50 miles farther from the old residence than was the former place of employment. Reg. § 1.121–3(c). Since Daniel's new place of employment is 400 miles from his previous place of employment, this requirement also is met.

Under § 121(c), the amount of the maximum exclusion is $250,000. This is determined by a ratio, the numerator of which is the shorter of the period during which the property has been owned and used by the taxpayer as a principal residence or the date of the most recent sale or exchange of property to which § 121(a) applied, and the denominator is two years. Daniel and Donna owned the property for 18 months but used it as a principal residence only for one year. Since the one-year period in which they used the property as a residence is shorter than their previous sale period of 18 months, the numerator is one and the denominator is two. This ratio is then multiplied by their maximum exclusion of $500,000. Thus, $250,000 of their $400,000 realized gain may be excluded. The Davises will have to recognize the remaining $150,000 of gain.

The basis in their new property, purchased in 2009, is $1 million. Donna realizes $200,000 on this residence when she sells it in April 2010. Since her sale occurs because of the death of her husband, this is an unforeseen circumstance under the regulations. Reg. § 1.121–3(e)(2). Section 121(c) again provides that a ratio be applied to determine the maximum exclusion. Since Donna owned and used the residence for one year, this is the numerator, and the denominator is two. Thus, the ratio is 50 percent. The question is to what limitation does this ratio apply? Donna is single at the end of the 2010 taxable year. However, § 6013(a)(3) allows Daniel's executor (or Donna if there is not one) to elect to file a joint return for the taxable year of Daniel's death. If such a return is filed, the maximum exclusion is $250,000 ($500,000 x 50 percent), so Donna's entire $200,000 gain will be excluded under § 121. If there is no joint return filed for this taxable year, the maximum limitation will be $125,000, and Donna will have to recognize $75,000 of her gain. Her basis in her new residence is its cost, $600,000, under § 1012.

5. TOOLS FOR SELF-ASSESSMENT

Under current § 121, the rules are much easier to apply and record keeping also is much easier than it was under former § 1034.

[1] In the first transaction in which both Daniel and Donna sell their respective residences, § 121(d)(1) at first blush appears to allow the exclusion of the full $500,000 of gain, instead of $450,000 as in the sample essay ($200,000 for Daniel and $250,000 for Donna). But under the more specific language of § 121(b)(2)(B), if two married taxpayers together do not meet all three threshold requirements, but one of the taxpayers does meet them, the exclusion is determined on an individual basis as though the taxpayers were not married. Since Daniel, presumably, does not meet the use test on the sale of Donna's residence, and she does not meet the same test on the sale of Daniel's residence, the combined $500,000 exclusion attributable to spouses filing a joint return does not apply. Instead, the taxpayers will be considered separate parties for this purpose. While § 121(b)(2)(B) provides that each spouse will be treated as owning property during the period that either spouse owned the property, this does not mean that the use test is satisfied.

A close reading of § 121(d) provides that if either spouse meets the ownership and use requirements, the benefits of § 121(a) are available even if the spouses file a joint return. Note, however, that § 121(d) does not refer to § 121(b), which provides the limitations for taxpayers filing a single or joint return. Therefore, the limitations are determined under § 121(b)(2)(B) and apply to each spouse as though the spouses had not been married. The result is that if the spouses file a joint return, and both sell their respective residences in the same taxable year, the limitations will be applied to each separately.

[2] While former § 1034 required a basis adjustment for excluded gain, § 121 provides a true exclusion rather than a deferral of gain. Thus, the application of § 121 has no effect on the basis of the new property. Also, new § 121 does not require the taxpayer to purchase a more expensive residence in order to obtain the benefit of the exclusion. So if Daniel and Donna sell their residence and buy a less expensive one, as they did in 2007, they still may obtain the benefit of § 121. The same applies to Donna when she sells the residence after Daniel's death and purchases a much less expensive one.

[3] When the Davises sell their residence in March 2009 because of Daniel's change in employment, the two-year look-back period does not apply because § 121(c)(1) provides that a sale within the two-year period to which that subsection (i.e., § 121(c)) applies, the ownership and use requirements of subsections (a) *and (b)(3)* shall not apply.

[4] When Daniel dies, and Donna decides to sell the residence and move, this circumstance is addressed under the regulations at § 1.121–3(e) and (f). While § 121(d)(2) provides that the period of ownership and use by a deceased spouse will be considered for purposes of determining the ownership and use requirements, that will not help Donna in her last sale because Daniel's ownership and use overlapped with her own. See Reg. § 1.121–4.

6. VARIATIONS ON THE THEME

What result if, in the alternative, the final sale had occurred because Daniel was in the armed forces and had been transferred overseas for an extended period? Would the Davises be required to recognize any gain? Why or why not?

5 DISSOLUTION OF A MARRIAGE

1. OPENING REMARKS

Marriage and its dissolution are determined under state law. But transfers of property between spouses and payments between the parties pursuant to a divorce may be taxed under federal law, depending upon the type of payment being made. In general, a transfer of property between spouses is a tax-neutral event that does not result in taxable income. When the parties divorce, however, payments or transfers of property between them may result in a tax consequence, depending upon the type of payment being made. In a divorce, there are three types of payments generally encountered: alimony, property settlements, and child support. Alimony payments are intended to provide support and separate maintenance for the less-affluent spouse. Since 1942, alimony payments have been deductible by the payor and includable by the payee. Because of this specific tax treatment, there are limitations on what payments constitute alimony under § 71. The parties may allocate the tax liability, however, by designating the payments as taxable to the payor (i.e., nondeductible) and nontaxable to the payee. Thus, the tax treatment of alimony payments may be negotiated between the parties.

Property settlements generally are treated the same as other transfers between spouses and are tax-neutral events. For the transferee, this is a more favorable result than an alimony payment (under the general rules) whereas for the transferor, the result is less favorable because there is no deduction generated on the transfer. In order to prevent taxpayers from attempting to disguise property settlements as deductible alimony and obtaining tax benefits to which they are not entitled, the alimony provision contains some safeguards to prevent this abuse. Section 71(f) provides rules to "recapture" the tax benefits and reallocate those to the payee if it is determined that the payments look more like a property settlement than alimony and separate maintenance payments.

Congress also was concerned about sham divorces that would enable the wealthier spouse to obtain an alimony deduction. Thus, § 71 provides that if the parties are divorced, they must live separate and apart. They cannot reside in the same household and take advantage of the alimony deduction provision.

Child support payments are tax neutral: they are neither deductible by the payor nor includable by the payee. The rationale behind this treatment is that child support is a legal obligation. Thus, child support payments, while nontaxable to the recipient, are not considered gifts.

2. HYPOTHETICAL

Edward and Ethel Everson had been married for 12 years and during this time, they had two children, Eddie and Edna, ages 10 and 8 respectively. The Eversons divorced two years ago in June, and in their divorce decree, Ethel was given custody of the children. Under the decree, Edward agreed to give Ethel his share of their house, which they jointly owned and had purchased 10 years ago at a price of $450,000. The house is now worth $900,000 but is subject to an outstanding mortgage of $250,000. The decree also required Edward to make the monthly mortgage payments of $2800 directly to the mortgage company and to pay Ethel $2500 per month for her support and maintenance. In addition, the decree required Edward to pay all medical and educational expenses of the children.

Edward began making these payments in July, following the finalization of the divorce in June. He made all required payments for the first 18 months, but then his business suffered a financial downturn and he was unable to pay the full amount that he owed Ethel. He agreed to continue making the mortgage payments and to pay the expenses for the children, but he asked Ethel if she would accept some stock in lieu of his cash payments to her for the next 10 payments, and she agreed. The stock had a total value of $25,000 but had been purchased by Edward in two lots. The first lot was purchased eight years ago for $20,000 and is now worth $15,000, while the second lot was purchased three years ago for $7,500 and it is now worth $10,000. He transferred both lots of stock to Ethel and after 10 months, he resumed making the stipulated cash payments.

In the current year, Edward has made payments of $6500 for the children's education and $850 for medical expenses.

Discuss the tax treatment to both Edward and Ethel of these payments and transfers. Do you have any advice for them?

3. LIST OF READINGS

Internal Revenue Code of 1986: §§ 71; 215; 1012; 1041; 1223
Regulations: Temp. Reg. § 1.71–1T(b)

4. SAMPLE ESSAY

Alimony: Alimony payments generally are included in the recipient's gross income under § 71 and are deductible by the payor under § 215. Section 71(b) lists the requirements for payments to be considered alimony and separate maintenance payments for federal income tax purposes. These requirements are strictly construed, and each one must be met, or the payments fail to qualify as alimony payments. The first requirement is that the payment must be made in cash. See § 71(b) and Temp. Reg. § 1.71–1T(b), Q&A 5. The payment also must be made pursuant to a divorce or separation instrument that does not designate the payment as nontaxable to the recipient, and there must be no obligation to continue the payments (or transfer cash or property in lieu of such payments) after the death of the payee. If the divorce decree in this problem does not contain a provision for termination of the payments upon the death of Ethel, or if the operation of local law does not provide that such payments cease upon the death of the payee spouse, the payments to Ethel will not constitute alimony. Instead they will be considered a property settlement, and they will not be taxable to Ethel as they are made, nor will they deductible by Edward. If the decree meets the requirements of § 71(b) (i.e., the decree does not designate the payments as nontaxable to Ethel and nondeductible to Edward, and Edward's obligation to make such payments ceases upon the death of Ethel), the $2500 per month cash payments made in the first 18 months following the divorce will be includable by Ethel under § 71(a) and deductible by Edward under § 215.

The monthly mortgage payments that Edward makes to the mortgage company may constitute alimony, provided that he has deeded his interest in the house to Ethel. Payments to a third party can constitute alimony if they are solely for the benefit of the alimony recipient. In this case, the mortgage payments can potentially constitute alimony, provided that Edward has deeded his interest to Ethel, and he has no further interest in the house. If he continues to have such an interest (i.e., if he has not yet deeded his interest to Ethel), the payments will not constitute alimony and instead will be considered a property settlement.

Property settlements: Transfers of property between current spouses or as a property settlement pursuant to a divorce fall under § 1041, which makes the transfer a tax-neutral event. Section 1041(a) provides that no gain or loss is recognized on the transfer of property between spouses or former spouses pursuant to divorce. If property is transferred pursuant to a divorce decree, it clearly is considered a transfer pursuant to divorce.

This means that the transfer will not be taxable to either party, and the transferee will take the basis and holding period of the transferor. There are two transfers in this hypothetical that fall into this category. The first is Edward's transfer of his half of the house to Ethel. The market value of the house is $900,000, and the couple's basis in this property is $450,000, determined under § 1012. If the property were sold for its market value, the couple would realize $450,000 ($900,000 less the $450,000 basis). Since they each own half of the house, Ethel realizes half of this amount, or $225,000, on the transfer of the house to her. Section 1041(a) provides that no gain or loss is recognized on the transfer of property between spouses or former spouses pursuant to divorce. Ethel's basis in the house after the transfer is $450,000, determined in part by § 1012 with respect to her half and § 1041(b) with respect to the portion that she receives from Edward. Her holding period in the entire property is 10 years because that is how long they have owned the property, and Edward's holding period carries over to her along with the basis. See § 1223(2).

The stock transfer is made in lieu of the support payments that were ordered by the court under the divorce decree. Thus, it occurs pursuant to the divorce, but it does not constitute alimony because it is not a cash payment (see Temp. Reg. § 1.71–1(b), Q&A 5), even if Ethel were immediately to sell the stock for cash. Instead, this transfer also will be considered a property settlement and will be a tax neutral event to both Edward and Ethel. Thus, it will not be includable by Ethel and will not be deductible by Edward. Ethel will take Edward's basis in the stock under § 1041(b) and will realize a gain or loss when she sells the stock. Edward's holding period in the stock also will carry over to Ethel under § 1223(2).

The problem that the stock transfer raises is that since the transfer is not considered an alimony payment, and the transfer occurs within the first three post-separation years following their divorce, it may trigger the recapture provision of § 71(f). This provision is designed to reverse the tax consequences between the payor and the payee if alimony payments are sufficiently front-loaded in the first three years following the divorce. This prevents high-income taxpayers from structuring property settlements as alimony payments in order to take advantage of the alimony deduction.

Under those provisions, the first post-separation year is the first calendar year in which the payor makes alimony payments to the payee. See § 71(f)(6).

This would be the year in which Edward and Ethel are divorced. In that year, Edward makes six payments of $2500 each, or $15,000, to Ethel. In the second post-separation year (the following calendar year), Edward makes payments of $30,000 to Ethel, and in the third post-separation year, he will make cash payments of $5000 to her.

Applying the rules of § 71(f), the excess payment for the second post-separation year must be calculated first under § 71(f)(4). This results in an excess alimony payment of $10,000 ($30,000 amount paid during second post-separation year less $20,000—the sum of the $5000 amount of alimony paid during the third post-separation year and $15,000). There is no excess payment from the first post-separation year under § 71(f)(3) ($15,000 payments in the first post-separation year less $32,500—$30,000 amount paid during the second post-separation year plus the $5000 amount paid during the third post-separation year, divided by two, plus $15,000).

The adjustment under § 71(f) occurs in the third post-separation year. Edward will be required to include $10,000 in income in the third post-separation year, and Ethel will be entitled to a deduction of that amount. Note that Edward also will be able to deduct the $5000 that he pays to Ethel as alimony in the third post-separation year.

The transfer of the stock was not a good deal for Edward. He was not able to obtain a deduction for the $25,000 value of the stock that he transferred to Ethel in fulfillment of his obligation to support her, and as a result of this transfer, he has an unanticipated tax liability. While he also would have had a tax liability upon the sale of the stock, that liability would have been negligible compared to the $10,000 inclusion that he has as a result of the transfer of the stock to Ethel. If Edward had sold the stock himself, he would have been able to recognize his realized $5000 loss, and his realized gain of $2500 would have been a long-term capital gain, if recognized. But § 1041 provides that no gain or loss will be recognized on a transfer of property between former spouses pursuant to divorce. Instead, Edward will incur a tax liability on $10,000 of ordinary income inclusion.

Child support payments: The medical and educational expenses that Edward pays for the children will constitute child support. Child support payments have no special tax consequences, so they will not be includable by either Ethel or the children and will not be deductible as such by Edward. The payments for the medical care of the children may be deductible under § 213, although these deductions are subject to severe restrictions. If the noncustodial parent provides more than half of the children's support and wishes to obtain a deduction for medical expenses and/or a dependency exemption under § 151, the custodial parent can sign a release to the exemption claim, and the noncustodial parent may take the tax benefits. See § 152(e). If Ethel signs such a release, Edward may claim the children as dependents on his tax return, and if he otherwise is able to take a deduction for the medical expenses, he may take that as well.

5. TOOLS FOR SELF-ASSESSMENT

[1] Although Temp. Reg. § 1.71–1T(b), Q&A 11 and 12 provide that the decree or agreement must specifically provide that payments cease upon the death of the payee spouse, this was invalidated by the Tax Reform Act of 1986.

Now, if local law provides that the payments terminate upon the death of the payee spouse, the payments will be considered alimony, despite the fact that the decree does not require the payments to cease. Often, the regulations are not amended in a timely manner to reflect changes in the law. Be aware that in any inconsistency between the Code and the regulations, the Code controls.

[2] The transfer of Edward's share of the house to Ethel results in a realization to her to the extent of the value of Edward's interest, but she has no recognition of income because § 1041(a) specifically provides that no gain or loss shall be recognized on a transfer of property between spouses or former spouses incident to divorce. Students often are inclined to look to the equity in the property as the amount realized, rather than the fair market value of the property transferred, as determined under § 1001. In economic terms, Ethel receives the equity in the property, or $325,000, upon the transfer of Edward's interest to her ($450,000 market value of Edward's half interest less the mortgage of $250,000 x one-half). In terms of the tax consequences, though, the mortgage is ignored because it was included in the basis of the property. The equity in the house is $650,000 ($900,000 market value less the outstanding mortgage of $250,000), and the total realization under § 1001, if the property were sold for its market value ($900,000 less the basis of $450,000), is $450,000. Both figures consider the appreciation in the property over the initial purchase price. The difference between the two is the $200,000 down payment that the Eversons made when they purchased the property initially. This is part of their equity in the property, along with the appreciation in the value of the property during the time they have owned it, but it is not part of the realization because the taxpayers are given credit for this down payment in their basis. Since realization is a tax term that considers the basis in the property in order to prevent double taxation, the equity in the property, while important to Ethel, has no relevance in terms of realization.

[3] It is important to keep straight the different types of payments that may occur in the dissolution of a marriage. It also is important to note that while a payment, such as the stock transfer, may satisfy the legal requirement of support in the divorce decree and may constitute alimony for purposes of state law, federal law has a very specific definition of alimony that may not coincide with the state law definition. Thus, while for purposes of state law Edward may have met his obligation to pay Ethel $2500 per month for her support when he transfers the stock to her, this transfer is not considered alimony for purposes of federal law.

[4] Since the transfer of the stock was made pursuant to a divorce between the parties, the tax consequences of this transfer must be determined. If it is not an alimony payment, the only other category under which it would fit is a property settlement. Although § 1041 provides that property transferred between spouses or former spouses incident to divorce is to be treated as a gift, the special basis rule that applies to property transferred by gift that has a basis greater than its fair market value (see § 1015(a)—basis for purposes of determining loss) does not apply under § 1041. Thus, Ethel will take

Edward's basis in both lots of stock, even though one lot has a basis that is greater than its fair market value at the time of the transfer.

[5] Even though Edward is being relieved of a legal obligation to pay cash when he transfers the stock in lieu of cash alimony payments to Ethel, this is not a discharge of indebtedness because he is satisfying the full amount of his obligation with property instead of cash. Edward is satisfying a legal obligation with appreciated property (for the portion that is appreciated), and therefore he realizes a gain on that portion (and a loss on the other portion). Under § 1041, neither is recognized since this is considered a property transfer pursuant to a divorce.

[6] Section 71(f) is a trap for the unwary. While there are some exceptions to the recapture of the alimony deductions, such as fluctuating payments beyond the control of the payor under § 71(f)(5)(C), this provision does not apply in this problem because § 71(f)(5)(C) applies specifically to obligations to pay a fixed portion of income from a business or property, or from compensation for employment or self-employment. In the case of Edward and Ethel, there was a general obligation for Edward to make support payments to Ethel. There was no specific delineation as to where this money was to be found. Edward could easily have sold the stock himself and transferred the cash to Ethel and indeed, for tax purposes, he should have done so. Therefore, the fluctuating payment, technically, was not beyond his control.

6. VARIATIONS ON THE THEME

Assume that in addition to the transfer of Edward's share of the house to Ethel and the payment of the monthly mortgage, the divorce decree requires Edward to make payments of $6000 per month to Ethel. These payments are to be reduced to $4000 per month when Eddie reaches age 18 and further reduced to $2000 per month when Edna reaches age 18. Discuss the tax consequences.

6

EMPLOYEE FRINGE BENEFITS

1. OPENING REMARKS

Fringe benefits are incidental benefits (for instance, they do not include health care or retirement benefits) for employees. Since these items constitute economic benefits, their value normally would be included as compensation income in the gross income of the employee receiving them. In some cases, though, the tax Code authorizes an exclusion from income, at least for certain types of benefits. There are several provisions that exclude the value of certain fringe benefits, such as §§ 79, 125, 127, and 129, but the primary exclusionary provision for incidental benefits is § 132, enacted in 1984 after much debate about whether and how to tax these benefits.

The policy rationale behind § 132 falls generally into two general categories: de minimis or business purpose. Thus, certain types of benefits may be of de minimis value so that accounting for them is administratively impracticable. Other types of benefits under § 132 primarily serve a business purpose of the employer. In order to prevent inconsistency in treatment of these types of benefits, § 132 authorizes their exclusion from the employee's gross income.

Section 132 applies to a variety of incidental employee benefits and is a very favorable provision because it authorizes a true exclusion rather than a deferral of recognition. But as with any provision that bestows a tax benefit, § 132 is strictly construed.

2. HYPOTHETICAL

Francine Fox and her husband, Fred, are both employed by the ABC Corp., a company that owns hotels in several different cities. Francine is an attorney for the company, and Fred is a general manager of one of the hotels and a vice president of the company. The company has a policy in which any employee can stay free in any of its hotels for up to five nights per year. Francine, Fred, and their two children took advantage of this policy on their vacation last summer by staying three nights at one of the company's hotels in Florida and another two nights at one in Savannah, Georgia. They needed two rooms each night, one for them and one for their children, so they paid the full cost of the extra room.

The company also gives its employees a 10 percent discount on certain items in the gift shop at all of the hotels. Francine and her daughter both purchased bathrobes for $90 each using the discount at the Florida hotel. The gift shops last year had gross sales of $300,000, and the employer's cost of the goods was $180,000.

Francine and Fred both are provided free parking while lesser paid employees must pay $100 per month to park. Normally, parking would cost $300 per month. In addition, both Francine and Fred are provided free coffee and pastries each day and, occasionally, lunch during a business meeting at work. They also both receive free access to the health club at Fred's hotel, which was recently upgraded to a state-of-the-art facility for the guests.

Are any or all of these benefits taxable to Fred and/or Francine? Discuss fully.

3. READING LIST

Internal Revenue Code: §§ 132; 414(q)
Regulations: §§ 1.132–2; 1.132–4; 1.132–6; 1.132–8
Article: McCoy, *Executive Perks and the Fringe Benefit Rules,* 42 N.Y. U. Inst. on Fed. Tax'n, ch. 39 (1984)

4. SAMPLE ESSAY

Section 102(c) provides that amounts transferred by an employer to or for the benefit of an employee are not excluded from the employee's gross income as a gift. However, § 132 excludes the value of employee fringe benefits from income if certain requirements are met. There are several such benefits that Fred and Francine receive. First are the free hotel accommodations. Obviously, Fred and Francine do not receive a financial benefit for the extra room because they paid full cost for it. The free room, however, constitutes an economic benefit to them because they otherwise would have had to pay to stay in the hotel. Section 132(a)(1) excludes the value of a "no-additional-cost service," provided certain requirements are met. Section 132(b) requires that the service be provided to the employee "in the ordinary course of the line of business . . . in which the employee is performing services." Since this employer has only one line of business, that requirement is not a problem. Section 132(b)(2) requires that the employer incur no substantial additional cost, including forgone revenue, in providing the service. This may be a problem for the Foxes because if both requirements (i.e., line of business and no-additional-cost to the employer) are not met, the value of the benefit is taxable to the employee. Reg. § 1.132–2(a)(5) provides that there is no exclusion allowed under § 132(a)(1) if the employer forgoes other income by displacing a paying guest. In order to avoid this problem, a prudent employer usually places certain restrictions on the right to stay cost free at any of its facilities. Usually these restrictions require the booking to be made within a certain narrow time frame during the less busy times of the year, and they usually provide explicitly that the reservation is subject to room availability. If the employer forgoes income to accommodate the Foxes, the fair cost of the "free" rooms for the nights that they stay there are subject to tax. If there is no revenue forgone, then they meet this part of the requirement and provided the other requirements are met, they may stay cost free and tax free in the room. The ultimate vacation!!

The final requirement under § 132 is that this type of benefit (i.e., § 132(a)(1)) must be provided on a nondiscriminatory basis to the employees. Thus, even if the other requirements are met, the value of the benefit is not excludable if the benefit is offered primarily to highly compensated employees. See § 132(j)(1). For this purpose, a highly compensated employee is one who is a 5 percent or greater owner, or who in the preceding taxable year had compensation of greater than $80,000 and was in the top 20 percent of the compensation range. See § 414(q). If the benefit fails to meet the antidiscrimination requirement, the entire amount of the benefit is includable, not just the apportioned amount. See Reg. § 1.132–8(a)(2).

It can be reasonably assumed that both Fred and Francine are highly compensated employees, although that is not entirely clear. If the employer offers this benefit on a nondiscriminatory basis to its employees, the value of the rooms will be excludable. If not, and Fred and Francine are highly compensated employees, the value of the rooms will be includable in their gross income, and they will incur a tax cost.

The discount in the gift shop falls under § 132(a)(2) as a qualified employee discount. Since the bathrobe is personal property, the excludable amount cannot exceed the employer's gross profit percentage, determined under § 132(c)(2). The ABC Corp.'s gross profit percentage is 40 percent ($300,000 less $180,000/ $300,000). Since the 10 percent discount that the company allows the employees is well under that, the entire amount of the discount is potentially excludable under § 132(a)(2). Section 132(a)(2) has the same line-of-business and antidiscrimination requirements as § 132(a)(1). So the same analysis applies to the § 132(a)(2) benefit.

The term "employee" in both §§ 132(a)(1) and (a)(2) refer to spouses and dependent children, as well as retired and disabled employees and surviving spouses. See § 132(h). Thus, the fact that the Foxes' daughter benefits from the discount will not cause that portion of the benefit to be taxable.

The parking probably constitutes a qualified transportation fringe benefit under § 132(a)(5), which encompasses three types of benefits: (1) transportation in a commuter vehicle, (2) transit passes, and (3) qualified parking. Section 132(f)(5)(C) defines qualified parking as parking provided to an employee on or near the business premises and not on or near property that the employee uses for residential purposes. The parking provided to the Foxes appears to meet this requirement. Note that unlike §§ 132(a)(1) and (a)(2), which are both subject to the nondiscrimination requirement, § 132(a)(5) is not subject to this requirement. See § 132(j)(1). Thus, the fact that parking is free for the more highly compensated employees and not for the lesser-compensated employees does not transform the benefit into a taxable benefit. There is, however, a ceiling on the amount of this benefit. Section 132(f)(2)(B) provides that the exclusion is limited to $175 per month (indexed for inflation). Thus, currently the Foxes each will have to include $70/month in income attributable to the parking perk.

The free coffee, pastries, and occasional lunch probably are excludable under § 132(a)(4) as a de minimis fringe benefit. This benefit is defined in § 132(e)(1) as any property or service with a value so small as to "make accounting for it unreasonable or administratively impracticable." See Reg. § 1.132–6(b)(2) and (e)(1).

The value of the use of the health club probably will be included in the Foxes' gross income. Section 132(j)(4) excludes the value of an on-premises athletic facility provided by the employer, but there are three requirements, all of which must be met for the exclusion to apply. First, the facility must be located on the premises of the employer, which this one is. Second, it must be operated by the employer, which presumably is the case here. Third, substantially all the use must be by employees, spouses, and dependent children. Since this facility is open to the general public/paying guests, that requirement is not met. Thus, the Foxes will be taxed on the value of their use of the facility.

5. TOOLS FOR SELF-ASSESSMENT

[1] When addressing an employee benefit problem, the first task is to determine the type of benefit in issue because the term "employee benefits" encompasses a multitude of benefits with various values and tax treatment that may differ depending on the benefit. The benefits at issue in this hypothetical all fall under § 132 as "incidental fringe benefits." Section 132(l) provides that with the exception of de minimis fringe benefits and a qualified moving expense reimbursement, § 132 shall not apply to any benefit if the tax treatment of that benefit is expressly provided for in another Code section. So, in the event of an overlap, the specific provision will trump § 132, except for these two exceptions.

[2] Generally, §§ 132(a)(1) and 132(a)(2) are the most complicated of the § 132 benefits. Thus, they usually will require the most analysis and discussion. For this reason, it is best to begin with these benefits because that will give you more time to reflect on them and to provide a better organized answer. Regardless of the order in which they are discussed, there is some overlap between these two benefits, and that makes it more efficacious to discuss them together. If a reduced price or free hotel room does not pass the no-additional-cost test (for example, because the company bumped a paying guest to allow the employee to stay in the room), the employee may be able to exclude the value of the benefit under § 132(a)(2) as a qualified employee discount. Both §§ 132(a)(1) and (a)(2) have the same line of business test and require that the benefit not discriminate in favor of the highly compensated employees, so if the benefit fails either of those tests, no other alternative under § 132 is available. In order to be considered a qualified employee discount, though, the discount (for services) must not exceed 20 percent of the price at which the services are being offered by the employer to customers. See § 132(c)(1)(B). This means that a free room can never pass the qualified employee discount test. Since the Foxes pay nothing for their rooms, § 132(a)(2) is not available as a fallback if their free room benefit should fail to meet the requirements of § 132(a)(1).

[3] Section 414(q) formerly included officers within the definition of highly compensated employees, but that is no longer the case. Since some companies (banks, for instance) have several vice presidents and other officers who may not fall within the highly compensated range for this purpose, the term "officer" was removed from the statute in 1996 in recognition of this phenomenon. However, Reg. § 1.132–8(f) has not been updated to exclude officers, so beware of relying on this portion of the regulation. Remember that the Code trumps the regulations in the event of a conflict between the two.

[4] An astute student may argue that the gift shop is a separate line of business for purposes of the qualified employee discount, but the regulations provide that where it is uncommon in the industry for one line of business to be operated without the other, the separate lines of business are treated as a single line. See Reg. § 1.132–4(a)(3).

[5] The de minimis fringe benefit provision may raise the issue of what exactly is a de minimis benefit. For instance, if Fred is an avid coffee drinker and

consumes gallons of coffee each day, the amount that he consumes may not be so de minimis over the course of a taxable year. On the other hand, it may pose an onerous burden on the company to monitor the frequency with which an employee actually uses the proffered benefit. Under Reg. § 1.132–6(b)(2), the determining factor is the frequency with which the employer provides the benefits to the workplace as a whole. If that is de minimis, individual use is irrelevant. Reg. § 1.132–6(e)(1) mentions coffee, doughnuts, and soft drinks as permissible de minimis benefits. However, there is not a plethora of guidance on this issue, and in some cases, it may not be as clear whether a benefit is de minimis or not.

6. VARIATIONS ON THE THEME

Assume the same facts except that ABC Corp. is an airline that also operates some hotels in close proximity to the airports. The airline permitted all employees and their families to fly free anywhere that the airline flies as long as there are spare seats available. The hotels also have agreements with other hotels in select cities whereby employees of both hotels can stay for free in the others as long as there are vacant rooms.

Fred and Francine fly to Florida with their children, stay three nights in one of the other hotels, and then fly to Savannah and stay two nights in an ABC-operated hotel. How, if at all, will this change your answer?

7

MEALS AND LODGING FURNISHED TO AN EMPLOYEE

1. OPENING REMARKS

In certain situations, an employee may be required to render services that require him to remain on the business premises for an extended period of time. In such a case, the employer may provide meals and, in some situations, lodging to the employee. In other cases, the employer may provide meals to employees on a regular basis because of the nature of the employment. The value of these benefits may be considerable over the course of a taxable year, so they may not be excluded as "fringe benefits" under any of the provisions of § 132.

Previously, there was some confusion over whether these benefits were taxable. The issue was not valuation or accountability but the aspect of forced consumption combined with the fact that the benefit was tied directly to the generation of taxable income. In 1954, Congress enacted §119, which provides that the value of meals and lodging provided by an employer to an employee may be excluded from the employee's gross income if certain stringent requirements are met. Section 119 provides that if the meals and lodging are provided for the convenience of the employer and on the business premises, their value is excluded from taxation. With lodging, the Code imposes the additional requirement that the benefit be required as a condition of employment. As with all exclusionary provisions, the terms of § 119 are strictly applied.

2. HYPOTHETICAL

Glenn Gladsome is an employee of the Big Oil Company in Houston, Texas. His specialty is the repair of oil rigs. Four months ago, Big Oil sent Glenn to the North Sea to repair a rig. The job was a big one and was expected to take about six months. Big Oil has furnished an apartment in Aberdeen, Scotland, for Glenn to use. The apartment is large enough for him to be able to host his family. The apartment is owned by Big Oil and has been used to house rig workers from time to time. It is located very close to the dock where Glenn goes each day to be taken out to the rig. His breakfast and lunch are provided for him on the rig, free of charge. He pays for his own dinners, but at the end of each week, he submits receipts to the employer and is reimbursed for these meals.

Is the value of the apartment and/or the meals included in Glenn's gross income?

3. LIST OF READINGS

Internal Revenue Code: § 119
Regulations: § 1.119–1

Cases: Commissioner v Kowalski, 434 U.S. 77, 98 S.Ct. 315 (1977); Commissioner v. Anderson, 371 F.2d 59 (6th Cir. 1966); Erdelt v. United States, 715 F.Supp. 278 (DND 1989); Lindeman v. Commissioner, 60 T.C. 609 (1973); Sibla v. Commissioner, 611 F.2d 1260 (9th Cir. 1980)
Rulings: IRS Announcement 99–77, 1999–2 C.B. 243

4. SAMPLE ESSAY

Section 119 excludes the value of meals and lodging furnished to an employee for the convenience of the employer, on the business premises of the employer, and in the case of lodging, as a condition of employment. The convenience of the employer requirement connotes a substantial noncompensatory business reason for requiring the employee's presence on the business premises. See Reg. § 1.119–1(a)(2). Thus, there is an element of forced consumption for the employee that justifies the exclusion.

In this case, Big Oil Co. has a substantial reason for requiring Glenn to remain close to the rig in case he is needed urgently. Thus, his continuous availability is required by the employer. The other question, though, is whether the apartment is considered to be "on-the-business premises." Courts have interpreted this term to mean (1) property that is an integral part of the business or (2) property on which the business conducts some of its activities.

The Sixth Circuit in *Anderson* denied the exclusion to a motel manager who resided two blocks away from the motel and was required to be on call 24 hours a day. The court determined that Anderson did not perform a significant part of his duties at the residence. On the other hand, the tax court in *Lindeman* permitted a hotel manager who lived in a separate residence on hotel property to take the exclusion because he made at least part-time business use of the residence.

Here, the apartment is owned by the employer, but otherwise, no business use seems to be made of the apartment other than allowing employees to live there. While it is conveniently located close to the dock, it is not property that is an integral part of the business. On the other hand, if Glenn can show that there was no other suitable housing available, that the apartment is located as near as practicable to the job site, and that he is required to be on call 24 hours a day, he may be able to claim the exclusion, although this seems doubtful. However, in *Erdelt*, the court allowed an exclusion to a rural school superintendent who was provided housing one block away from the school. If Glenn is not successful with this argument and the lodging is included in his income, it is included at its fair rental value, irrespective of whether he would have preferred to live in cheaper housing.

The final test is the condition of employment test. According to Reg. § 1.119-1(b), the employee must be required to accept the lodging in order to enable him to properly perform the duties of his employment because the employee is required to be available for duty at all times or because the employee could not perform the services required of him unless he is furnished such lodging. In order to determine whether this test is met, we would need to know whether Glenn is required to be available for work on the rig 24 hours per day. The IRS typically will look to the employer's reasons for providing the benefits and to what is standard in this business and how other businesses treat similarly situated employees.

If the lodging is excludable, meals generally are excludable as well. Clearly, the meals provided to Glenn while he is on the oil rig in the North Sea will be considered on the business premises and clearly, they are furnished for the convenience of the employer. There does not appear to be any feasible alternative for the employees on the oil rig because it is not feasible for them to leave the rig for lunch and return afterward. Section 1.119–1(a)(2)(C) provides that meals will be regarded as furnished for a substantial noncompensatory business reason when they are furnished during the employee's working hours because "there are insufficient eating facilities in the vicinity of the employer's premises." The only problem here is whether the breakfasts fit into that category. If Glenn is required to be on the rig prior to breakfast or very early in the morning, this requirement may be met. If so, then the meals on the oil rig appear to be furnished for a substantial noncompensatory business reason, and the value of these meals (breakfasts and lunches) should be excluded from Glenn's gross income.

But the dinners are more complicated. They are not furnished on the business premises and they are reimbursements, as opposed to meals in-kind. In *Kowalski*, the Supreme Court held that meal allowances for state highway patrolmen were not excludable under § 119. However, the patrolmen were given cash allowances at the end of each month, regardless of whether they had eaten the meals or not. Thus, there was a compensation flavor to the payments. The Court in *Kowalski* seemed to imply, though, that meal allowances could be excludable if they met the requirements of § 119. The Ninth Circuit has distinguished *Kowalski* in *Sibla*, in which firemen who made mandatory payments into a firehouse mess fund were able to obtain a § 119 exclusion. Unfortunately, in *Kowalski*, the Supreme Court did not address the issue of whether the meals the patrolmen ate in restaurants adjacent to the state highways were considered on the business premises, so we do not know how strictly the courts will define that term. It appears, though, that restaurants close to the dock will not meet the business premises test.

Another problem for Glenn is whether these dinners occur during working hours. If they do not, the convenience of the employer test is not met unless Glenn is required to be on 24-hour call while he is in Aberdeen. If so, then this requirement may be met. If the employer has placed any restrictions on where Glenn may eat his meals (because the employer requires him to be available if he should receive an emergency call), this would help as well. If, however, Glenn is able to eat dinner wherever he chooses and is reimbursed by the employer, this looks like bonus compensation rather than forced consumption for the convenience of the employer.

If any of the benefits are not excluded under § 119, they may be excluded under § 132(a)(3) if they are considered working condition fringe benefits.

5. TOOLS FOR SELF-ASSESSMENT

[1] In a real life situation (and on some final examinations), an employer who provides meals and lodging to its employees is also likely to provide some incidental benefits as well. As you have seen in the previous problem, § 132 operates differently than § 119, so these benefits must be clearly separated and dealt with independently of one another.

[2] The requirements for the exclusion of lodging are the same as those for the exclusion of meals, with an additional requirement: it must meet the condition of the employment test under § 119(b)(2). There does not appear to be much difference between the convenience of the employer test and the

condition of employment test. What is clear is that a mere term in the employment contract that housing and/or meals are being furnished for the convenience of the employer and that the employee is required to accept the lodging as a condition of employment will not control. While the IRS generally does not question contract terms, it can and does if there is a substance-over-form argument to be made. The determination of whether a benefit is offered for the convenience of the employer is a facts-and-circumstances test that becomes more difficult where the employer is a closely held company, and the employee is also a shareholder/owner. In general, the IRS will look to whether the policies of the employer are reasonably related to the legitimate needs of the business. If there is a substantial noncompensatory business reason for providing meals and/or lodging to the employee, this will control regardless of the fact that there might be a compensatory reason as well. Reg. § 1.119–1(a)(2)(i) and 1.119–1(b). The IRS assured employers in Announcement 99–77 that it would "not attempt to substitute its judgment for the business decisions of an employer as to what specific business policies and practices are best suited to addressing the employer's concerns." But it went on to add that it would examine all facts and circumstances behind the provision of the benefit, including the employer's past practices.

[3] Note that the term "business premises" may have a different meaning under § 119 than under § 162. So even though the apartment may not be considered on the business premises for purposes of the exclusion under § 119, the employer, Big Oil, may be able to deduct the rentals on the apartment as a business expense, or it may be able to take depreciation deductions if it owns the apartment.

[4] Note that ordinarily § 162 does not apply to this problem because the question is whether the value of any or all of these benefits is includable in Glenn's *gross income*. However, if § 119 does not exclude the value of the benefits, that value may be excluded under § 132(a)(3) as a working condition fringe benefit. Section 132(a)(3) applies only if the benefit otherwise is deductible under § 162. In this case, the value of any includable benefit probably would be deductible for Glenn because he is temporarily away from home for a business reason. Thus Glenn probably could exclude under § 132(a)(3) the value of any benefit not excluded under § 119. Since § 162 has not yet been discussed, however, the sample answer does not discuss this aspect of the problem. Note also that any reimbursement for an otherwise deductible expense under § 162 will be a de facto exclusion because § 62(a)(2)(A) provides a favorable above the line deduction that will directly offset the includable reimbursement. A thorough answer should take this into consideration if § 162 has been discussed.

6. VARIATIONS ON THE THEME

Assume that Big Oil charged all employees a set monthly fee for the meals served on the rig, regardless of whether the employee ate all the meals or not. This monthly fee, however, was considerably less than the cost of the meals. What are the tax consequences to Glenn with respect to those meals?

LIFE INSURANCE

8

1. OPENING REMARKS

There are two general types of life insurance policies: term and whole life. Term insurance is a policy for a specific term, usually one year, on the life of the insured. This also is referred to as "pure insurance," because it is solely an insurance policy on the life of the insured. It represents a bet by the insurance company that the insured will live longer than the term. If so, the premium payments represent profits for the company, and the beneficiaries get nothing. Whole life is a policy insuring the entire life of the insured, and it has a savings feature, which is reflected in the policy's cash surrender value. The earnings attributable to the savings feature accumulate tax free unless the insured "cashes in" the policy by surrendering it and receiving the proceeds. If the insured does not cash in the policy, the benefits payable at the death of the insured are excluded from the beneficiary's gross income under § 101. Section 101 provides an exclusion only for amounts paid under a life insurance contract by reason of the death of the insured. This is consistent with § 102, which excludes amounts received as inheritances, devises, or bequests because by its nature, life insurance proceeds also are received because of death. Also, like § 102, § 101 applies regardless of who the beneficiary is. Thus, the beneficiary does not have to be a family member, employee, or related to the insured in any way.

Section 101 excludes only the amount of the proceeds payable by reason of the death of the insured. Any amount of interest or other earnings or additional amounts payable after the death of the insured will be taxable to the beneficiary. By broad definition, whenever insurance proceeds are received by a beneficiary after the death of the insured, the payment is made by reason of the death of the insured. The IRS looks beyond this broad definition, however, in determining the tax treatment of the proceeds. For instance, if the insured pledged the policy as security for a debt, the receipt of the proceeds by the creditor is not considered a receipt by reason of the death of the insured. By the same logic, if the insured sells the policy to a third party, the receipt of the proceeds is not considered paid by reason of the death of the insured.

Some individuals facing a life threatening illness in which their expenses have not been adequately covered by medical insurance have turned to the savings component of their life insurance policies. There are companies, called viatical settlement providers, that buy such policies, profiting from them after the death of the insured. Section 101(g) provides that the amount received by the terminally ill insured (defined under § 101(g)(4)(A) as an individual who has been certified by a physician as having an illness that is reasonably expected to result in death within 24 months or less from the date of certification) is treated as an accelerated death benefit. Thus, it is excludable under § 101(a) because it is treated as an amount paid by reason of the death of the insured. See § 101(g)(1). The viatical settlement provider is treated as any other third-party purchaser of a life insurance policy. Thus, when the insured dies, and the company collects under the policy, the amount that it receives will be offset by its basis (i.e., the amount that it paid for the policy), and the remainder will be a realized gain that will not be excludable under § 101(a).

2. HYPOTHETICAL

Hope Hamrick's father died last year at the age of 92. He had a life insurance policy for $150,000, payable to Hope. The insurance company has offered Hope the choice of several forms of payments. She can elect to receive the entire $150,000 in a lump sum immediately, or she can leave the money with the company, and it will pay her $4500 per year for five years. At the end of five years, the company will pay her $150,000 in a lump sum. A third option is to receive payments of $12,000 per year for 15 years. Under options two and three, if Hope should die before receiving the lump sum payment, that amount would be payable to her beneficiaries or to her estate. A fourth option is to receive payments of $7500 per year for the remainder of her life. She currently has a 25-year life expectancy under the insurance mortality tables. If she dies prior to recovering the entire principal amount, she will forfeit the remainder of the principal. Discuss the tax consequences to Hope of each of these options.

3. LIST OF READINGS

Internal Revenue Code of 1986: §§ 61(a)(4); 101
Regulations: § 1.101–3; 1.101–4

4. SAMPLE ESSAY

Section 101 provides an exclusion for amounts received, whether in a single sum or otherwise, under a life insurance contract if such amounts are paid by reason of the death of the insured. In this case, Hope is the sole beneficiary of her father's life insurance policy, and she will receive the proceeds because of his death. Thus, regardless of which option she chooses, she will exclude the $150,000 face amount of the policy under § 101(a).

The first option is the easiest in terms of the tax consequences. If Hope elects to receive the entire $150,000 in a lump sum, she will not have to include any of this amount in income because § 101(a) excludes the entire amount.

The second option is to leave the principal amount with the company and to receive a payout of $4500 per year for five years and then to receive the entire principal amount at the end of that time. Section 101(c) will include each of the $4500 payments in income as they are received. Since the entire principal amount will be payable to Hope at the end of the five-year period, the interim payments are considered interest under § 61(a)(4).

The third option is to receive $12,000 per year for 15 years. At the end of that period, Hope will receive nothing further under the policy. Section 101(d) prorates the amount of the exclusion over the period in which payments are made. Since Hope's payments will extend over 15 years, her excludable amount will be $10,000 per year. She will receive $12,000 per year, so she will have to include $2000 of that amount in her gross income each year. Over the 15-year period, Hope will receive total payments of $180,000. She will include $30,000 of this amount in gross income ($2000 per year for 15 years). Thus, her total tax-free recovery will be $150,000, the amount of the principal that was excluded from income under § 101(a).

The fourth option is to receive an annuity of $7,500 for the remainder of her life. An annuity is a series of payments spread out over a period of time, usually exceeding a year. Section 101(d) again applies to prorate the exclusion ratably over the term of the payout. Since Hope has a 25-year life expectancy, her excludable amount ($150,000) will be prorated over her life expectancy of 25 years. Thus, $6000 of the $7500 that she receives each year under this option will be excludable under § 101(a). If Hope lives beyond her life expectancy, she will continue to exclude $6000 of the $7500 payment, even though she will have recovered all of her excludable amount. See Reg. § 1.101–4(c). The trade-off is that if Hope dies before the end of the 25-year period, neither she nor her estate will be able to claim a deduction for the unrecovered amount of the exclusion.

If we examine each of the first three options under a broad view, Hope will be able to exclude the entire $150,000 amount under § 101(a), regardless of the option she chooses. The difference among the options is in the ultimate amount that she receives, which is, in turn, a difference of timing. The longer she leaves the principal with the company, the more she stands to receive in the long run. The fourth option is a little different than the others because the risk for Hope is much greater with this option. If she elects this option, she will be gambling that she will outlive her life expectancy of 25 years. If she does, then this is a good option for her because she will receive more money than under any of the other options, and her exclusion continues after she has recovered her $150,000 principal amount. Thus, from a tax perspective, this is the best option. If, however, she does not outlive her life expectancy, this obviously would be the worst choice for her because she not only will forfeit the remainder of the principal, but she (or her estate) also will have no further tax advantage from the unrecovered amount. Thus, Hope will be taking both a financial risk and a tax risk if she chooses this option.

5. TOOLS FOR SELF-ASSESSMENT

[1] In addressing a question involving life insurance proceeds, the first issue is whether the proceeds were payable by reason of the death of the insured. If not, then § 101(a) does not apply. If so, then the second issue is to determine what amount of proceeds are excludable under § 101(a), and how are those proceeds to be paid. As you can see from this problem, the method of payment will make a difference both in terms of the ultimate amount that the beneficiary receives and in terms of the tax consequences during each year of the payout.

[2] The taxation of annuities generally is determined under § 72 of the Code. Where the annuity is funded with life insurance proceeds payable by reason of the death of the insured, however, § 72 defers to the more specific provision of § 101. In general, the two provisions operate much the same way, with the "investment in the contract" (the excludable amount) prorated over the payout term. Can you discern any differences between these two sections?

[3] Subsections (c) and (d) of § 101 both anticipate that amounts will be held by the insurer, but they work in slightly different ways. Section 101(c) considers

the entire payment interest until the principal amount is paid. Section 101(c) applies to the second option in the hypothetical, because it covers the situation in which the insurer holds amounts "without a substantial diminution of principal" during the period in which the payments are made. See Reg. § 1.101–3(a). Section 101(d) applies to the third and fourth options because the payments that Hope is to receive will consist of both principal and interest.

[4] The trade-off for the continuation of the § 101(a) exclusion beyond her life expectancy is the forfeiture of the deduction for Hope's estate if she fails to outlive her life expectancy. Does this make sense?

6. VARIATIONS ON THE THEME

Would any part of your answer change if Hope's father had named her the beneficiary under his policy in repayment of a $100,000 loan that she had made to him 10 years ago?

DISCHARGE OF INDEBTEDNESS

9

1. OPENING REMARKS

A taxpayer does not realize income when she borrows money, regardless of how she spends the funds, because she assumes a corresponding obligation to repay the borrowed amount. If she ultimately does not repay the full amount that she borrowed, she will realize an economic benefit to the extent of the unpaid amount because of the freeing of assets that otherwise would have been used to pay the debt. (Note that there may be tax consequences to the lender as well if the borrower fails to repay the full borrowed amount, but at this point, we are focusing only on the borrower.)

Since nonrealization of income hinges on the obligation to repay, realization arises when the lender agrees to forgive all or a portion of the debt. There are several reasons why this may occur. First, the debtor may be in financial trouble and unable to repay the full amount. Second, if the loan is a mortgage on real property, the value of the underlying property may have declined below the amount of the outstanding mortgage, a phenomenon that is becoming all too common. In that case, if the lender agrees the debtor simply may transfer the property back to the lender in satisfaction of the debt. Third, the borrower and the lender may reach an agreement to reduce the amount of the debt in return for an increase in the interest rate or the borrower's promise to pay off the debt early.

The income inclusion attributable to a discharge of indebtedness often is referred to as *Kirby* income (from the case of *U.S. v. Kirby Lumber Co.*, 284 U.S. 1 (1931)) or C.O.D. income (cancellation of debt) or discharge of indebtedness income. Section § 61(a)(12) specifically includes discharge of indebtedness income. The inclusion applies to a forgiveness of a legally enforceable obligation. An obligation that is not legally enforceable does not give rise to *Kirby* income and is not included under § 61(a)(12). See *Zarin v. Commissioner,* 916 F.2d 110 (3rd Cir. 1990).

Because forgiveness of indebtedness often occurs in a business context in which the debtor/business owner is experiencing financial problems, the additional tax liability attributable to the forgiveness may imperil the debtor's ability to repay the creditor. Section 108 alleviates the harshness of the income inclusion by providing amnesty for struggling taxpayers. Particularly in our current economic climate, the tax laws should not act as an impediment to the economic recovery of a struggling individual (or business).

Section § 108 provides protection against the harshness of income recognition in several situations, not solely where the taxpayer is struggling financially, but it is not a freebie if the taxpayer feasibly can "pay" for the benefit. Thus, § 108 generally does not provide a true exclusion (although in some cases it may). Instead, the "cost" of the immediate exclusion of the income realized is the swap of a deferred tax benefit, such as a reduction of basis or the reduction of another tax attribute, such as a net operating loss.

2. HYPOTHETICAL

Ian Iverson owns a limousine service. He has three limousines, two of which he purchased three years ago for $100,000 each and which now are worth $60,000 each. Ian borrowed the money from a bank to buy these limos, paying $20,000 down and financing the remainder of the purchase prices, $180,000 total, through a recourse loan on which he has personal liability. Last year, Ian purchased the third limousine at a cost of $110,000. He paid $10,000 cash down, and this time he financed the remainder of the purchase price through the dealer. This limousine has a current value of $90,000. Nothing has been paid on the principal amount of the indebtedness of any of these three loans.

Ian also owns three office buildings, one of which he uses as his current office. This building (Building # 1) was purchased five years ago for $260,000. Ian paid $15,000 down and financed the remainder through a recourse mortgage. This building has a current value of $215,000, and the outstanding principal amount of the mortgage is $230,000. The second office building (Building # 2) is a smaller building that he rents to a third party. Recently, however, his tenant has given Ian notice that she will be leaving soon. This building was purchased three years ago for $200,000, and Ian financed the entire price through a nonrecourse mortgage on which he does not have personal liability. This building currently is worth $180,000, and the outstanding principal amount of the mortgage remains at $200,000. Building # 3 was purchased 10 years ago for $160,000. This building currently has a value of $210,000, and the outstanding amount of the recourse mortgage is $125,000. This office recently was rented under a six-month lease.

After depreciation deductions on the limos and buildings, Ian's basis in each of the assets is as follows:

Limos # 1 and # 2—$40,000 each
Limo # 3—$80,000
Building # 1—$210,000
Building # 2—$185,000
Building # 3—$90,000

Recently, Ian's business suffered a downturn, and he is having difficulty meeting his financial obligations. He has approached all of the lenders asking for help because without it, he soon would be forced to file for bankruptcy. The limo dealer agrees to reduce Ian's indebtedness (on Limo # 3) by $5000. The banks that are holding the notes on the other two limos both have refused to help. The recourse lender holding the mortgage on Building # 1 has agreed to reduce Ian's indebtedness by $25,000. The bank holding the nonrecourse mortgage on building # 2 has offered to forgive the entire indebtedness if Ian will execute a quit claim deed and surrender the property to the bank. After much thought, Ian decides to do this. The lender holding the recourse mortgage on Building # 3 refuses to reduce the indebtedness.

Ian has a $5000 net operating loss but no other tax attributes (no capital loss carryovers, general business credit carryovers, minimum tax credit, passive activity loss, or foreign tax credit carryovers). Discuss the tax consequences of these transactions to Ian. Ignore issues of depreciation recapture.

3. LIST OF READINGS

Internal Revenue Code of 1986: §§ 61(a)(12);108; 1017

Regulations: § 1.1001–2(a)

Cases: Crane v. Commissioner, 331 U.S. 1 (1947); United States v. Kirby Lumber Co., 284 U.S. 1 (1931); Commissioner v. Tufts, 461 U.S. 300 (1983); Estate of Delman v. Commissioner, 73 T.C. 15 (1979); Yarbro v. Commissioner, 737 F.2d 479 (5th Cir. 1984).

4. SAMPLE ESSAY

A reduction or forgiveness of indebtedness that gives rise to cancellation of indebtedness income under *Kirby Lumber Co.* will be included in ordinary income under § 61(a)(12), unless an exception applies to exclude it. Ian's total amount of debt reduction on the limos and the buildings is $50,000, but not all of it constitutes *Kirby* income. The $5000 forgiveness on Limo # 3 by the limo dealer results in a realization of $5000 of *Kirby* income. The forgiveness of the $25,000 of recourse mortgage amount on Building # 1 also results in a realization of $25,000 of *Kirby* income.

The indebtedness discharge on building # 2, however, is different from the other discharges. For one, this indebtedness is nonrecourse, so Ian does not have personal liability under this loan. For another, it involves the property being deeded back to the lender. If property subject to a nonrecourse mortgage is deeded to the lender in lieu of foreclosure, no discharge of indebtedness income results, even if the debt exceeds the value of the property at the time of the transfer. See *Yarbro*. Instead, the transfer is treated as a sale of the property. The U.S. Supreme Court held in *Commissioner v. Tufts* that the full amount of the nonrecourse indebtedness is included in the amount realized, even if the property is worth less than the indebtedness at the time of the discharge. Thus, Ian realizes a gain of $15,000 on the transfer of the property back to the lender ($200,000 outstanding nonrecourse indebtedness less his basis of $185,000) under *Tufts* and *Estate of* Delman. *See* § 1.1001–2(a). Since it is not considered a discharge of indebtedness, this amount will not be included under § 61(a)(12), and it will not be eligible for § 108 treatment. Instead it will be considered a gain realized under § 1001(a). See J. O'Connor's concurrence in *Tufts*.

Section 108(a)(1)(B) provides an exception to income inclusion in the case of a taxpayer who is insolvent but has not filed bankruptcy. The amount of the exclusion is limited, however, to the amount of the insolvency. Insolvency is determined under § 108(d)(3) and requires the taxpayer's liabilities (immediately before the discharge) to exceed the fair market value of any assets. In this case, Ian's total indebtedness amounts to $835,000, immediately before the discharge, while the total value of his assets is $815,000. Thus, he is insolvent to the extent of $20,000, and under § 108(a)(2)(B) he may exclude $20,000 of his $30,000 of *Kirby* income that he realizes on the forgiveness. The remaining $10,000 will be included under § 61(a)(12), unless there is an exclusionary provision that applies. Note that under § 108(a)(2)(B), the insolvency exception takes precedence over the qualified real property business (QRPB) indebtedness exception under § 108(a)(1)(D), provided Ian is not a corporate taxpayer.

Next, Ian must determine whether he will incur a tax cost for this exclusion. Section 108(b) requires a taxpayer who receives an exclusion under § 108(a)(1)(A), (a)(1)(B) or (a)(1)(C) to reduce any tax attributes in the order provided under subsection (b). Ian has net operating losses of $5000 and no other tax attributes under § 108(b), except the bases in his assets. Ian has a choice at this point. He may reduce his net operating loss to zero under § 108(b) and then reduce the bases in his assets in accordance with § 1017(b), or he may elect to keep his net operating loss and reduce the bases of his depreciable assets under § 108(b)(5) by the entire $20,000 that was excluded under § 108(a).

Section 1017 provides the mechanism for making the basis adjustment. If Ian elects to reduce his net operating loss to zero and then reduce the basis in his remaining assets (in other words, if he does not make a § 108(b)(5) election), the basis reduction for an amount excluded by reason of his insolvency under § 108(a)(1)(B) is limited to an amount that does not exceed the aggregate of the bases of the property of the taxpayer immediately after the discharge over the aggregate of the liabilities immediately after the discharge. See § 1017 (b)(2). In this case, the aggregate amount of liabilities ($615,000) exceeds the aggregate bases of the property ($460,000) immediately after the discharge. Thus, no basis adjustment is required under § 1017 if Ian does not make a § 108(b)(5) election. If he does make such an election, the § 1017 (b)(2) limitation does not apply, and the basis of his depreciable property will have to be reduced, regardless of the liabilities.

As a practical matter, Ian will fare better by reducing his net operating loss and not making a § 108(b)(5) election. That would mean that his "cost" of the $20,000 exclusion would be the reduction of his $5000 net operating loss. No other reduction of tax attributes would be required. If he makes the §108(b)(5) election, he can keep his net operating losses, but he must reduce the bases of his depreciable assets by $20,000. Thus, the total tax "cost" of the § 108(b)(5) election is the $20,000 reduction in the bases of his properties, whereas the "cost" of not making such an election is the loss of his $5000 net operating loss.

The remaining $10,000 of *Kirby* income would normally be included in income under § 61(a)(12). However, the $25,000 mortgage reduction represents QRPB indebtedness under § 108(a)(1)(D), provided Ian elects to have the indebtedness treated as such under § 108(c)(3). Section 108(c)(3) defines QRPB indebtedness as acquisition indebtedness, incurred after January 1, 1993, secured by real property used in a trade or business. The provision applies only if the taxpayer elects to have the indebtedness treated as QRPB indebtedness, and it cannot include qualified farm indebtedness.

If Ian had not been insolvent, he would have been able to make an election to exclude this entire amount of mortgage reduction as income from QRPB indebtedness under § 108(a)(1)(D). See also § 108(c)(3). However, he is insolvent, so to that extent, the insolvency exception takes precedence over the QRPB indebtedness exception but only to the extent of the insolvency. See § 108(a)(2)(B). Since the first $20,000 of the *Kirby* income was excluded under the insolvency exception, and the entire amount of the insolvency offset the $20,000 of *Kirby* income, §108(a)(1)(D) should be available for the remaining $10,000, provided that Ian elects to use this provision.

There are two limitations to § 108(a)(1)(D), however. The first is that the amount of the QRPB indebtedness eligible for exclusion cannot exceed the excess of the principal amount of the indebtedness (immediately before the discharge) over the fair market value of the real property securing the indebtedness, reduced by the outstanding principal amount of any other QRPB indebtedness secured by that property. See § 108(c)(2)(A). The second limitation is that the exclusion cannot exceed the aggregate adjusted bases of the depreciable real property held by the taxpayer immediately after the discharge, determined after the § 108(b) basis adjustment. See § 108(c)(2)(B).

The first limitation applies to exclude an amount of refinanced mortgage or other indebtedness incurred because of the decline in the value of the property. In Ian's case, the principal amount of the outstanding indebtedness before the discharge was $230,000, while the fair market value of the property was $215,000. This is sufficient to cover the remaining $10,000 of *Kirby* income after the application of § 108(a)(1)(B). The second limitation is applied after the basis reduction attributable to the insolvency exclusion. If no § 108(b)(5) election is made, that reduction is zero.

The § 108(a)(1)(D) exclusion also requires a basis adjustment under § 1017(b)(3)(F) and does not have a comparable limitation to that of § 1017(b)(2). Thus, the basis in Building # 1 will have to be reduced by $10,000 if Ian makes the § 108(c)(3) election.

5. TOOLS FOR SELF-ASSESSMENT

[1] It is important to distinguish the relationships among *Kirby*, § 61(a)(12) and § 108. In a forgiveness of indebtedness problem, the first step generally is to determine whether the indebtedness is genuine and legally enforceable. If it is not, *Kirby* does not apply. If it is, the next step is to determine whether *Kirby* applies and if so, what amount of income is realized. If there is no realization, neither § 108 nor § 61(a)(12) applies. If there is *Kirby* income realized, the next step is to determine whether any or all of that income is recognized. If § 108 does not apply and no other exclusionary provision (such as § 102) applies, then the income is included under § 61(a)(12). If § 108 does apply, the final step is to determine the cost of the exclusion to the taxpayer. Section 108(b) directs the reduction of tax attributes.

[2] In the hypothetical above, all of the indebtedness appears to be legally enforceable, including the nonrecourse indebtedness. The next step is to determine the income realized in the various transactions. This is a relatively simple matter because the amount of the forgiveness generally triggers a realization of income under *Kirby Lumber Co.* and, of course, under *Glenshaw Glass*. Students are inclined to bypass this step and to jump straight into § 108. Resist this temptation because if there is no realization of income under *Kirby*, there is no need to discuss § 108. *Kirby* addresses the realization of discharge of indebtedness income, while § 108 addresses the recognition of that income. If § 108 applies, there is no recognition under § 61(a)(12) to that extent. If there is *Kirby* income realized that is not excluded under § 108 or under any other provision (such as a gift under § 102), then the income is included under § 61(a)(12).

[3] The next step is to determine whether any or all of the amount realized will be recognized. Section 61(a)(12) specifically recognizes forgiveness of indebtedness income, but § 108 overrides § 61(a)(12). Section 108 is a complex provision, probably because it is taxpayer friendly. After all, the

taxpayer already has received a significant benefit from the indebtedness (i.e., no initial realization, the proceeds increase the basis of the asset he purchased, and the taxpayer is entitled to depreciation deductions if the property is depreciable). It is best to read carefully through § 108 first to familiarize yourself with its various permutations. This hypothetical presents several issues, and you should identify and separate these issues because § 108 may treat them differently.

[4] Normally, when a creditor who also is the seller of property agrees to forgive a portion of the indebtedness, the debtor does not recognize income because the debt reduction is treated as an adjustment in the sales price of the property. Thus, the basis in the property is reduced to reflect the adjustment. Section 108(e)(5) is a recognition of this general principal. However, when the debt reduction occurs because the taxpayer is insolvent (within the definition of § 108(d)(3)), the general principal does not apply. See § 108(e)(5)(B). It is important also to realize that the insolvency exception overrides the QBRP exception to the extent of the taxpayer's insolvency. See § 108(a)(2)(B).

[5] The insolvency definition under § 108 seems a bit strange at first blush. The normal inclination is to assume that a taxpayer is either insolvent or not. The definition under § 108(d)(3) is akin to being a "little pregnant." But the purpose of § 108 is to provide relief to taxpayers from income inclusion under certain circumstances. The relief, however, is limited in the case of insolvency outside of bankruptcy.

[6] Section 108 is tied to § 61(a)(12). This means that the forgiveness of the indebtedness must generate ordinary income for § 108 to apply. The nonrecourse indebtedness means that the taxpayer does not have personal liability on the mortgage. While Mrs. Crane had a tax liability when she sold her apartment building subject to a nonrecourse mortgage, careful consideration of the *Crane* case shows that her tax liability was attributable to the depreciation deductions she had taken previously.

[7] Note that another difference between making a § 108(b)(5) election and not making the election is in the timing of the adjustment. While making the § 108(b)(5) election will mean that Ian ultimately will pay four times more for the cost of his exclusion, the trade-off is that the net operating loss will produce a greater tax benefit to Ian in the near future. He may need this loss now and not really care about the $15,000 difference in the basis adjustment much later on. In fact, he may never realize much of a benefit from his basis anyway if his finances do not improve, and if he does obtain a benefit from his basis, he is not likely to see this benefit until much later.

6. VARIATIONS ON THE THEME

How, if at all, would your answer differ if the nonrecourse mortgage on Building # 2 had been a recourse mortgage?

7. OPTIONAL READINGS

Geier, "*Tufts* and the Evolution of Debt-Discharge Theory," 1 Fla. Tax Rev. 115 (1992).

ASSIGNMENT OF INCOME

10

1. OPENING REMARKS

While the tax rates have varied considerably over the years, the basic principal underlying the rates has remained relatively constant: the rates increase as taxable income increases. This is known as "progressivity." Occasionally, taxpayers attempt to exploit this principal by shifting income to family members in lower tax brackets. While it is possible to shift income to family members or others in lower tax brackets and to completely avoid any further tax consequences, if the transferor retains too much control over the property, the transferor will suffer the tax consequences. This is referred to generally as an anticipatory assignment of income, and several provisions in the Internal Revenue Code prevent such assignments by taxing the transferor instead of the transferee on the income. Outside of these specific provisions, the general judicial doctrine of anticipatory assignment of income is designed to tax income to the proper party. This doctrine can be divided into two parts: assignment of income and assignment of property. It is important to differentiate between the two parts because the rules are slightly different, although the ultimate outcome may be the same: the transferor assumes the tax liability, and the property or income is considered a tax-free gift to the transferee.

The general assignment of income rule is that income should be taxed to the taxpayer who earned it. Thus, if a taxpayer assigns earned income to a third party, the taxpayer generally will be taxed on this income, and it will be considered a gift to the third party. See *Lucas v. Earl*, 281 U.S. 111 (1930). This means that the taxpayer may be responsible for both an income tax and a gift tax, depending on the size of the income transferred.

An assignment of property generally is more complicated because the property may have an income component, such as stocks and dividends. For a successful assignment so that the transferor will avoid being taxed on the income from the property, the transferor will have to transfer the property outright, with no "strings" attached. If this occurs, the transferee generally will be taxed on any income generated by the property after the transfer.

Note that a successful assignment means initially that the transferor may be liable for gift taxes but not for subsequent income taxes, while an unsuccessful assignment means that the transferor may be liable for both, depending on the size of the transfer. The reason is that an assignment of property or income may represent a completed transfer under state law, which determines whether title to property has passed and if so, would trigger the gift tax liability. However, the same transfer may not be considered a completed transfer for purposes of federal income tax. Thus, if the assignment is not successful, the property or income is treated as vesting, even for a brief moment, in the party who owned the property or earned the income or was entitled to it, and this triggers the income tax liability. Then that person is treated as having transferred the property to the recipient, triggering the gift tax liability.

2. HYPOTHETICAL

Janie Johnson is a middle-aged widow with three children ages 27, 24, and 22. Andy, who is 27, was married two years ago, and he and his wife recently had a baby. Barbara, age 24, has recently received her masters in nursing and is beginning her first real job. Charlie, age 22, has recently graduated from college and is looking for work.

Janie decided that since each of her children had some recent event to celebrate, she would transfer property to each of them. She purchased 200 shares of stock in the XYZ Corporation and transferred this to Andy to be used for the benefit of his baby as he saw fit. Some years ago, Janie had purchased 1500 shares of stock in a national bank. This stock has been paying good dividends during the period that Janie has owned it. She assigned these dividends to Barbara for a period of three years. Janie also had a small piece of real property that she had owned for about 10 years. Recently, someone contacted her about buying this property. Janie had preliminary discussions with the buyer, and she determined that the buyer was serious about purchasing the property. While there had been some discussion about the purchase price, a final figure had not been agreed upon. Janie deeded the property to Charlie, and the sale went through a short time later. Charlie made a handsome profit on the sale.

Discuss fully the general tax implications of each of these transfers. Are there any further facts you will need to know?

3. LIST OF READINGS

Internal Revenue Code: §§ 102; 1001; 1015; 1222

Cases: Blair v. Commissioner, 300 U.S. 5 ((1937); Helvering v. Horst, 311 U.S. 112 (1940); Smith's Estate v. Commissioner, 292 F.2d 478 (3d Cir. 1961); Estate of Stranahan v. Commissioner, 472 F.2d 867 (6th Cir. 1973); Ferguson v. Commissioner, 108 T.C. 244 (1997), *aff'd,* 174 F.3d 997 (9th Cir. 1999); Susie Salvatore, 29 T.C.M. 89 (1970).

Article: Kayle, *The Taxpayer's Intentional Attempt to Accelerate Taxable Income,* 46 Tax. L. 89 (1992).

4. SAMPLE ESSAY

Each of these transfers presents separate assignment of income issues. The transfer of the bank stock dividends to Barbara presents the easiest case because this clearly is an anticipatory assignment of income. It is a gratuitous transfer of the dividends, and Janie has retained the underlying stock. See *Estate of Stranahan v. Commissioner.* Thus, it is Janie who has the legal right to the dividends, even if she directs the company to pay those dividends directly to Barbara. Since Janie retains the "tree" (the income producing property), the "fruit" (the income from the property) will be taxed to her as the dividends are paid to Barbara. See *Blair v. Commissioner*. The dividends then will be considered a gift from Janie to Barbara. Barbara will receive the dividends tax-free as a gift under § 102. See *Helvering v. Horst*. If the dividends exceed the annual per donee exclusion ($13,000 for taxable years beginning in 2009), Janie will owe a gift tax on the dividends as they are paid to Barbara. Thus, depending upon the amount of the dividends, Janie may owe both a gift tax and an income tax on these dividends as they are paid to Barbara.

The transfer of the XYZ stock to Andy involves two components: the stock and the dividends on the stock. In this transfer, Janie's entire interest in those shares has been transferred to Andy, so here she transfers the tree as well as the fruit. If the value of the stock exceeds the annual per donee exclusion, Janie will have to pay a gift tax on the transfer of the stock to Andy. While Andy realizes an economic benefit to the extent of the value of the stock, he will not recognize that benefit because the value of the stock will be excluded from his gross income as a gift under § 102. He will take Janie's basis as a carryover basis under § 1015, adjusted for any gift tax liability that Janie may incur. (But note the special rule under § 1015(a) for purposes of determining a loss on property in which the fair market value at the time of the transfer is less than the donor's adjusted basis.) Andy will realize a gain or loss under the principles of § 1001 when he subsequently sells the stock.

The treatment of the dividends is a bit more complex. Since Janie gives Andy the tree (the stock), she avoids further tax liability on the fruit (the dividend income from the stock) unless the tree has "ripe fruit" on it at the time of the transfer. This will occur if a dividend is payable to Janie at the time of the transfer of the stock to Andy. When a corporation declares and pays a dividend to its shareholders, there are several dates that may be relevant. Generally, a company will declare a dividend on the "declaration date." This dividend will be payable to shareholders of record on a certain date, called the "record date," which may be same date as the declaration date. The date on which the dividend is paid is the "payment date." If a dividend recently was paid to Janie prior to the transfer, she is taxed on that dividend, and there is no further problem. If the stock is transferred after the declaration date and before the record date (assuming these are two separate dates), Andy will be taxed on the dividend because he will be the shareholder of record on the record date, and Janie will have no right to receive that dividend. If the stock is transferred after the record date and before the payment date, Janie is taxed even if Andy receives the dividend because she is the shareholder of record on the record date and is legally entitled to receive the dividend. Thus, she will be treated as having received the dividend and then having transferred it as a gift to Andy. See *Smith's Estate v. Commissioner*.

The issue of ripe fruit arises only on the first dividend paid after the transfer of the stock to Andy. After the payment of the first dividend, Andy clearly will be taxed on any other dividends (*see* §102(b)(1)), and Janie will have no further tax consequence. If Janie is taxed on this dividend and it exceeds the amount of the annual per donee exclusion, she also will have a gift tax liability on the dividend.

The transfer of the real property to Charlie presents the most difficult question. Clearly, the underlying property (the "tree") has been transferred since Janie deeded the land outright to Charlie. The question again is whether there was income ("ripe fruit") inherent in the property when it was transferred. If so, the gain on the sale will be taxed to Janie and then will be considered a gift to Charlie. If not, then Charlie will be taxed on the gain and Janie's only tax consequence on the transfer will be a possible gift tax liability if the value of the property exceeds the amount of the annual per donee exclusion ($13,000).

The important aspect of this case is the element of control. If the details of the sale had been set so that Charlie would have no say in the terms and nothing to do but to sit back and transfer the property to the buyer, then this would be considered an anticipatory assignment of income, and Janie would be taxed on the gain while Charlie would receive the proceeds tax free as a gift from Janie. According to *Ferguson*, the "ultimate question is whether the transferor, considering the reality and substance of all the circumstances, had a fixed right to income in the property at the time of transfer." If, though, Charlie actively negotiated the terms of the sale and had the final say in whether or not the sale proceeded, then he will be considered the owner of the gain from the sale, and he will be taxed on it.

In *Ferguson*, the Tax Court stated:

> A transfer of property that is a fixed right to income does not shift the incidence of taxation to the transferee. The reality and substance of a transfer of property govern the proper incidence of taxation and not formalities and remote hypothetical possibilities. In determining the reality and substance of a transfer, the ability, or the lack thereof, of the transferee to alter a prearranged course of disposition with respect to the transferred property provides cogent evidence of whether there existed a fixed right to income at the time of transfer. Although control over the disposition of the transferred property is significant to the assignment of income analysis, the ultimate question is whether the transferor, considering the reality and substance of all the circumstances, had a fixed right to income in the property at the time of transfer.

108 T.C. at 259.

In this case, it does not appear that the terms of the transaction had been set at the time that Janie transferred the property to Charlie. But more facts will be necessary to determine how far the negotiations had advanced prior to the transfer and whether Charlie had the ability to walk away from the sale with no consequences from the prospective buyer. If there had been only preliminary discussions between the buyer and Janie prior to the transfer, it is likely that the transfer of the property to Charlie will be considered a successful transfer of the property, and Charlie will be taxed on the gain realized when the property is sold. But that is not entirely clear. This is a substance-over form-question and if Janie purposely deferred any discussion of the final sales price to avoid the anticipatory assignment of income rules, but otherwise there was a general understanding of the price, the transfer will not be a successful assignment of the gain from the sale, and Janie will taxed on this gain. See *Susie Salvatore*.

If this is a successful assignment of property, Janie may have a gift tax liability on the value of the property at the time of the transfer but otherwise will have no further tax consequence. If it is not a successful assignment, she not only will have a gift tax liability, but she also will have an income tax liability on the gain from the sale of the property. This is a terrible result for Janie, who may not have anticipated being taxed twice.

Whether the assignment is successful or not, the transfer of the property to Charlie is considered a gift, so he will not be taxed on the receipt of the property. The question is: who is taxed on the gain on the sale of the property? If the assignment is successful, Charlie will be taxed on it. He would take a carryover basis from Janie under § 1015, adjusted for any gift tax paid on the transfer. This basis would offset the amount realized on the sale to produce the gain. Charlie also would take Janie's holding period in the property, so if she has held the property for longer than a year, Charlie also will be considered to have held the property longer than a year and thus the gain on the sale would be a long-term capital gain. See § 1222(3). If, on the other hand, the assignment is not successful, Charlie will not be taxed on the gain because Janie will assume the income tax liability on this gain, and it will be considered an excludable gift to Charlie under § 102.

5. TOOLS FOR SELF-ASSESSMENT

[1] Since the question is not specific as to which party's tax consequences are at issue, a full discussion of the tax consequences must involve a discussion of each of the parties: the transferor and the transferees. The tax consequences of the transferor generally must be discussed first because those consequences determine the transferee's tax consequences. A full discussion of the tax consequences entails not only a discussion of the gain or loss on the transfer and who is taxed on the gain but also the basis in the property to the transferee as well because that is a tax consequence to the transferee just as a realization is a tax consequence. Many students tend to forget this fact.

[2] While the problem can be answered in the order in which the transfers are presented, it is easier and logical to begin with the easiest issue, which is the transfer of the dividends to Barbara. Some students have difficulty comprehending the fact that a gift tax and an income tax may be payable on the same income. This is not impermissible double taxation because these taxes are different taxes from which liability arises for different reasons. The gift tax is a transfer tax that arises because of the successful transfer of property, determined under state law. As long as the value of the gift exceeds the annual per donee exclusion, a gift tax liability arises. This liability is separate and distinct from the income tax liability, and it arises because of the assignment of income principles discussed above.

[3] In a problem involving an assignment of income or property, the primary consideration is substance over form. This is particularly clear in the case of the transfer of the real property to Charlie. As the tax court stated in the case of *Susie Salvatore*, ". . . the form of a transaction cannot be permitted to prevail over its substance." In addition, the individual transfers must be analyzed from the perspective of whether they are income transfers or property transfers. If the assignment is not successful, and the transferor is taxed on the transfer, this is good news to the transferee because that party initially will not be taxed on the income or gain realized from the property. Instead, the transfer of the income or gain on the sale will be considered a gift. If, on the other hand, the transfer is successful so that the transferor avoids any further tax consequence other than a possible gift tax liability, the transferee will be taxed on any income or gain generated by the property or the sale of the property.

[4] If the anticipatory assignment of income doctrine applies, it taxes the income or gain to the donor instead of to the donee. It is like a rubber band around the property that snaps the income back to the donor for purposes of federal income taxation. In determining whether that rubber band applies, the assignment of income doctrine uses another metaphor, that of the "fruit"

and the "tree." If the tree (the income producing property: in this case, the stock) is transferred to a third party, any fruit (income, such as dividends) that it produces is taxed to the owner of the tree. If the transfer involves income, the general inquiry is who earned the income, or who had the right to receive the income? If the transfer involves property, the inquiry is whether the property contains any "ripe fruit."

6. VARIATIONS ON THE THEME

Assume instead that Janie was an author who contracted with her publisher to transfer the royalties from her yet-to-be-written book to her three children. Who would be responsible for the taxes on the royalties, and why?

11

EDUCATION INCENTIVES

1. OPENING REMARKS

The treatment of tax benefits to defray the costs of education invokes the proverbial good news and bad news. The good news is that there are a myriad of tax benefits available for all types of education, particularly for lower and middle income taxpayers. The bad news is that the operation of these benefits can be very confusing and complicated, and in most cases, the use of tax benefits for education requires some forethought and careful planning, particularly for the costs of higher education.

Tax benefits, in general, fall into three categories: exclusions, deductions, and credits. The same is true of education benefits, which also fall into these three categories. Some benefits are currently available to offset the present cost of education, while others work better over time to provide funds to pay the cost of higher education at a later date. These benefits have different requirements and apply to different costs; some provisions are more liberal, and others are more restrictive. Because of the relatively large number of tax benefits available to help defray the cost of education, Congress may decide in the future to limit or eliminate some of them. Note that some of these benefits may have state tax consequences, but this problem addresses only the federal tax aspects of benefits to defray the costs of education.

2. HYPOTHETICAL

Ken and Kathie Klein married three years ago, and they have a blended family. It was a second marriage for each of them, and both of their respective former spouses have died, leaving him with three children and her with two. Ken has twin boys from his previous marriage, currently age 18 and ready to attend college. He also has a younger child, a girl named Katy, who now is age 15 and in private school. Kathie has a boy and a girl, both younger than Ken's children. Kathie's children currently are ages 13 and 7, and they are both in public school.

Ken is an accountant with a local accounting firm, and Kathie is a teacher in the local public school. Their modified adjusted gross income is $160,000.

The twins each have academic scholarships of $20,000 to defray the cost of their college tuition. One of the twins also has a $5000 tennis scholarship. The Kleins have some savings that they plan to use for their children's education. Otherwise, they plan to get by on student loans and hopefully, scholarships.

The Kleins recently have learned that there may be significant federal tax benefits to help defray the costs of their children's education, and they seek your advice on whether any of these benefits might be feasible for them. They also want to know whether the twins' scholarships will have a tax consequence either to the twins or to them. What advice would you give them?

3. LIST OF READINGS

Internal Revenue Code of 1986: §§ 25A; 62; 102; 117; 135; 170(b); 221; 529; 530

Regulations: § 1.221–1(b)(4)

Rulings: Rev. Rul. 77–263, 1977–2 C.B. 47; Rev. Proc. 2009–21, 2009–16 I.R.B. 860

Legislative History: Conf. Rep. No. 105–220, 105th Cong., 1st Sess. 363 (1997)

Cases: review Commissioner v. Glenshaw Glass Co., 348 U.S. 426, 75 S.Ct. 473, 99 L.Ed. 483 (1955)

Articles: McCoskey, *Saving and Paying For A College Education, Part I: Vehicles for Saving for a Child's College Education,* 80 Taxes–The Tax Magazine 47 (Nov. 1, 2002); McCoskey, *Saving and Paying For A College Education, Part II: Paying For A Child's College Education,* 80 Taxes–The Tax Magazine 23 (Dec. 1, 2002)

4. SAMPLE ESSAY

There are significant benefits available to offset the various costs of education, but these benefits have different limitations and requirements. The twins present the most pressing issue because they are about to begin college. Section 117 excludes amounts received as qualified scholarships by individuals who are degree candidates at an educational organization that regularly carries on educational activities, has a regular faculty and enrolled student body, and a regular curriculum. See § 170(b)(1)(A)(ii).

A qualified scholarship is a scholarship that is used for a qualified purpose, defined under § 117(b)(2) as tuition and fees for enrollment or attendance and fees, books, supplies, and equipment required for courses of instruction. To the extent that the twins use their scholarships for a qualified purpose, the scholarship is tax free to them. Note that room and board is not included in this definition of qualified expenditures, so if the twins use any of their scholarship for room and board, they will be taxed on that amount. If any of their scholarship or fellowship is attributable to a grant-in-aid, they will have to include an amount attributable to the amount they otherwise would have earned by doing the same type of work. See § 117(c)(1).

The tennis scholarship raises the same issues as the academic scholarship (it must be used for a qualified purpose), but it also raises other issues, such as whether the scholarship is awarded as compensation for the athletic ability of the twin. The IRS declared in Rev. Rul. 77–263 that an athletic scholarship was excluded under § 117 where the school expects but does not require the student to participate in a particular sport, requires no particular activity in lieu of participation, and does not cancel the scholarship if the student does not participate. It is unclear whether these requirements are met in this problem. If they are, then the scholarship is excludable to the extent that it does not exceed the qualified expenditures (when combined with the academic scholarship). If they are not, then the amount of the scholarship is included in the twin's gross income either as compensation for services or as general gross income under the principals of *Glenshaw Glass*.

If the scholarships do not pay all of the college expenses for the twins, the Kleins will have to find the money to pay these expenses. While it is too late for the twins to take advantage of any tax benefits that require advance planning, there are some current benefits to lessen the costs of higher education. The twins can, of course, apply for student loans if they have not already done so. The interest on a student loan is deductible up to $2500 under § 221 (subject to phaseouts) through the 2012 taxable year (although Congress may decide to extend the provision). This deduction is a more advantageous above-the-line deduction, so it is available whether or not the individual itemizes. See § 62(a)(17). This deduction is phased out for married taxpayers having modified adjusted gross income (mAGI) between $120,000 and $150,000 (between $60,000 and $75,000 for single taxpayers). Since the Kleins' adjusted gross income exceeds the phaseout amount, they will not be able to obtain the benefit of the deduction, so it would be better for the twins to pay off their own loans after they graduate and then take the deduction themselves. The regulations permit someone other than the person who is legally obligated on the loan (such as a parent) to make payments on behalf of the obligor, and those payments will be treated as a gift to the obligor, who will be treated as having paid the interest. Thus, the obligor will be entitled to the deduction. See Reg. § 1.221–1(b)(4)(I). If the twins take the deduction, they cannot be claimed as dependents on their parents' return. If the twins are married by then, they must file a joint return in order to be eligible for the deduction.

Through 2011, an above-the-line deduction of up to $4000 is available for qualified tuition and related expenses (defined as tuition and fees required for the enrollment of the taxpayer, taxpayer's spouse, or any dependent at an eligible educational institution). See §§ 222 and 62(a)(18). The deduction is phased out for single taxpayers having adjusted gross income between $65,000 and $80,000 and for joint filers having adjusted gross income between $130,000 and $160,000. In order to take this deduction, the student cannot be claimed as a dependent and neither the student nor the student's parents can claim a §221 deduction. So the §221 and §222 deductions are mutually exclusive. Also, if the §222 deduction is taken, no §25A credits may be taken and qualified expenses considered for purposes of § 222 will reduce the qualified expenses that may be considered for purposes of §§135, 529, and 530.

Another option for the Kleins is to take out a home equity loan and use the proceeds for their children's education. To the extent that the loan does not exceed $100,000, the interest on it will be deductible under § 163, although the Kleins will have to itemize their deductions in order to take advantage of this. Note that if a taxpayer uses a home equity loan to pay education expenses, the taxpayer may not take a § 221 deduction for those expenses. See § 221(e)(1).

Another possible current option is that a taxpayer can take an early distribution from a Roth or a regular IRA (Individual Retirement Account) without the usual 10% penalty on early withdrawals if the distribution is used to pay qualified higher education expenses of the taxpayer, taxpayer's spouse, child or grandchild. See § 72(t)(2)(E). Qualified higher education expenses include tuition, fees, books, supplies, and equipment at a post-secondary educational institution; graduate level expenses also qualify. If the student is at least half-time, room and board are also considered qualified expenses. If a tax benefit is obtained for any qualified educational expenses (such as a tax free scholarship or fellowship), these expenses are reduced in determining qualified educational expenses for purposes of the IRA.

Section 25A provides two credits that the Kleins may use currently for the twins' education. These are the Hope scholarship and Lifetime Learning credits.

There are, however, restrictions on the use of these credits. First, for either credit, the student must be carrying at least half of a full-time workload and must not have been convicted of a felony drug offense. See § 25A(b)(2)(B) and (b)(2)(D). The second restriction involves the availability of the credits. The Hope credit normally is available only for the first two taxable years of postsecondary education. However, the American Recovery and Reinvestment Act of 2009 (ARRA) (also known as the Economic Stimulus Act) extended the credit to four years of postsecondary education for taxable years beginning in 2009 and running through 2012. See § 25A(i)(2). This new beefed up Hope credit is called "the American Opportunity" credit. The Lifetime Learning credit is a per taxpayer credit rather than a per student credit, so only one credit is allowed per return. Unlike the Hope credit, the Lifetime Learning credit was not affected by the ARRA. However, the Lifetime Learning credit applies to any year of postsecondary education, including graduate education. The third restriction is in the amount of the credit. Normally, the Hope credit is limited to $1800 per student (100 percent of the first $1200 of qualified expenses and 50 percent of the second $1200), after being indexed for inflation (see Rev. Proc. 2009–21). The ARRA also increased the amount of the Hope credit to $2500 (100 percent of the first $2000 of qualified expenses and 25 percent of the second $2000) for taxable years 2009 through 2012. After that, it returns to its former limitation of $1800. The Lifetime Learning credit (which is unaffected by the ARRA) is limited to $2000, which is 20 percent of the first $10,000 of qualified expenses. The fourth restriction is the phaseout of the benefit that applies to higher income taxpayers. For married taxpayers filing a joint return, the phaseout of the Hope credit (which has been increased under the ARRA for taxable years 2009 through 2012) applies to those taxpayers with modified adjusted gross income (mAGI) between $160,000 and $180,000 (between $80,000 and $90,000 for single taxpayers). The phaseout limit for the Lifetime Learning credit applies to joint filers with mAGI between $80,000 and $100,000 ($40,000 and $50,000 for single taxpayers).

Clearly, the Hope credit is a better credit, at least if used in taxable years 2009 through 2012, for those taxpayers who are eligible to use it. Not only is it a larger amount of credit, but it also is a per student credit, rather than a per taxpayer credit, so it can apply to each of the twins if their parents take the credit on their return. Moreover, the ARRA has transformed the normally nonrefundable Hope credit into a partially refundable one (up to 40 percent) during the extension period. The Lifetime Learning credit remains nonrefundable.

The Kleins' mAGI falls just at the increased phase-out limitation for the Hope credit. Thus, they will not have to reduce their credit until their mAGI rises above $160,000, provided they use the credit in the 2009 through 2012 taxable years when the phase-out limit is increased. After that, the phaseout limits return to their former range of $40,000-$50,000 of mAGI for single taxpayers and $80,000-$100,000 of mAGI for joint filers. This will mean that the Kleins' will not be able to take the credit after the 2012 taxable year unless the increased limitations are extended by Congress. They can get around this limitation (to an extent) by making a gift to the twins that they can use to pay their own qualified expenses. In that case, the twins would be eligible to take the Hope credit and could get up to 40% of the credit refunded to them if they use it in taxable years 2009 through 2012. If the twins choose to take the credit, they may not be claimed as dependents on their parents' return. The other limitation is in determining qualified expenses. Qualified expenses are defined as tuition and fees for enrollment or attendance (also increased in taxable years 2009 through 2012 to include textbooks and course materials). See § 25A(f)(1). They do not include the expenses covered by a scholarship or fellowship that are excludable from gross income under § 117. They also do not include expenses covered by an educational assistance allowance or any other amount used for education that is excluded from gross income, except for gifts and inheritances. See § 25A(g). Students loans and private savings can be used, though, to pay qualified expenses without a reduction under § 25A.

If grandparents or other family members wish to make a gift to the twins to help with their college costs, this will not be taxable to the twins under § 102. The donor can give up to $13,000 per donee per annum (in 2009 and after) without paying a gift tax on this amount ($26,000 per donee for a married couple donor). Any amount of the gift that the twins use to pay qualified college costs will not reduce the amount of the qualified cost that may be considered for the Hope or Lifetime Learning credits.

If the twins decide to continue their education after college, they may elect the Lifetime Learning credit (since their parents cannot pass the phaseout limitation). If one of the parents should retire or no longer work at that point so that their mAGI is below the phaseout limitation, they may be eligible to take the Lifetime Learning credit, but it will apply only to one child, since it is a per taxpayer and not a per student credit. (If the parents file a joint return they are considered one taxpayer). The parents could take the credit for one twin and give the other a gift to pay his own tuition and fees so that he then could take his own credit. Note that if the student elects to take the credit, the student may not be claimed as a dependent on any other return.

Both the Hope and Lifetime Learning credits apply to the costs of higher education, so they will not be available for Katy, who is in a private secondary school. The Kleins' primary concern with respect to the younger children will be funding the cost of their higher education. Any tax consequences likely will be of secondary consideration with respect to these children. Nevertheless, there are several tax-favored investment vehicles available to help defray the costs of higher education for these younger children.

First is the § 135 Series EE and I savings bonds. These bonds must be purchased by someone who is at least 24 years of age and held by that person. Thus, the bonds must be purchased generally by someone other than the student, such as a parent, grandparent, uncle, or aunt. There is no restriction on the amount of bonds that can be purchased, and the full amount of interest on the bond generally is excludable under § 135, provided that the proceeds are used to pay the cost of tuition and fees. To the extent any of the interest is taxed, it is taxed to the bondholder. However, the interest exclusion is subject to phaseouts in the year of the distribution. For a couple with young children, this makes planning difficult because their mAGI may be greater than the phaseout limitation by the time they are ready for a distribution. For this reason, it is better for someone who is retired or living on a fixed income to purchase the bonds because that person's tax liability will be more easily determined at the time of the distribution. The purchase of these bonds is not considered a gift since they must be purchased by and in the name of someone at least 24 years of age. Therefore, gift taxes are not a concern with this type of vehicle. Also, the proceeds can be used for graduate level education as well.

Second is a § 529 qualified tuition plan. These are state education plans, but they offer a federal tax advantage. The state creates a fund under § 529, and the eligible colleges can participate individually with participants purchasing tuition credits from the college of their choice. The participant makes after-tax contributions to the plan on behalf of a designated beneficiary. These contributions are considered gifts, so the gift tax rules apply, but the contributions accumulate tax free to cover the costs of the beneficiary's higher education. One advantage of this type of plan is that there are no phaseouts, so anyone can contribute regardless of income level. Later, when the beneficiary begins college or postsecondary education, he or she then can take a tax-free distribution from the account to cover qualified education expenses. There is a liberal definition of "qualified education expenses" under § 529. These expenses include tuition, fees, room and board, books, supplies, and equipment. In 2009 and 2010, the cost of a computer also was included within the definition.

The earnings on any excess distribution that are not spent on a qualified expense are taxed to the beneficiary at the beneficiary's tax rate. The tax liability is determined under § 72, and the investment in the contract (i.e., the nontaxable portion) will be the amount of the initial contribution that was considered a gift to the beneficiary. See § 529(c)(3). Thus, § 72 taxes the interest portion only. Any unused amount that is subject to tax is also subject to a 10 percent penalty, although both the tax liability and the penalty can be avoided by rolling the unused portion over to an eligible family member or to another plan. See § 529(c)(5); § 529(c)(6); § 530(d)(4).

If the beneficiary dies before completing postsecondary education, the unused portion may be rolled over to another beneficiary, or if it was used by the decedent, it will be taxed at the decedent's rate but will not be subject to the penalty. If the beneficiary should be fortunate enough to receive a scholarship, the beneficiary may take a distribution only for the amount of qualified expenses not covered by the scholarship. Such a distribution will be tax free. If the scholarship covers all expenses, and there is no other family member to roll the contributions over to, the beneficiary will be taxed under § 72 on the amount of any distribution but the 10 percent penalty will not apply. See § 529(c)(6); § 530(d)(4)(B).

Third is an Educational Savings Account or Coverdell Educational Savings Account (named for the late Senator Paul Coverdell) that is used exclusively for purposes of education. Under this account, up to $2000 may be contributed annually through 2012 for each child until the child reaches age 18 (unless the child has special needs). See § 530. The child does not have to be a dependent of the donor, so grandparents, uncles, aunts, etc., can contribute up to $2000 per year per child. Note that the $2000 limitation is a limitation on the account, not on the donor, so each child may receive only $2000 per year regardless of how many donors there are. Unlike a regular IRA, the amount of the contribution is not deductible, so contributions are made with after-tax dollars. However, the contribution accumulates tax free, and the withdrawals also are tax free, provided the money is used for a qualified education expense, which includes room, board and tuition. This is the same liberal definition as that of § 529. See § 530(b)(2)(A).

This vehicle is available for the costs of all education, from kindergarten through college and graduate school. The money must be withdrawn, though, within 30 days of the beneficiary's thirtieth birthday. See § 530(b)(1)(E). Any amount remaining in the account after that point, or any amount that is withdrawn and not used for a qualified expense will be subject to tax under § 72 and also will be subject to the 10 percent penalty. See § 530(d)(4). As with the Qualified Tuition Plan (QTP) under § 529, any unused portion may be rolled over to another educational savings account (ESA) for the benefit of another family member under the age of 30. See § 530(d)(5).

There also are some further limitations on contributions to this account. The $2000 maximum contribution is phased out for higher income taxpayers with mAGI between $95,000 and $110,000 for single filers and between $190,000 and $220,000 for joint filers. See § 530(c). However, a taxpayer with mAGI above those amounts may make a gift to another family member with income below the threshold amount, and this family member then may make the contribution to the ESA. Because of the relatively small amount of the contribution and because of the tax deferral aspect of this vehicle, it obviously works better for very young children in which contributions can be made early and can accumulate for a significant period of time.

After December 31, 2012, however, the Coverdell rules become much more restrictive, unless Congress should choose to extend the current rules. For instance, the maximum contribution to a Coverdell account will be reduced from $2,000 to $500; while the phaseout limits for single taxpayers will remain the same, those for joint filers will be reduced to $150,000 to $160,000 (thus reinstating the marriage penalty); the Coverdell will no longer cover expenses of elementary or secondary school; and there will no longer be an exception for children with special needs.

Although not specifically prohibited under the statute, Congress intended that contributions not be made to both a QTP and an ESA in the same year for the same beneficiary. See Conf. Rpt. 105–220. Thus, if a contribution is made to a QTP on behalf of a beneficiary, no similar contribution may be made to an ESA for that beneficiary, even though the contributors may be different. If distributions are received from both an ESA and a QTP, all amounts may be received tax free, provided they are all used to pay qualified expenses. If not used entirely for qualified expenses, allocations must be made in a reasonable manner between the two plans to determine the tax consequences. See § 530(d)(2)(C)(ii).

In general, there is no double dipping with respect to tax benefits for education. Thus, qualified expenses considered for purposes of the Hope and Lifetime Learning credit may not be considered for purposes of other tax-favored benefits. For instance, if a student or parent takes a deduction for student loan interest under § 221, that student or parent may not also take the Hope or Lifetime Learning credit for those same expenses. However, if the qualified education expenses are reduced by the amount considered for the Hope or Lifetime Learning credits, the interest deduction may be taken under § 221 for the remaining expenses that are paid with a student loan.

5. TOOLS FOR SELF-ASSESSMENT

[1] Because there are so many provisions that apply to help defray education costs, and because each benefit is subject to its own limitations and cover

different expenses, the area is very complicated. In a real life situation, the Kleins generally will be concerned about three things: (1) the funding alternatives available to them with respect to the twins' college education, (2) the tax benefits available to them for each of the funding alternatives, and (3) the planning opportunities with respect to the younger children.

[2] The best way to approach this problem is to address the twins' situation first because they present the most immediate and pressing problem since they are ready to enter college. It is too late for any advance planning to defray their college costs. Therefore, the only feasible sources of funding will be scholarships and fellowships, gifts, loans, and current savings. The twins may get jobs to help defray their costs, and the sample essay does not address this issue because any income that they derive will be taxed under the general rules. If the student pays his or her own expenses, either from earned income, savings, loans, or gifts, the student may take the tax benefits discussed above. Usually, for a student who is paying her own expenses, the student must not be a dependent of any other taxpayer and if married must file a joint return with her spouse. The former restriction prevents higher income parents from avoiding the income phaseout limitation by shifting the deduction/credit to the child. The latter prevents double dipping by the couple because married taxpayers are considered one taxpayer for this purpose.

[3] It is logical to consider scholarships and fellowships first because these amounts, to the extent that they fall under § 117 and are tax exempt, will reduce the amount of qualified expenses that may be considered for other educational benefits. From a practical perspective, if money is a consideration, as it is to most families facing the high costs of higher education, the Kleins probably will be more interested in the scholarships and student loans at this point because these amounts can be used directly to defray their costs, whereas the other benefits are solely tax benefits that are available only after a payment has been made. They may also be interested in the home equity loan, but with other children to educate, they probably will want to avoid this route if they have any other alternatives. If they decide on a home equity loan, they should check with their accountant as to the full tax and financial ramifications.

[4] After the financing of the twins' college education, the Kleins then will be concerned about the tax consequences. This problem encompasses each type of general tax benefit: exclusions, deductions, and credits. Gifts present the best of all worlds because the taxpayer/student will not have to come up with the funds herself. Instead, the funds will be excludable from her gross income, and the payment of any qualified expenses with the gift will not reduce the qualified expenses that may be considered for other purposes. Thus, a gift or inheritance presents the only situation in which the taxpayer may "double dip" and obtain two tax benefits for the same amount. The gifts may be made over a period of time under the state Uniform Gifts to Minors Act, and the savings then may be used to defray the costs of education. Bear in mind, however, that any earnings on the gift are taxable.

[5] An above-the-line deduction, such as §§ 221, is a very beneficial deduction for three reasons. First, it may be taken by any eligible taxpayer regardless of

whether that taxpayer itemizes deductions. This means that a student who is the obligor on a student loan will be able to deduct the interest even though the student does not own a residence and is not deducting interest on a qualified residence indebtedness. Second, above-the-line deductions are not subject to the limitations and phaseouts to which itemized deductions often are subject. Third, an above-the-line deduction reduces gross income to produce adjusted gross income. This has the added benefit of reducing the threshold limitation on other deductions, such as medical expenses and miscellaneous itemized deductions, both of which may be taken only if they exceed a percentage of adjusted gross income. This is called a "floor."

Itemized deductions, such as the interest on a home equity loan, are subject to more limitations than the other types of tax benefits in this problem. First, the taxpayer must be able to itemize deductions, so the deductions must exceed the standard deduction; and second, itemized deductions may be subject to a phaseout depending upon the income level of the taxpayer.

[6] Credits reduce the taxpayer's tax liability dollar for dollar. Some states have arrangements to help defray the costs of higher education, such as the Hope scholarship, funded by the state lotteries. These scholarships are excluded from income if they meet the requirements of § 117. While § 25A of the Code provides a Hope scholarship credit, this is not tied to the Hope scholarships offered by the states. In other words, § 25A can apply regardless of whether the student has a state Hope scholarship.

[7] Credits are usually subject to strict limitations, as is the case with § 25A. No more than $2500 in Hope credit may be taken per student in taxable years 2009 through 2012, and no more than $1800 may be taken in taxable years thereafter (subject to index for inflation), unless Congress chooses to extend this benefit. For taxable years 2009 through 2012, the Hope credit is more advantageous than the Lifetime Learning credit. Note that the effect of the ARRA increases in the Hope credit is that if a student entered college in 2007, the student will be able to take an extra four years of Hope credit for a total of six years. If the student entered college in 2008, the student may take an extra three years of Hope credit (through 2012). After that, the normal rules apply, and the student will be limited to two years of Hope credit.

[8] As to the long-term benefits for the other Klein children, there are several considerations. First is the amount that can be contributed. There is no restriction on the amount of § 135 bonds that may be purchased, but the purchase is made with after-tax dollars. If not used for a qualified expense, the interest will be taxable to the bondholder. There also are no restrictions on the amount that can be contributed to a § 529 QTP except that the contributions must be reasonably related to the amount the beneficiary will need for higher education. See § 529(b)(6). Since the amount of the contribution is considered a gift, the donor will be concerned about the gift taxes. Currently, the donor may contribute up to $13,000 per beneficiary per year without incurring a gift tax. (This is increased to $26,000 in the case of a joint return). In the case of a § 529 QTP, however, the donor may

contribute up to $65,000 in one year and then spread the contribution over five years without a gift tax consequence to the donor. See § 529(c)(2)(B). Contributions to an ESA are limited to $2000 per year per beneficiary, subject to the phase-out limitation, although after 2012 the contribution limits drop precipitously. The advantage of all of these vehicles is that the interest accumulates tax free.

[9] Second, the donor will be concerned about phaseouts. If the savings bond holder's mAGI is above the phaseout limitation under § 135(b)(2), the bond holder will be taxed on all or a portion of the interest when the bond is redeemed. Section 529 QTPs are the most advantageous in this regard because they are not subject to any phaseouts, either on contributions or on distributions. Contributions may be reduced or completely phased out under § 530, although the phaseout limitation is higher than it is under § 135.

[10] Third, the donor will be concerned about control of the funds to ensure that the maximum amount will be available for the education of the donee. Sections 135 and 530 provide guaranteed returns on the investment while § 529 does not. Thus, when a taxpayer contributes to a § 529 QTP, there is no guaranteed return on the investment, and the donor loses all control. Instead, the contributed amount is completely subject to fluctuations in the market.

[11] Fourth, the donor will be concerned about the flexibility of the contribution. Both § 529 plans and § 530 accounts can be rolled over for the benefit of another family member. While there is no such rollover provision under § 135, the feature is available as a practical matter, because the savings bonds are held by the bondholder and are not restricted to a particular beneficiary. The bonds can be used by the taxpayer, spouse, and dependents. However, the definition of family member under § 135 is more restrictive than under either § 529 or § 530.

[12] A fifth consideration is the amount and type of costs that qualify for the exclusion. The § 135 bond has the most restrictive definition of costs because it encompasses only tuition and fees. See § 135(c)(2)(A). Thus, no room and board expenses or other expenses may be paid with the proceeds of this bond. A distribution from a §529 QTP may be used for tuition, fees, books, supplies, equipment (including a computer in 2009 and 2010), room and board, and any special educational needs. See § 529(e)(3). The § 530 ESA has the most liberal definition of costs because it encompasses all the same costs as the § 529 plan, but it also covers elementary and secondary education expenses at least through 2012. See § 530(b)(2)(A) and (b)(4).

[13] A sixth consideration will be the overlap with other benefits. All three provisions require a reduction in qualified expenses by any amount that overlaps with §§ 25A, 135, 529, 530, 117, 127, etc. None of them require a reduction in qualified expenses that are paid from gifts, inheritances, or student loans.

6. VARIATIONS ON THE THEME

Assume that Ken Klein had purchased $10,000 of Series EE bonds when the twins were small. The bonds are now redeemable for $16,000. Each twin has a scholarship that will pay $5000 of their tuition costs. The twins' tuition costs, after the scholarship, are $30,000 ($15,000 apiece). Their fees are $5000 apiece. The Kleins decide to take the Hope credit for each of the twins, and their mAGI is $170,000. Discuss the Klein's tax consequences.

12

CASUALTY LOSSES, MEDICAL EXPENSES, AND THE TAX BENEFIT RULE

1. OPENING REMARKS

Casualty loss deductions are among the very few loss deductions allowed to nonbusiness individual taxpayers. The deduction, however, is limited and in some cases can be quite complicated. First, the tax Code specifically defines a casualty loss for individual, nonbusiness taxpayers under § 165(c)(3). Casualties under 165(c)(3) must occur at a definable point so that there is no problem determining the point of realization of the loss. A loss that does not take place at a single definable point may not be deducted as a casualty loss. For instance, taxpayers have not been successful in arguing that subterranean termite damage is a deductible casualty loss because termite damage is better characterized as progressive deterioration. The second complexity for taxpayers is determining the amount of the loss, and this depends upon whether the property was totally or partially destroyed. The burden is on the taxpayer to prove the correct amount of the loss and the rules for deductibility vary depending upon whether the destruction is total or partial. Third, the deduction is an itemized deduction, so it is not available unless the individual has enough deductions to exceed the standard deduction. Fourth, there is a floor of $100 on the casualty loss deductions of individuals under § 165(h)(1). Fifth, net casualty losses can be taken only to the extent of net casualty gains plus the excess net loss over 10 percent of adjusted gross income. See § 165(h)(2).

Section 213 allows a deduction for medical expenses, but this deduction is only available for "extraordinary" medical expenses that exceed a floor of 7 1/2 percent of the taxpayer's adjusted gross income. The deduction includes dental expenses, prescription drugs, and insulin. It also includes transportation expenses to receive medical care. Again, this is an itemized deduction so it is available only if these and any other itemized expenses of the individual exceed the standard deduction.

While the medical expense deduction is very separate from the casualty loss deduction, in real life the two often occur together. Note that the medical expense deduction also must be coordinated with the exclusion for personal injury recoveries under § 104 because the taxpayer cannot "double dip" and claim both an exclusion and a deduction for the same item. Any amount of medical expense compensated by insurance is not eligible for the deduction. If a medical expense deduction was taken in a prior taxable year, and there is a subsequent recovery of that amount (whether through insurance or through a lawsuit or a settlement), the recovery must be included in the taxpayer's income under the "tax benefit doctrine" to the extent of any actual tax benefit taken previously.

2. HYPOTHETICAL

Larry Lawson is a single, calendar year taxpayer who uses the cash method of tax accounting. In October of year one, Larry was heading to the grocery store when his SUV was rear-ended by a beer truck. He was taken to the hospital and treated for a concussion, a broken arm, a ruptured spleen, and a displaced kneecap. He spent a week in the hospital, underwent surgery for his spleen and kneecap, and had to undergo physical therapy for the knee. Larry's hospital bill was $185,000; his physical therapy bill was $2500; and his pain medication, after his release from the hospital, cost $200. In the year of the accident and in the following two years, Larry had an adjusted gross income of $150,000.

In the year of the accident, his insurance company paid $100,000 of his hospital bills, and another $70,000 was paid by the insurance company the following year (year two). Larry paid the remaining $15,000 from his own funds in the year following the accident (year two). Larry incurred $700 of the physical therapy expenses in the year of the accident (year one), but he had a $400 deductible so he paid this amount himself in that year. The remaining $300 was paid by his insurance company in year one. The remaining $1800 of physical therapy expenses were incurred in the year following the accident and the insurance company paid all of this amount. The insurance company paid none of the cost of the pain medication following his release from the hospital.

Larry found that he suffered from post-traumatic stress disorder after the incident, so he sought the services of a psychiatrist. He spent $3000 on psychiatric visits, $500 of which was paid by him in year one and the remaining expense was paid by him in year two. His insurance paid none of that bill.

In addition, Larry also suffered property damage to his vehicle, which was less than a year old. He had purchased the vehicle new for $55,000, and its blue book value before the incident was $47,000. It cost $16,500 to repair the car to restore it to good working condition. His auto insurance company paid this entire amount, less a $500 deductible, in year one when the repairs were made. Once the car was repaired, its blue book value was $42,000.

In an unrelated incident, someone broke into Larry's house in early November, shortly after the accident and stole $5000 of silver and jewelry. His basis in this property had been $2500, and he received $1000 in compensation from his homeowner's insurance policy.

During the winter months in the year following the accident, Larry's knee bothered him. His physical therapist said arthritis had set in after the trauma he had suffered. The therapist suggested that a warmer climate might help. Larry rented a condominium in Florida for the month of June (in year two) at a cost of $4000. He drove himself to Florida and back, and his total transportation expenses were $270, which included gas, meals, and lodging for one night. He found that his knee did seem better after his month in Florida.

Larry had been in negotiations with the company that owned the beer truck but was not able to reach a satisfactory settlement. In August of the year following the accident (year two), Larry brought suit against the beer company to recover his costs. The company made another effort to settle, but Larry rejected the offer. The case went to trial in February of the following year (year three), and a jury awarded Larry $200,000 in actual damages and another $50,000 for pain and suffering.

What are Larry's tax consequences in each of these three years?

3. LIST OF READINGS

Internal Revenue Code: §§ 55; 56(b)(1)(B); 68; 104(a); 111; 165; 213
Regulations: §§ 1.165–7
Rulings: Rev. Rul. 93–72, 1993–2 C.B. 63

4. SAMPLE ESSAY

Year One: In the year of his accident, Larry incurs total medical costs of $186,400 attributable to his hospital stay ($185,000), his prescription drug medication ($200), psychotherapy expenses ($500), and physical therapy ($700). His insurance company paid $100,300 of this amount in year one (for the hospital bills and the physical therapy expense above the amount of the deductible), and Larry paid $1100 ($200 for prescription medication, $400 for physical therapy, and $500 for psychotherapy). Section 104(a)(3) excludes amounts received from a personal insurance policy that pays expenses of personal illness or injury. Since Larry's insurance policy paid $100,300 of his hospital and physical therapy expenses in the year of the accident (year one), this amount is fully excludable by Larry under § 104(a)(3).

Section 213 authorizes a deduction for medical expenses paid during the taxable year, provided that the expenses are not covered by insurance or otherwise and provided that they exceed 7.5 percent of the taxpayer's adjusted gross income. Thus, Larry will be able to deduct his medical expenses only to the extent that they exceed $11,250 (7.5 percent x $150,000). Another problem is that Larry will be able to deduct the excess amount only if he is able to itemize his expenses because § 213 deductions are itemized (below the line). In year one, he will not be able to deduct any of the $1100 of medical expenses that he pays because those expenses do not exceed the 7.5 percent floor.

The medical expenses authorized under § 213 are the amounts paid for "the diagnosis, cure, mitigation, treatment, or prevention of disease, or for the purpose of affecting any structure or function of the body." See § 213(d)(1)(A). Ordinarily, there is no problem with hospital expenses falling under this provision unless they relate to an elective cosmetic procedure. Prescription drugs and insulin may be deducted under § 213(b), but the taxpayer must produce receipts to verify the cost of the medication(s). Since § 213(a) provides that only the qualifying expenses that are actually paid by the taxpayer are eligible for the deduction, the amounts incurred in the year of the accident that are paid by the insurance company are not considered § 213 expenses.

Larry suffers two casualty losses during year one: the accident and the theft. The property damage to his car constitutes a casualty loss under § 165(c)(3). Section 165(c)(3) allows a deduction for a loss incurred by an individual taxpayer who suffers a casualty attributable to fire, storm, shipwreck, theft, or other casualty. A car accident constitutes an "other casualty" under Reg. § 1.165–7(a)(3) since the damage resulted from the faulty driving of the other driver and not from the intentional act or willful negligence of Larry.

In the automobile accident, Larry's car repair costs were $16,500, of which $16,000 was covered by his insurance and $500 was paid by Larry as a deductible. Thus, Larry's direct casualty loss under (section) 165 was $500. However, he also suffered a loss on the value of the car because the blue book value after the repairs was $5000 less than it had been before the repairs. In general, the deduction for a partial casualty loss is the lesser of (1) the difference between the fair market value of the property immediately before the casualty less the fair market value of the property immediately after the casualty or (2) the adjusted basis of the property. Reg. § 1.165–7(b)(1). The estimate of the fair market value of the property must be made by a competent appraiser, although the cost of repairs is acceptable as evidence of the loss of value if the taxpayer shows (1) the repairs are necessary to restore the property to its condition immediately before the casualty, (2) the amount spent on the repairs is reasonable, (3) the cost of the repairs does not cover more than the damage attributable to the casualty, and (4) the value of the property after the repairs does not exceed the value before the repairs. Reg. § 1.165–7(a)(2).

The loss in value of Larry's car probably is attributable to the fact that, despite the repairs, the car has been in an accident, so its value after the accident will be less than its value before the accident. The regulations allow this devaluation to be taken into account in determining the loss. See Reg. § 1.165–7(a)(2). Applying these rules to Larry, his car was worth $48,000 before the accident and $43,000 afterward. Adding this $5000 difference to the cost of the repairs brings the total loss to $21,500. However, Larry's out-of-pocket loss is only $5500, attributable to the decline in the value of his car after the accident and the amount of his deductible. Applying the threshold floor to this loss brings the potentially deductible loss to $5400 ($5500 less $100).

His second casualty is the theft loss from the break-in. With a theft loss, the taxpayer must be able to prove that the theft occurred. A police report is proof of a loss but is not absolutely necessary if the taxpayer has other proof. The rules discussed above under § 1.165–7(b)(1) apply to determine the amount of the deduction. After the theft, the fair market value of the property is zero for this purpose, but the "lesser of" amount is Larry's basis of $2500, which is less than the $5000 fair market value of the property stolen. The amount of the insurance recovery must be subtracted from the deductible amount, less the $100 floor, which applies to each casualty. This brings Larry's preliminary tax loss from the theft to $1400 ($2,500 basis less $1000 insurance recovery less $100 threshold floor).

Larry's total preliminary tax loss in year one is $6800 ($5400 attributable to the auto accident plus $1400 attributable to the theft). However, there is a floor on the amount of casualty losses that may be deducted, similar to the medical expense deduction, but in the case of a casualty loss, it is a double floor. First, the eligible losses must exceed $100 per casualty. See § 165(h)(1). Then, a net casualty loss is allowed only to the extent that it exceeds 10 percent of the individual's adjusted gross income. See § 165(h)(2)(A). Since Larry's preliminary tax loss of $6,300 does not exceed 10 percent of his adjusted gross income ($150,000 x 10 percent = $15,000), Larry is not able to deduct any of his casualty losses in year one. Note that a casualty loss, like the medical expense deduction, also is an itemized deduction.

Year Two: The following year (year two), Larry pays $17,500 in medical expenses ($15,000 for hospital care and $2500 for psychotherapy). The insurance company pays the final $70,000 of the hospital bill and $1800 of the physical therapy expense. Again, the insurance recovery is excluded from Larry's gross income under § 104(a)(3). Since his threshold amount (i.e., floor) under § 213 is $11,250, he may deduct $6250 of his $17,500 medical expenses that he paid in that year as an itemized deduction. See § 63(d).

Also in the year following the accident, Larry takes a trip to Florida on the advice of his physical therapist, who tells him that he will benefit from milder weather. The expenses that Larry incurs on this trip are not deductible because he travels to Florida for his general well-being, not because a doctor specifically recommended Florida as a treatment. Further, his trip to Florida had a significant element of personal pleasure, recreation, or vacation. This means that it is not an eligible expense under § 213. See § 213(d)(2).

Year Three: The $250,000 recovery from the beer company in year three (provided Larry actually receives this amount) normally would be excludable under § 104(a)(2) because it is a compensatory damage award that is entirely attributable to a physical personal injury. But § 104(a) excepts any amount attributable to deductions allowed under § 213, so to the extent that Larry previously took a deduction attributable to an item of recovery, he may not also obtain an exclusion. This is called "double dipping," and it is not permitted under the tax Code. Larry had eligible medical expenses under § 213 in year two of $6250 for the medical expenses that he incurred and paid in that year. To the extent that he received a deduction in a prior taxable year, any recovery in the current taxable year must be included in income. None of Larry's medical expenses were eligible to be deducted in year one because they did not exceed the 7.5 percent floor. Therefore, any amount of the recovery attributable to those expenses may be excluded.

While $6250 of Larry's medical expenses were eligible for deduction under § 213 in year two, itemized deductions are subject to phaseouts for higher income taxpayers, of which Larry would be considered one. See § 68. Thus, if he was able to take this deduction, he will have to include the recovery but only to the extent of the actual reduction in tax liability attributable to that amount. This inclusion will be reduced by any amount by which Larry's itemized deductions were phased out. This amount may be further reduced by any portion of his medical expense deduction that was taxed under the alternative minimum tax. See §§ 55 and 56(b)(1)(B). The IRS has issued guidelines in Rev. Rul. 93–72 on how to determine the inclusion.

5. TOOLS FOR SELF-ASSESSMENT

[1] Since this problem involves several discrete issues over several taxable years, careful attention must be paid to the issues and to the Code sections and individual rules pertaining to each issue. A floor means that the amount of the limitation must be subtracted from the eligible expenses, and that amount will not be deductible. Casualty losses and medical expenses are among the most severely limited of the deductions allowed to individual taxpayers. The best way to organize this problem is to take each year separately and analyze the tax consequences of the expenses incurred in those years because different limitations will apply in each of the years.

[2] Section 104(a)(2) excludes the amount of *any* damages received on account of a *physical* personal injury. Thus, damages received on account of emotional distress related to a physical personal injury are excludable.

[3] No deduction is allowed for a casualty loss attributable to the intentional act or willful negligence of the taxpayer. This does not mean that another person

must be at fault for the taxpayer to obtain a casualty loss deduction. It simply means that if the taxpayer intentionally or willfully brought about the result, no loss deduction attributable to the casualty will be allowed.

[4] The loss in value of the vehicle is also a casualty loss that potentially is deductible, provided that it exceeds the floors on deductibility when combined with the other loss(es) from that casualty. Remember that the $100 floor is a *per casualty* limitation, not a per year or per taxpayer limitation.

[5] The natural tendency in a casualty loss is to assume that the fair market value of the damaged property, less any amount of insurance recovery should be deductible, subject to the floors. However, students must realize that there is a difference between financial accounting and tax accounting. For financial accounting purposes, Larry suffers a loss equal to the fair market value of the stolen property ($5000) less the amount of any insurance recovery ($1000). For tax purposes, however, the difference between the fair market value of the property and the adjusted basis in the property represents untaxed appreciation. To allow a deduction for an amount on which the taxpayer was never taxed is considered impermissible double dipping. Also, it is possible to have a casualty gain if the insurance recovery exceeds the adjusted basis of the stolen property.

[6] Larry's trip to Florida has three problems for purposes of deductibility. The first problem is that it was recommended by his physical therapist, who is not a doctor. The second is that the expense is the type that is regarded with suspicion by the IRS, especially where the location is a prime vacation spot, and the rental cost of the condominium is expensive. The third is that the physical therapist *suggested* the trip because it *might* help Larry's leg. Thus, even though the recommendation was made for a specific ailment, it was only a general suggestion.

[7] Section 213(a) is an example of a specific tax benefit (no double dipping) rule. Section 111 is the codification of the general tax benefit rule. There are two ways to look at this rule. The first is that in order for the taxpayer to obtain a tax benefit (i.e., to deduct the item), the taxpayer must have paid the amount (in this case, the medical expense) and must not have been compensated *by insurance or otherwise*. See § 213(a). This requirement ensures that the tax benefit is balanced by an actual economic detriment. The second is that § 213(a) cannot be avoided by tax accounting manipulation. To illustrate these principals: If Larry had paid his medical expenses and received an insurance recovery compensating him for those expenses in the same taxable year, he would not be able to deduct his medical expenses because he did not incur an economic detriment for those expenses. The amount of the insurance recovery also would not be included in Larry's income because it would be excluded under § 104(a). But if Larry had paid the medical expenses in year one and received no insurance recovery in that year, he would be able to deduct his expenses (subject to the limitations) in that year. If he receives a recovery (whether through insurance or settlement) in the subsequent year, he must "pay" for that earlier tax benefit by including the amount of the recovery in income (to the extent that it produced a tax benefit). When this amount is included in

income, it balances both the economic and tax benefits and detriments (e.g., the medical expense payment in year one is balanced by a tax deduction in that year, and the recovery in year two is balanced by the income inclusion in year two).

[8] Note that § 111, which includes the recovery of tax benefit items, only addresses deductions and credits, not exclusions. Therefore, the amount of the recovery attributable to the insurance-paid hospital costs that were excluded under § 104(a)(3) are not included in Larry's income under § 111. Note also that there are exclusionary provisions that address both the insurance payment of the medical expenses (§ 213) and the recovery from the tortfeasor (§ 104).

6. VARIATIONS ON THE THEME

What would result if Larry's insurance policy had been capped at $100,000, and he had to pay the remainder of his hospital bill himself in year one? Also, what would result if Larry had traveled to Florida to a specialized clinic recommended by his doctor for treatment for his leg?

7. OPTIONAL READINGS

Cases: Montgomery v. Commissioner, 428 F.2d 243 (6th Cir. 1970); Hunt v. Commissioner, 31 T.C.M. 1119 (1972)

13

CHARITABLE DEDUCTIONS

1. OPENING REMARKS

Section 170 of the tax Code allows a deduction for contributions to charities that are considered qualified organizations. Many nonprofit organizations are qualified charities under § 170, and they derive an important part of their resources from contributions. A deductible contribution may be made either in cash or in property, but services do not qualify under § 170. In addition, the contribution must be a true donation, so if the taxpayer receives anything of value in return, the taxpayer is not entitled to a deduction to the extent of that value. Sometimes this issue is obvious, such as a donation in which the donor receives a tangible item of property—a coffee mug, an umbrella, or a book. In other cases where the benefit is intangible, the quid pro quo may not be as obvious: for example, when the taxpayer receives concert or theater tickets that he neither uses nor wants. Courts look to the *Duberstein* rationale to determine whether the contribution was made from detached, disinterested generosity. Thus, the contribution must constitute a gift, rather than a quid pro quo.

Since the inception of the tax Code, Congress has permitted taxpayers to take a charitable deduction. But there are limitations to prevent taxpayers from eliminating their tax liabilities entirely through charitable deductions. First, the deduction is an itemized deduction and therefore is not available to taxpayers who are not eligible to itemize. Second, it is subject to the general phaseout of itemized deductions for higher income taxpayers under § 68. Third, certain contributions are further subject to limitations within § 170 that are based on a percentage of the donor's adjusted gross income.

While the charitable deduction has been the subject of much debate over the years, on occasion Congress has used it to encourage taxpayers to support certain projects. An example of this special legislation occurred in 2005 in the wake of the Hurricane Katrina disaster when Congress lifted the percentage limitation on contributions for that year and increased the standard mileage allowance for the use of a vehicle for charitable purposes.

2. HYPOTHETICAL

Mark and Mary McLemore have three children, all of whom attend a private Catholic school, although they themselves are not Catholic. The McLemores contributed $3000 to the school during its annual fund raising drive. The school had announced that the majority of these donations would be spent on "student enrichment" programs.

Mary has been on the board of the local humane society for the past five years. Each year she has spent approximately 100 hours working on various projects for the society. But her term on the board is coming to an end this year. Mary decides to donate her three-year old van that she has used for personal purposes to the organization because it has been looking for a reasonably priced vehicle to transport the animals. Mary initially paid $60,000 for the van, fully loaded, and it is currently worth $25,000. She arranges for the organization to buy her van for $5000, and she intends to donate the remainder.

Mark owned some publicly traded stock that he had purchased five years ago for $10,000 that currently is worth $20,000. He donated this stock recently to State University (SU), his alma mater. SU wrote Mark, thanking him for his donation and offering him the privilege of purchasing skybox seats for the coming football season. According to the letter, this is a privilege that SU offers its "major donors."

The McLemores have adjusted gross income of $180,000 and no net operating losses. Their home mortgage interest and state and local taxes allow them to itemize their deductions. Will they be able to obtain a charitable deduction for their donations? If so, how much will they be able to deduct? Discuss.

3. LIST OF READINGS

Internal Revenue Code: §§170; 1011(b)
Regulations: §§ 1.170A-1; 1.170A-13(a); 1.1001–1(e)
Rulings: Rev. Rul. 83–104, 1983–2 C.B. 46

4. SAMPLE ESSAY

Section 170 authorizes a deduction, within certain limits, for any charitable contribution made within the taxable year to an organization defined in § 170(c). As a religiously affiliated institution, the children's private school should qualify. A contribution for purposes of § 170 is "a voluntary transfer of money or property . . . made with no expectation of procuring a financial benefit commensurate with the amount of the transfer." Rev. Rul. 83–104.

When a parent makes a donation to a child's school, the threshold question for purposes of § 170 is whether the donation is made with the expectation of deriving a benefit or whether there is any degree of coercion involved. To some extent, every parent expects or hopes that his or her child will have a better educational experience as a result of such donations.

Rev. Rul. 83–104 provides that if a reasonable person, taking all relevant facts and circumstances into consideration, would conclude that the payment was entirely voluntary, with no expectation of a specific benefit such as continued enrollment for a specific child or children contingent upon the payment, the contribution should be deductible, subject to the limits under § 170(b). There are several factors that the IRS is likely to consider: (1) whether the McLemores otherwise have paid their children's tuition at the school, (2) whether there is any substantial or unusual pressure applied to them to contribute, (3) whether the fundraising drive occurs as part of the admissions or enrollment process, (4) what sources of revenue the school derives for operations, and (5) any other indications that the "fundraising drive" is designed to avoid the characterization of payments as tuition. Rev. Rul. 83–104.

This fact pattern is similar to that of Situation Five in Rev. Rul. 83–104. There, the IRS allowed the deduction, stating that under these circumstances, taxpayers generally will be able to claim a charitable deduction. This appears to be a routine fundraising campaign, and the fact that the McLemore's children attend the school will not create a specific inference that the benefits enjoyed by their children depend upon contributions from the parents. Even though the school states that the majority of the contributions will be used for a specific purpose–enrichment programs—this should not be significantly different than a school stating what it costs to educate each student. Thus, the McLemore's $3000 charitable contribution to their children's school is potentially deductible, subject to the limits of § 170(b).

Only contributions of cash and property are deductible under § 170. Thus, the value of Mary's time spent working with the local humane society is not deductible, and neither is any time she may have spent performing services at the children's school. See Reg. § 1.170A-1(g).

Mary's sale of her van to the local humane society is a bargain sale to a charity that must be bifurcated into a sale portion and a charitable donation portion. See §§ 1011(b); 170(e)(2). The burden will be on Mary to prove the value of the van at the time of the sale. The price set by the parties will not control in this situation because the sale is a "bargain" sale at less than fair market value, with the difference between the value of the van and the amount paid being a charitable contribution. Since the van is worth $25,000 and Mary is paid $5000 for it in the sale, she has sold 20 percent of the van and donated the remaining 80 percent. This means that 20 percent of her basis ($60,000 x 20%), $12,000, will offset the $5000 that she receives on the sale. She thus realizes a loss of $7000 on the sale portion of the van ($12,000 basis less $5000 amount realized), which she will not be able to recognize because it is a sale of personal use property. See also Reg. § 1.1001–1(e). The remaining portion attributable to the charitable donation is potentially deductible. In the case of a donation of property to a charity, the amount of the donation is the fair market value of the property at the time it is given to the charity. Reg. § 1.170A-1(c)(1). Thus, Mary should be able to deduct $20,000 ($25,000 value of the van less $5000 payment by the charity) in the year of the donation.

In the case of the stock that Mark donates to SU, the first question is whether this donation constitutes a quid pro quo. In other words, did Mark donate the stock to get the skybox seats? Did he make this donation for business purposes? Section 170(l) takes the guesswork out of this question because it provides that 80 percent of a donation to an institution of higher education is deductible if the amount of the donation otherwise would be deductible, except for the fact that the taxpayer receives the right to purchase tickets at an athletic event at the institution. The next question is: what is the amount of the donation? In this case, the donation is appreciated stock that Mark was holding for investment. Thus, if he were to sell the stock, he would recognize a long-term capital gain. Since the stock is publicly traded, its value can be readily determined. Thus, the amount of Mark's donation is $20,000, the fair market value of the stock. See Reg. § 1.170A-1(c)(1). Since 80 percent of this amount is deductible under § 170(l), Mark will be able to deduct $16,000 of this donation.

After the various donations have been determined, the next step is to consider whether there are any limitations on the amount of the overall deduction. Section 170(b) divides charitable organizations into two groups: 50 percent charities and 30 percent charities. This refers to the percentage limitation on the charitable deduction. In the case of a 50 percent charity, the deductible contribution is limited to 50 percent of the individual's contribution base, which is the individual's adjusted gross income (computed without regard to any net operating loss carry-back). § 170(b)(1)(G).

The 50 percent charities are described under § 170(b)(1)(A). They include churches, educational organizations, governmental units, private foundations, and organizations receiving a substantial portion of their support from a governmental unit or the general public. All of the charitable organizations to which the McLemores have donated appear to fall into the 50 percent range. All charities not listed under § 170(b)(1)(A) are limited to 30 percent of the individual's contribution base. § 170(b)(1)(B). The McLemore's contribution base is $180,000 (i.e., their adjusted gross income), and since their donations are all to 50 percent charities, their § 170(b) limitation is $90,000. Thus, their total charitable contributions in any taxable year cannot exceed $90,000. Since the stock donated to SU is appreciated property, § 170(b)(1)(C) requires the limitation to be reduced further to 30 percent. This reduces the limitation to $54,000 for contributions of capital gain property, but the stock value is well under this amount. The McLemore's total charitable donations of $38,000 are well under the amount of the limitation, so their entire donations should be deductible under § 170(a), subject to any phase-outs of itemized deductions for higher income taxpayers under § 68.

Note that the McLemores must be able to substantiate their donations in order to take them. See Reg. § 1.170A-13(a)(1). This can be done in the form of a canceled check or a statement from the charity. In the case of property, a qualified valuation also must be substantiated. This is easier in the case of publicly traded stock.

5. TOOLS FOR SELF-ASSESSMENT

[1] There is a general tendency among students to immediately jump in and begin discussing the amount of the deduction, particularly if the donation is made to an educational institution, a church, or a well-known charitable organization. When examining the deductibility of charitable contributions, however, the IRS generally considers two threshold issues: whether there was a direct benefit or promise of a direct benefit as a result of the contribution, and whether the taxpayer is attempting to transform nondeductible payments (such as tuition) into deductible charitable contributions (always a no-no!).

[2] Normally, bargain sales or part-sales-part-gifts do not require apportionment for income tax purposes but are considered straight sales with no recognition of any realized loss. See § 1.1001–1(e). In the case of a bargain sale to a charity, though, the taxpayer must apportion or bifurcate the transaction between the sale portion and the donation portion.

[3] In the case of a donation of appreciated property to a charity, it seems counterintuitive that a taxpayer should be able to obtain a deduction for appreciation that has not been subject to tax. After all, that is the reason why donated services to a charitable organization are not deductible. But in the case of appreciated property, the Code and regulations permit a taxpayer to obtain a deduction equal to the fair market value of the donated property. So Mark may obtain an initial deduction of $20,000, the fair market value of the stock, even though if he were to sell his stock on the open market, he would realize a long-term capital gain of $10,000 ($20,000 amount realized

less $10,000 cost basis) and would be taxed on this gain. This appears to violate a fundamental principle of federal income taxation.

Section 170(e) addresses this problem and provides that a taxpayer such as Mark may take a deduction equal to the full fair market value of the stock, even though he has never been taxed on the appreciation (i.e., the difference between the market value of the stock, $20,000, and his adjusted basis, $10,000). Section 170(e)(1) provides four exceptions to this rule, but Mark does not fall into any of them. Because § 170 permits a deduction of untaxed appreciation, there are special limits imposed on the deduction under § 170(b). If appreciated capital gains property is donated to a 50 percent charity and is not subject to any of the exceptions under § 170(e)(1)(B), the 50 percent limit is reduced to 30 percent (and the 30 percent limit is reduced to 20 percent) under § 170(b)(1)(C). A taxpayer instead may elect to reduce the amount of the deduction by the amount that would have been a long-term capital gain if the property had been sold. Then the limit will remain at 50 percent. If there is any amount of charitable deduction that is not deductible in any given year because of the limits of § 170(b), the excess amount may be carried over to the next succeeding five taxable years. See § 170(d)(1).

[4] This reduced limit will make no difference to the McLemores, though, because Mark's donation is below the reduced limitation of $54,000 ($180,000 contribution base x 30 percent). Therefore, he is able to deduct the full $20,000 fair market value of his donation to SU. This is a good deal for Mark because he avoids the tax liability on the appreciation while obtaining a full tax benefit attributable to the contribution.

6. VARIATIONS ON THE THEME

In the alternative, assume that Mark and Mary have adjusted gross income of $75,000, and instead of the Humane Society, Mary donates the van to a "30 percent charity" within the meaning of § 170(b)(1)(B). Assume further that the stock that Mark donates to SU has a fair market value of $5000 instead of $20,000. What amount of charitable deductions may the McLemores take? Do you have any advice for them?

7. OPTIONAL READINGS

Article: For a thought-provoking article that examines the effect on various charities of the Obama administration's proposal to reduce the charitable deduction, see Robert J. Yetman & Michelle Yetman, *Does the Incentive Effect of the Charitable Deduction Vary Across Charities?*, Available at SSRN: http://ssrn.com/abstract=1435150, (July 22, 2009).

14 MOVING EXPENSES

1. OPENING REMARKS

We live in a mobile society, and Congress has recognized that fact by allowing a favorable above-the-line deduction under § 217 for moving expenses incurred in a work-related move, provided certain requirements are met. First, the expenses must be incurred in connection with work, whether starting a new job or changing jobs and whether self-employed or an employee. Second, the taxpayer must meet the distance and time limitations. In order to qualify for the deduction, the new principal place of work must be at least 50 miles farther from the former residence than was the former principal place of work. Thus, the new place of work must involve a commute that is 50 miles farther than the one the taxpayer had with the previous place of work. If the taxpayer is an employee, after she arrives in the new location, she must be employed full time for at least 39 weeks during the 12-month period following the move. If she is self-employed, she must work full time, either as a self-employed individual or as an employee for at least 78 weeks during the 24-month period following the move, and she must either be a full-time employee or self-employed during 39 weeks of the first 12-month period.

2. HYPOTHETICAL

Ned and Nancy Norris live in Midville, where Ned is a self-employed shoe store owner, and Nancy is a receptionist for a group of doctors. Toward the end of last year, the shoe business began to slow down, and Ned considered closing the store. This year, business has not improved, and Ned has been considering other options. After much thought and discussion, he decided to close the store and move his family to Suburb, 40 miles away from Midville, where he plans to become the sales representative of a manufacturing company based in nearby New Township, while Nancy will stay home, at least at first, with their three young children. Ned's new job will require some travel, but he will be based primarily in New Township, which is 60 miles away from Midville. Although his new commute to work will be farther each day (3 miles in Midville as opposed to 20 miles in Suburb), he thinks the school system in Suburb is better than in Midville and that his family will be happier in the idyllic Suburb than in New Township.

The Norrises incur the following expenses in their move: $3500 for a moving van, $60 for a meal along the way, $20 for gas and $20 for wear and tear on their car, $150 for two motel rooms for the first night in Suburb because they could not move into their house until the following day, and $250 in utility deposits. His new employer gave Ned a moving allowance/reimbursement of $1500 to help defray the cost of the moving van.

Discuss the tax consequences of the Norrises' move.

3. LIST OF READINGS

Internal Revenue Code of 1986: §§ 62(a)(15); 132(a)(6) and (g); 217
Regulations: Regs. § 1.217–2(b)

4. SAMPLE ESSAY

Section 217 authorizes a deduction for moving expenses paid or incurred during the taxable year in connection with the commencement of work. Section 217 encompasses taxpayers beginning work for the first time, employees who are transferred by their employers or who transfer jobs on their own initiative, and self-employed taxpayers who change their job location or become employees.

In order to take the deduction, however, the taxpayer must meet two threshold requirements: distance and time (length of employment). The distance requirement is met if the new principal place of work is at least 50 miles farther from the taxpayer's former residence than was his former principal place of work. (If there had been no previous principal place of work, the new place of work must be at least 50 miles from the former residence.) This means that since Ned's former principal place of work was three miles from his residence in Midville, the new principal place of work in New Township must be at least 53 miles from his former residence. Since New Township is 60 miles from Midville, the distance requirement appears to be met. In making this determination, § 217(c) provides that the shortest of the more commonly traveled routes between the two points shall be used.

The second threshold requirement is a length of employment requirement. Since Ned is an employee in the new location, he must be employed full time for 39 weeks during the 12-month period immediately following the move. If the move occurs later in the year, and this condition has not been satisfied by the end of the taxable year, it may be satisfied in the following taxable year, and the expenses may be deducted in the year in which they were incurred or paid, depending on the taxpayer's accounting method. See § 217(d)(2). If Ned does not ultimately satisfy the length of employment condition in the following taxable year, the Norrises will have to include the amount that they deducted in the prior taxable year, unless Ned's failure to meet this requirement is due to death, disability, or involuntary separation from full-time employment where he otherwise reasonably expected to meet the requirement. See § 217(d).

Since the Norrises appear to meet the threshold requirements under § 217, the next issue is the amount of the deduction. Section 217(a) allows a deduction for moving expenses, defined in § 217(b). For this purpose, moving expenses include reasonable expenses of (1) moving household goods and personal effects from the former residence to the new residence and (2) traveling (including lodging) from the former residence to the new place of residence. It does not include meals. Thus, provided the Norrises meet the reasonableness requirement under § 217(b), their deductible § 217(b) expenses include the cost of the moving van ($3500), the $20 for their gas used en route, and the $150 for the motel rooms. See § 217(b) and Reg. § 1.217–2(b). Their meals and utility deposits are not deductible expenses.

The $3500 expense for the moving van, if reasonable, is a qualified moving expense under § 217(b). The cost of moving all family members and pets are included in the allowable expenses. The employer reimburses $1500 of the Norrises' moving van expense. This is considered a tax-free fringe benefit under § 132(a)(6) as a "qualified moving expense reimbursement" since the cost of the moving van, if reasonable, is a valid § 217(b) expense that would be deductible otherwise by the taxpayer because the move is incurred for business reasons. Since this amount is excludable, the taxpayer cannot obtain a double benefit by deducting it as well, so the $1500 reimbursement will reduce the expense of the moving van and that, in turn, will reduce that portion of the § 217 deduction to $2000.

The expenses of traveling to the new residence are deductible, and all family members need not travel together. The gas expense is clearly deductible, provided the Norrises have a receipt to verify their expenditure. If not, they can claim a federal mileage allowance. They also may deduct reasonable repairs on the car but otherwise may not obtain a depreciation deduction or an allowance for wear and tear on their car.

As a result of the move, the Norrises incur total expenses of $3800. Ned obtained a $1500 moving expense reimbursement from his employer on which the Norrises are not taxed because of § 132(a)(6), which excludes the amount of any qualified moving expense reimbursement. This is defined under § 132(g) as any amount received from an employer for reimbursement of expenses that would be deductible under § 217 if directly paid or incurred by the individual. The amount of the reimbursement reduces the deductible expense of the moving van to $2000. Their expense for wear and tear on their car and the utility deposits are not deductible. Thus, their total § 217 expenses are $2170 ($2000 for the moving van, $20 for gas, and $150 for the motel rooms). This amount may be deducted above the line under § 62(a)(15).

5. TOOLS FOR SELF-ASSESSMENT

[1] Section 217 is the authorizing provision for the deduction of qualified moving expenses. Section 62(a)(15) directs the taxpayer to take the deduction above the line. Resist the urge to cite § 62(a)(15) as the authorizing provision, because it is not. The requirements of § 217 must be met before the taxpayer (or the student) can move to § 62(a)(15). The two threshold requirements under § 217 are the work time and the distance requirements. While there are some very limited exceptions to the work time requirement, § 217 is generally an "all-or-nothing" provision. If the taxpayer fails to meet either of the threshold requirements, no deduction is allowed.

[2] Some students find the time requirement confusing in its application to self-employed individuals. The time period is extended from 39 weeks during the first 12 months for employees to 78 weeks during the first 24 months for self-employed individuals, with full-time employment (either as a self-employed or as an employee) during 39 weeks of the first 12-month period. The purpose behind this is recognition by Congress that self-employed individuals may be in a more precarious financial position than employees. On the other hand, as a self-employed individual, it is easier to manipulate the tax system and obtain a deduction for a personal moving expense. Therefore, the time period is doubled for self-employed individuals to avoid the latter problem, and the Code provides that the employment period may be either as a self-employed individual or as an employee. This addresses the

first problem, so if the business does not do well, the self-employed individual still may be able to deduct the moving expenses above the line if she finds full-time work as an employee.

[3] The more confusing requirement is the distance requirement, which involves a comparison of two measurements. The first is the distance from the former residence to the former principal place of employment, and the second is the distance from the former residence to the new place of employment. The second measurement must be 50 miles farther than the first measurement. The 40-mile distance from Midville to Suburb is a red herring, so do not be tricked by this. The distance from the old residence to the new residence is irrelevant for this purpose. Thus, as we see in this problem, the new residence may be within the 50-mile radius, yet the moving expenses will still be allowed, provided that the new principal place of employment is outside of that radius. By the same token, the new residence may be more than 50 miles from both the old residence and the former place of employment, but the expenses will not be deductible if the new principal place of work falls within the 50-mile radius. A simpler way to explain the distance requirement is to ask whether the taxpayer's commuting distance to the new place of work would be at least 50 miles longer than the taxpayer's previous commute if the taxpayer had stayed in the former residence? If so, the distance requirement is met.

[4] Note that the regulations provide that *meals* and lodging (emphasis added) en route are deductible. See Reg. § 1.217–2(b)(4). These regulations conflict with § 217, which specifically disallows any deduction for meals en route. See § 217(b)(flush language). The discrepancy is due to the fact that § 217 previously authorized a deduction for meals en route. When this provision was changed, there was no corresponding change in the regulation. Periodically, this will happen. Congress will amend a Code section, and if there is not an otherwise significant change in the regulations, the Treasury Department will leave the regulation without any amendment. Beware of this practice! In the event of a discrepancy between the Code and the regulations, the Code trumps the regulations. Lodging is allowed en route and for one night at the old place of residence and one night at the new location. See Reg. § 1.217–2(b)(4). The deduction of the lodging expenses in Suburb require careful reading of the regulations because Reg. § 1.217–2(b)(4) provides that eligible expenses do not include "living or other expenses *following the date of arrival* at the new place of residence and while waiting to enter the new residence or waiting for household goods to arrive." But the same regulation also says that lodging en route is deductible under § 217, *including the date of arrival*.

6. VARIATIONS ON THE THEME

What results if Ned decides after 40 weeks that the job is not for him, so once again he opens a shoe store, this time in New Township?

15 BUSINESS EXPENSE DEDUCTIONS

1. OPENING REMARKS

Tax liability is determined by multiplying the applicable tax rate times the taxpayer's taxable income. Taxable income is gross income less allowable deductions and exemptions. There must be an authorizing Code provision to deduct an item because deductions are matters of legislative grace. This means that taxpayers have no constitutional right to a deduction unless it is specifically authorized under the Internal Revenue Code. Allowable deductions include expenses incurred in producing income. The so-called "workhorse" provision for business deductions is § 162, which authorizes a deduction for ordinary, necessary, and reasonable expenses incurred in carrying on a trade or business. A taxpayer may not deduct the personal expenses of day-to-day living, but the expenses incurred in a business or profit-oriented transaction are deductible. There are, however, some initial limitations on the deductibility of these expenses. First, the taxpayer must be engaged in a trade or business in order to take the § 162 deductions. Second, the expenditure must be an ordinary and necessary expense. Third, the expense must be a currently deductible expense and not a capital expenditure.

"Start-up" expenses incurred in establishing a business technically do not fall under § 162 because the taxpayer is not "carrying on" a trade or business at the time the expenses are incurred. Section 195 provides some relief to these taxpayers by allowing the expenditures to be capitalized and deducted currently, up to a limit of $5000, then amortized ratably over a 180-month period beginning in the month that the business becomes operative. Some expenses may be extraordinary and unnecessary, even though they are incurred in a business context. While most business expenses do not fall into this category, some do, and those expenses are not deductible. The seminal case defining the term "ordinary and necessary" is *Welch v. Helvering*, 290 U.S. 111 (1933), in which a taxpayer who worked for a bankrupt company decided to pay some of the company's debts in order to strengthen his own business standing. The U.S. Supreme Court held that he could not deduct these payments because they were not "ordinary and necessary" expenditures. The Court stated that the term "ordinary" does not mean that the expenses "must be habitual or normal in the sense that the same taxpayer will have to make them often," but rather the expense must be a "common and accepted" expense. The Court defined the term "necessary" to mean "appropriate and helpful." Even if the expense passes these tests, it will not be currently deductible if it is a capital expenditure. Instead, the expense will have to be capitalized (i.e., added to the basis of the asset) and recovered in either of two ways: (1) as a basis offset when the property is sold or otherwise disposed of, or (2) through amortization (i.e., written over gradually over a period of time), such as depreciation. But in order to amortize an expenditure, there must be an authorizing Code provision. Because of the time value of money, a current full deduction generally is more advantageous than either an amortized write-off over time or a deferred offset of the basis when the property is later sold. Thus, it is important to recognize the distinction between a currently deductible expense and a capital expenditure because this distinction raises timing issues that are important to business taxpayers. Finally, some business deductions are subject to limitations under the Code, so even if all the other tests are met and the deduction otherwise is allowed, the taxpayer may not be able to deduct the full amount of the expense.

2. HYPOTHETICAL

Oliver Oldman owns a heavy equipment leasing company. His wife, Olympia, owns a small clothing boutique that she started last year. Oliver has five employees in his business, and Olympia has two. Olympia owns the building in which her boutique is located, but Oliver rents his office. Both businesses are incorporated and are calendar year, cash method taxpayers.

Last year, Oliver purchased three acres of land adjacent to his office because he got a good deal on the property, and he thought that eventually his business might need the additional space. He paid $30,000 for this property. Oliver also leases a warehouse that he uses for equipment storage. The cost of one year's rental is $8400, and his lease period runs from October 1 through the following September 30. On September 15 of last year, he paid the entire $8400 when he signed the new lease. In addition, Oliver incurred advertising expenses of $20,000 last year. This included $3500 for a radio ad that ran for two weeks in November, $15,000 for a billboard ad for a year, and $1500 for a newspaper ad for a month. Finally, Oliver was sued last year for breach of contract by a disgruntled customer. He won this suit, but it cost him $18,000 in legal fees to defend himself. To show his appreciation to his long-time customers and to build goodwill after the lawsuit, he took four of his best customers and their spouses out to dinner at a new restaurant that had opened in town and then to a concert. The tab for the meal was $650, including drinks, tax, and tip, and the cost of the concert tickets was $950.

Olympia started her business last year after investigating several possibilities. She incurred travel costs of $2400 in traveling to New York to talk to designers and distributors after she made the initial decision to start the boutique. She also incurred legal expenses of $3000 for a market study and due diligence, $3000 in advertising expenses, and $3600 in accounting fees to set up the books. She also paid $40,000 for a franchise and incurred $45,000 in inventory costs. In the first half of her taxable year, she sold $96,000 of clothes, and she spent $15,000 on clothes, at wholesale, for her and her staff to wear at the boutique so that customers could see what the clothes looked like when worn. In the second half of the year, Olympia's sales slacked off, and in an effort to revive them, she started a delivery service for customers living within a 20-mile radius. She incurred costs of $500 in advertising this service, and she used her own car for the service and incurred costs of $500 for gas.

Last year, the roof of Olympia's boutique began to leak, so she hired a roofer to replace a portion of her roof. This replacement cost $3500. While she was having the roof repaired, she decided to have some minor carpentry work done in the boutique and to paint the interior. This work cost $2500. She also installed a burglar alarm at a cost of $2000.

Discuss whether any of Oliver and Olympia's expenses will be currently deductible. Why or why not? Ignore specific issues of depreciation for the moment.

3. LIST OF READINGS

Internal Revenue Code: §§ 162; 165; 195; 197; 261; 263; 274(a); 280F; 461; 1012

Regulations: §§ 1.61–3; 1.162–4; 1.162–11; 1.162–14; 1.162–20(a)(2); 1.263(a)-4(f)(1); 1.263(a)-5(e); 1.274–2(c) and (d); 1.274–3; 1.461–1

Cases: Indopco, Inc. v. Commissioner, 503 U.S. 79 (1992); Welch v. Helvering, 290 U.S. 111 (1933); Bonaire Development Co. v. Commissioner, 679 F.2d 159 (9th Cir. 1982); Commissioner v. Boyleston Market Ass'n, 131 F.2d 966 (1st Cir. 1942); Zaninovich v. Commissioner, 616 F.2d 429 (9th Cir. 1980); Morton Frank v. Commissioner, 20 T.C. 511 (1953); Yeomans v. Commissioner, 30 T.C. 757 (1958); Deihl v. Commissioner, TCM 2005–287

Rulings: Rev. Rul. 92–80, 1992–39 I.R.B. 7

Articles: Evans, *INDOPCO–The Treasury Finally Acts,* 80 Taxes 47 (2002)

4. SAMPLE ESSAY

Section 162 authorizes a deduction of all ordinary and necessary expenses paid or incurred during the taxable year in carrying on a trade or business. This simple provision covers a multitude of business expenses. Section 162(a)(1) authorizes a specific deduction for "a reasonable allowance for salaries . . . ." The salaries that Oliver and Olympia pay their employees clearly will be a deductible business expense under § 162(a).

The $30,000 that Oliver paid for the three acres of land is a capital expenditure that is not currently deductible. See §§ 261 and 263. His basis in this property is $30,000, a straight § 1012 cost basis. The rent that he pays on the warehouse normally is considered a currently deductible business expense under § 162, provided the rent is reasonable. If any portion is considered unreasonable, the IRS would argue that portion is not a necessary expense, and no deduction should be allowed for it, although the remainder would be deductible. In this case, however, Oliver prepays the rent for the entire 12-month period, and that raises a timing issue because a portion of that payment is attributable to the lease period that runs beyond the taxable year. Section 461(a) provides that any deduction or credit must be taken in the proper taxable year under the method of accounting employed by the taxpayer. The regulations provide that a deductible expenditure by a taxpayer using the cash receipts method of accounting may be taken in the year paid unless the "expenditure results in the creation of an asset having a useful life which extends substantially beyond the close of the taxable year." Reg. § 1.461–1(a). Under *Boyleston Market*, prepaid rent (like prepaid insurance, which was at issue in *Boyleston Market*) can be clearly allocated to discrete periods of time. Thus, only a pro rata portion of the rental payment attributable to the year in which it relates may be deducted in the year in which the amount is paid. This would mean that Oliver would be able to deduct only $2100, the portion of the payment attributable to the rental period from October through December. This is consistent with

Reg. § 1.162–11, which states that the lessee may deduct "an aliquot part" of the total lease payment each year, "based on the number of years the lease has to run."

However, the Ninth Circuit in *Zaninovich* interpreted the "substantially beyond the close of the taxable year" language to allow the full deduction if the payment spans two taxable years but does not relate to a period of more than one year. *Bonaire* clarified that *Zaninovich* had involved an arm's length, negotiated lease in which advance payment was customary and required, and that there was no attempt by the taxpayer to evade or distort taxes.

Although the IRS initially disagreed with the result in *Zaninovich*, it apparently has conceded the issue in Reg. § 1.263–4(f)(1), which adopts a 12-month rule similar to that of *Zaninovich*. Under the regulations, a prepayment may be deducted in the year paid, provided the right or benefit that is the subject of the payment does not extend beyond the earlier of (1) 12 months after the date on which the right or benefit is realized, or (2) the end of the taxable year following the taxable year in which the payment is made. In this case, Oliver pays the full year's rent on September 15 of year one, but the rental period begins on October 1. Since that term does not extend more than 12 months beyond October 1 of year one, nor does the payment relate to a term that extends beyond the end of taxable year two, Oliver falls within the safe harbor of Reg. § 1.263(a)-4(f)(1), and thus he may deduct the full payment in the year that it is made.

Oliver's advertising expenses, to the extent they are recurring, relate directly to his business, and are ordinary and necessary are currently deductible. Despite initial concern after *Indopco*, the IRS has clarified in Rev. Rul. 92–80 that such expenses remain currently deductible. But the government's assurances in Rev. Rul. 92–80 do not mean that all advertising expenses may be deducted automatically. Some may have to be capitalized, depending upon their nature. Reg. § 1.162–20(a)(2) provides that expenditures for "'good will' advertising that keeps the taxpayer's name before the public are generally deductible as ordinary and necessary business expenses, provided the expenditures are related to the patronage the taxpayer might reasonably expect in the future." Since the expense of the billboard appears to fall within the safe harbor of Reg. § 1.263(a)-4(f)(1), this expense and the other advertising expenses should be currently deductible under § 162.

The $18,000 in legal fees that Oliver paid to defend his business from the lawsuit brought by the disgruntled customer will be deductible as an ordinary and necessary business cost under § 162. In *Welch*, the Supreme Court noted that "a lawsuit affecting the safety of the business may happen once in a lifetime," but it is considered an ordinary and necessary business expense under § 162. Defending one's business from disgruntled customers is, unfortunately, often a necessary part of business. Thus, it is considered an ordinary and necessary expense under § 162 and deductible in the year or years in which it is paid.

The $1600 that Oliver spends on dinner and the concert with his clients will not be considered an advertising expense but rather an entertainment expense. In order to prevent abuse of the tax system, § 274(a)(1)(A) provides that no deduction is allowed for an entertainment, amusement, or recreation expense unless the taxpayer establishes that the expenditure was "directly related to" or "associated with" the active conduct of the taxpayer's trade or business. Reg. § 1.274–2(c) clarifies that "directly related" means that the taxpayer must be actively engaged in a business discussion, meeting, negotiation, or transaction, although income or other business benefit is not required for every such expenditure. Reg. § 1.274–3(i) provides that the taxpayer must have "more than a general expectation of deriving some income or other specific trade or business benefit (other than the goodwill of the person or persons entertained)." Thus, the dinner to show appreciation does not appear to fit within the "directly related" category. If the expenditure does not meet that test, it may be deducted if it is "associated with" the active conduct of the taxpayer's trade or business. Reg. § 1.274–2(d)(2) provides that this test is met if the taxpayer establishes a "clear business purpose in making the expenditure," such as "encourag[ing] the continuation of an existing business relationship." If this test is met, expenses allocable to the spouses should be deductible as well. The stumbling block for Oliver is whether a "substantial and bona fide business discussion" took place at, before, or after the meal and/or concert. Such a discussion must be substantial in relation to the entertainment. See Reg. § 1.274–3(a). If Oliver can pass this hurdle, § 274 imposes other restrictions on the deductibility of the expense. First, § 274(k) provides that the meal must not be lavish or extravagant. If so, that portion of the expense is disallowed. Also, the taxpayer or an employee must be present at the meal, which Oliver was, so this requirement is not a problem. Second, § 274(n) provides that only 50 percent of the otherwise allowable expense may be deducted. Third, § 274(d) requires the taxpayer to substantiate the expense by adequate records, corroborating the amount of the expense, date, time, and place that the expense occurred; the name of those present and their business relationship to the taxpayer; and the business purpose of the expense. If the concert tickets are deductible, § 274(n) applies to the face amount of the tickets. So if Oliver paid more than the face amount for the tickets, the additional amount is not deductible. See § 274(l). Also, the 50 percent limitation applies to this as well, so only 50 percent of the face amount of the tickets is deductible under §§ 162 and 274(n).

Olympia's travel expenses to New York, accounting fees, attorney's fees, and advertising expenses ordinarily would be deductible under § 162 but for the fact that she is not "carrying on" an active trade or business at the time the expenses are incurred. See *Morton Frank*. However, § 195 allows her to expense $5000 of the $12,000 of expenses in year one if they are considered "start-up" expenses. These are defined as expenses incurred in (1) investigating the creation or acquisition of an active trade or business, (2) creating an active trade or business, or (3) expenses incurred before the business becomes operational. § 195(c)(1)(A). The expenses must be of a type that normally would be deductible under § 162 if the taxpayer were carrying on a trade or business. The legal, advertising, and accounting fees appear to meet this requirement. The remaining $7000 must be amortized over a period of not less than 180 months, beginning with the month in which her business actually begins. § 195(b)(1)(B). Any expenses incurred in the purchase of the business is an acquisition cost that must be capitalized and added to Olympia's basis in her business. The franchise is an intangible asset that is amortizable over a 15-year period (beginning with the month in which the intangible is acquired) using a straight line write-off under § 197.

The inventory expense is a cost of goods sold that will offset Olympia's income from the sales of the clothes to arrive at gross income. Thus, the cost of the inventory that she sells during the taxable year will offset her total amount realized from the sale of those clothes. See Reg. § 1.61–3(a). The other clothes that she purchases for her and her staff to wear in the boutique are deductible only if they meet three tests: (1) they must be required or essential in the taxpayer's employment, (2) they must not be suitable for general or personal wear, and (3) they must not be so worn. See *Deihl*. The clothes that Olympia purchases for wear in the boutique will not be deductible because they are suitable for everyday wear outside of the boutique, whether she wears them outside of the boutique or not. Indeed, they are being sold for that purpose. Thus, they do not meet the requirements for deductibility, so Olympia may not obtain any tax advantage for the cost of these clothes.

The advertising costs and gas for the delivery service are currently deductible, provided Olympia has adequate records to document the business use of her car. Section 274(d) requires substantiation for any business deductions involving the use of a car. See § 274(d)(4). The car will be depreciable if it is used for business purposes, but the personal use cannot be considered. Thus, Olympia will have to apportion the business use versus the personal use, and only with respect to the business use will she be able to obtain a deduction. In addition, an automobile is considered "listed property" that is subject to limits on depreciation under § 280F.

In order to be deductible, a repair must be an "incidental" repair that neither materially increases the value of the property nor appreciably prolongs its useful life but rather keeps it in an ordinarily efficient operating condition. However, repairs in the nature of replacements, to the extent that they arrest deterioration and appreciably prolong the property's life, must be capitalized and depreciated. See Reg. § 1.162–4. The tax consequence of the roof repair depends on the amount of the roof that was repaired. If it was a relatively small portion, it will be considered a true repair and thus deductible under § 162 (except to the extent of any insurance recovery). If, however, it "materially adds to the value of the building or prolongs its useful life," it will be considered a capital expenditure that must be added to the basis of the building and depreciated over its useful life. Of course, any repair of the roof arguably will prolong the useful life of the building, so the correct focus should be on whether the "repair" extends the life of the building beyond what would normally have been expected when the building was constructed. Since the problem is not specific as to exactly how much of the roof was repaired, it cannot be said with certainty whether this will be a capital expenditure or a currently deductible repair. This issue will involve a factual determination of the amount of the roof repair in question.

The $2500 that Olympia spends for the burglar alarm will not be currently deductible because it will be considered an acquisition cost and thus will be a capital expenditure. The amount that she spends for the monthly monitoring, though, will be currently deducible under § 162. The "minor" carpentry work and painting probably will be deductible. In general, minor repairs and painting are considered currently deductible expenses under § 162. Where the painting expense arises as part of a "renovation," though, it is not deductible and will be considered a capital expense. If the painting is simply a "refresh" of the interior, it will be a currently deductible expenditure.

5. TOOLS FOR SELF-ASSESSMENT

[1] Since their businesses are incorporated, Oliver and Olympia are considered separate taxpayers for business purposes. They each will file a separate corporate return in addition to their joint personal income tax return. Thus, their expenses must be considered separately although they will incur some similar expenses, such as the undisclosed salary expenses for their respective employees. While there are issues that can arise as to the reasonableness of the salaries under § 162(a)(1), these issues are unlikely to arise with Oliver and Olympia's employees. If they arise at all, it is likely to be with respect to the compensation of Oliver and/or Olympia, who are more highly compensated, and they control their respective businesses. Under the facts of this problem, though, there are no issues of reasonableness of compensation presented, so all the salaries, including those of Oliver and Olympia, should be deductible by their companies.

[2] Oliver will not be able to amortize the cost of his three acres because land is never depreciable, despite taxpayers' best arguments. Thus, this cost will be recoverable only when the property is later sold. At that point, it will offset any amount realized to either reduce the amount of the taxable gain or increase the amount of any loss.

[3] Although the rental cost of the warehouse seems high, the determination of reasonableness is a facts and circumstances determination, and the assumption that the cost is unreasonable cannot be made under these facts. Relevant considerations include: Is the warehouse located in an urban area or a rural area? How large is the facility? Does it have any special features (such as air conditioning, heating, burglar alarm, hydraulic lift, etc.)?

[4] The purpose of spreading the deduction for the prepayment of rent over the leasehold term is to prevent a distortion of income. However, the *Bonaire* court noted that a prepayment causes a distortion in the first and last years, and arises only because of the cash method itself. As the Ninth Circuit noted in *Zaninovich,* the proration method would require a partial deduction in the last year of the lease, even though no payment would be made then. In the face of such arguments, the government was persuaded to change its position on *Zaninovich* in the regulations.

In *INDOPCO,* the U.S. Supreme Court held that expenditures that produce "significant benefits" that extend "beyond the tax year in question" must be capitalized, even though they "do not create or enhance separate and distinct assets." This threw into question a slew of expenditures that previously had been considered currently deductible, such as advertising expenses, routine repairs, and maintenance. While the broad position of the Supreme Court was a clear win for the government, the Treasury Department has retreated somewhat from this view that each expense must be examined to determine if it produces significant benefits that extend beyond the taxable year. As a general rule, routine advertising expenses are currently deductible, even though the benefits may extend beyond the taxable year of the payment. The fact that an expense is attributable to advertising does not necessarily mean that the expense is deductible under § 162, however, because an expenditure to purchase, rather than rent, a billboard would be a capital expenditure.

[5] Separating the pleasure component from the business component when a taxpayer takes a client, customer or business associate to dinner, a play, a concert, a ball game, etc., is a very difficult task under the tax law, and § 274 is a very convoluted statute. The first thing to remember is that the deduction first must pass the requirements of § 162. Section 274 is not an alternative to § 162, but rather a limitation on it.

[6] A problem with Olympia's start-up expenses is that the expenses may be treated differently if she has decided to enter into this business and is beyond the initial investigation stage. If she is in the "transactional stage," then her expenditures for legal fees, organization costs, etc., must be capitalized. These include appraisals, tax advice on the structure of the transaction, legal fees in negotiating the transaction, preparing and reviewing documents, obtaining regulatory approval, obtaining shareholder approval, and expenses of conveying property (such as transfer taxes and title registration costs). See Reg. § 1.263(a)-5(e)(2).

[7] Note that in the first year, she may take more than the $5000 initial amount under § 195(b)(1)(A)(ii) because she also gets to amortize her remaining start-up costs over the 180-month period, beginning with the month in which the business becomes active. Note also that the $5000 initial amount is reduced dollar-for-dollar to the extent that the start-up expenses exceed $50,000. So, if her start-up expenses had exceeded $55,000, she would not get to take any of the $5000 additional amount in year one but she would be able to amortize her start-up expenses over the 180-month period.

[8] There is some authority for deducting the cost of clothes if the taxpayer can establish that she was required to purchase them, they are not the type of clothes she ordinarily would wear and indeed, she has not worn them outside of work. *See* Yeomans v. Commissioner, 30 T.C. 757 (1958). However, as the Tax Court explained in *Deihl,* the subjective test has been specifically rejected in favor of an objective test, "which denies a business expense deduction for the cost of clothing that is 'generally accepted for ordinary street wear' (i.e., for ordinary street wear by people generally rather than by the taxpayer specifically)." *Deihl*, quoting *Pevsner v. Commissioner*, 628 F.2d 467, 470 (5th Cir.1980).

[9] Since Olympia owns the building that houses the boutique, she will be able to take annual depreciation deductions against the basis of the building. However, the problem tells us to ignore specific issues of depreciation, so we do not need to discuss the depreciation of the building nor any specific issues that may pertain to the business use of Olympia's car, such as whether it is listed property under § 280F and whether it is a "luxury" automobile.

[10] The repair versus capital expenditure issue is a difficult one because so much depends upon factual determinations. Items that normally would be deductible, such as painting a room in an office or rental property, would be required to be capitalized if done as part of a renovation project. This is also a problem in the case of Olympia's building. The "repairs" may be considered capital improvements, depending on the extent of the overall work that is done. There are two issues to be concerned with: (1) the amount of the work

done and whether it results in an extension of the useful life beyond that anticipated when the building was constructed, and (2) whether there were any upgrades or improvements made to the building at the same time. If so, unless the upgrades were very minor, it looks like a capital improvement.

6. VARIATIONS ON THE THEME

How, if at all, would your answer change if Olympia's business folded in its third year and she sold everything? What if Oliver decided to pay two years' rent on the warehouse in year one?

16

NONBUSINESS, PROFIT-ORIENTED EXPENSES

1. OPENING REMARKS

Section 162 allows a deduction for ordinary and necessary expenses incurred in carrying on a trade or business. Thus, the costs of generating taxable income are taken out of the taxable equation. Under the early tax Code, there was no corresponding deduction for expenses incurred in generating investment (i.e., nonbusiness) income. In the early 1930s, however, a wealthy investor named Eugene Higgins sought deductions under the precursor of § 162 for expenses incurred in managing his extensive portfolio of stocks and bonds. Mr. Higgins argued before the Board of Tax Appeals (the forerunner of the U.S. Tax Court) that his expenses should be deductible as if he were engaged in a business because his investment activities were continuous, constant, regular and extensive, and he derived a great deal of income from them. He argued that these activities differentiated him from a smaller investor and thus should entitle him to deduct his expenses under § 162. The Board held for the Commissioner, denying Mr. Higgins his deductions. This decision was affirmed by both the Second Circuit and the U.S. Supreme Court. See *Higgins v. Commissioner*, 312 U.S. 212 (1941). These courts both reasoned that Mr. Higgins, despite the extensiveness and regularity of his activities, was not "carrying on a trade or business" in managing his personal investments and thus was not entitled to a deduction for the expenses incurred in the management of those investments. The following year, Congress enacted § 212, authorizing deductions for ordinary and necessary expenses "for the production or collection of income" or "for the management, conservation, or maintenance of property held for the production of income." In 1954, Congress added a third provision, allowing a deduction for expenses incurred "in connection with the determination, collection, or refund of any tax." See § 212(3).

While § 212 contains the same "ordinary and necessary" language as § 162 and is generally interpreted in the same manner (i.e., no deduction for capital expenditures), § 212 authorizes the deduction even though the individual is not carrying on a trade or business. Section 162 deductions generally are more favorable, though, than § 212 deductions because they are taken above-the-line (except for unreimbursed employee business expenses), while § 212 deductions are itemized deductions, except for expenses in connection with rents and royalties. In addition, most § 212 deductions are considered miscellaneous itemized deductions under § 67, which means that they are deductible only to the extent that they exceed the floor of 2 percent of the taxpayer's adjusted gross income.

2. HYPOTHETICAL

Paul Phillips owned 28 percent of the XYZ company, a publicly held corporation. Paul became very unhappy with the manner in which the company was run, so he decided to campaign to get himself and one other person elected to the XYZ board of directors in order to have more control over the running of the business. In particular, he was concerned about a decision of the management to sell a unit of the company. He incurred expenses of $20,000 in conducting mailing campaigns and in traveling to New York to attend the annual shareholders' meeting. Ultimately, he was successful in getting his other person elected to the board, but he was not successful in getting himself elected. While his friend was instrumental in bringing about a change in some of the company's policies, he was not successful in preventing the sale of the unit, which went forward as planned. Paul hired an attorney in an effort to prevent the sale, and after expending another $25,000, he was unsuccessful in this effort as well.

After his unsuccessful attempts to change the course of the company, Paul decided to sign up for two courses on corporate transactions and investment management at the business school of his local university. He took these courses for enlightenment and not for college or graduate credit.

The frustration of his failed attempts took a toll on his marriage. Shortly after the sale went through, Paul and his wife decided to divorce. He then spent $5000 in discussions with his attorney and accountant about the amount and tax ramifications of the alimony payments to his wife, and about the tax and investment consequences to him of the sale of the unit of the XYZ Company.

Discuss whether or not Paul may deduct any of his expenses. Are there any further facts you would need to know?

3. LIST OF READINGS

Internal Revenue Code: §§ 212; 274(h)

Regulations: Reg. § 1.212–1

Cases: U.S. v. Gilmore, 372 U.S. 39 (1963); Surasky v. United States, 325 F.2d 191 (5th Cir. 1963); Meyer J. Fleischman v. Commissioner, 45 T.C. 439 (1966)

Rulings: Rev. Rul. 64–236, 1964–2 Cum. Bull. 64; Rev. Rul. 72–545, 1972–2 C.B. 179

4. SAMPLE ESSAY

Section 212 allows a deduction for all "ordinary and necessary expenses paid or incurred during the taxable year for the production or collection of income or for the management, conservation, or maintenance of property held for the production of income." The regulations further provide that "such expenses must be reasonable in amount and must bear a reasonable and proximate relation to the production or collection of taxable income or to the management, conservation, or maintenance of property held for the production of income." Reg. § 1.212–1(d). The term "ordinary and necessary" has the same meaning as in § 162. See *Surasky*.

The facts of this hypothetical are similar to those of *Surasky,* in which the court directly addressed the extent to which it would require a proximate relation between the expenditure and the generation of a profit. In *Surasky*, the lower court had disallowed a § 212 deduction for the expenses of a proxy battle because of the speculative nature of the expenditure. In overturning the lower court's decision, the Fifth Circuit opined that the expenses should be allowed under § 212 if they are "genuinely incurred in the exercise of reasonable business judgment in an effort to produce income," even though the expenses "may fall far short of satisfying the common law definition of proximate cause." *Surasky,* at 195. Further, the court noted that it did not matter whether the expenses were incurred in an effort to increase the taxpayer's investment income or to prevent a loss. Note, though, that the IRS has stated in Rev. Rul. 64–236 that while it will follow the *Surasky* decision, it will not follow the portion of the opinion in which the court indicated that the deductible expenditures "need not be proximately related, either to the production or collection of income, or to the management, conservation, or maintenance of property held for the production of income." *Id.*

There are, however, some differences between this problem and *Surasky*. For instance, although the shareholder in *Surasky* was unsuccessful in his attempt to replace a majority of the board of directors, he was successful in precipitating the resignation of the chairman of the board and the president, and in increasing the value of his stock substantially. In this problem, it is unclear whether Paul has been successful in increasing either his dividend income or the value of his stock.

While the *Surasky* court thought the lower court had applied too strict a standard in requiring a proximate relationship between the expenditures and the increased dividends at the time the expenditures were made, it nevertheless engaged in an analysis of those expenditures compared to the results produced. The court discussed the *Alleghany Corporation* case, which involved similar facts to those of *Surasky,* where the tax court concluded on the basis of the facts that it was clear that the taxpayer had made the expenditures to protect the taxpayer's business.

It would be helpful in this problem to have a clearer understanding of Paul's purpose in opposing the sale of the unit. If his objection is a moral one, for example based on a belief that the employees would suffer needlessly because of a sale, this would not be a valid purpose under § 212. But if his objection is, for example that a sale would hurt the value of his stock or affect the amount of his dividends, this would be a valid purpose under § 212 and *Surasky*.

In order to be deductible under § 212, the expenses must be reasonable. See Reg. § 1.212–1(d). Here, Paul is a significant shareholder, and it is reasonable and ordinary to assume that he would be interested in protecting his substantial investment in the XYZ Co. In determining whether the amount of his expenditures is reasonable, a comparison must be made between the expenditures and Paul's investment in the company. We do not know the extent of his holdings in monetary terms, but if the XYZ Co. is publicly held and Paul owns 28 percent of the shares, we can assume that he has a significant monetary investment in the company. Presumably, his expenditures, which also were significant, are not out of line in relation to his investment. If they are, then they would not be considered ordinary expenditures. If they are not, then the expenditures of $45,000 should be deductible under § 212, provided that Paul can establish a proximate relationship between these expenditures and a profit motive.

The amount that Paul spends on the business courses is not deductible under § 212 because it is directly disallowed under § 274(h)(7), which provides that any expense incurred in attending a convention, seminar, or similar meeting is not deductible under § 212. In addition, a course of study such as that being pursued by Paul is not an ordinary expense in managing one's investments, and arguably, is not necessary for him to continue to manage those investments. Finally, the regulations disallow any § 212 deduction for the expense of taking special courses or training. See Reg. § 1.212–1(f).

The discussions with the accountant and the attorney about the tax consequences of the sale of the XYZ unit should be deductible under § 212(3), provided the discussions are about Paul's personal tax liability and provided the amount is reasonable. If the discussions centered around the effect of the sale of the unit on the value of Paul's stock, that amount should be deductible under § 212(1) or § 212(2). The amount of the professional fees that pertained to Paul's divorce will be considered personal in nature (see *Gilmore*) and thus will not be deductible except to the extent that they are attributed to advice about Paul's tax consequences on the divorce. See *Meyer J. Fleischman*.

Since some of the professional's fees are deductible and some are not, the burden will be on Paul to allocate and substantiate his deductions. See Rev. Rul. 72–545. This means that he will have to have a specifically itemized bill from the attorney and the accountant, clearly noting what the fees pertained to and what, in general, was discussed.

5. TOOLS FOR SELF-ASSESSMENT

[1] Generally, the best way to address a tax problem is first to state the Code section at issue and then apply the Code section to the facts. This produces a well-organized answer.

[2] The first thing to remember is that tax benefit provisions (such as those authorizing an exclusion or a deduction) are strictly construed by both the IRS and the courts. Expenditures under §§ 162 and 212 must first pass the threshold ordinary, necessary, and reasonableness tests under strict standards.

[3] The second point is more important because it is less obvious. When the tax consequences depend upon an examination of the facts, do not assume that the holding of the court in a case with similar facts will produce the same result in your case. Sometimes slight changes in the facts may produce different results. Thus, it is important to read the *Surasky* opinion carefully to see what the court considered significant in that case. This will make the difference between an "A" answer and a "B" answer on an exam, and in real life, it may make the difference between a win and a loss in court. Also, a related point is that sometimes you may not have enough facts and will have to make assumptions or discuss things in the alternative, so be specific if you are making assumptions. Again, this can make the difference between an "A" paper and a "B" paper.

[4] Although Paul does not own a majority of the outstanding shares of XYZ stock, he owns a significant share, and since the company is publicly held, he may be a majority shareholder. Do not gloss over the fact that this is a publicly held corporation. A 28 percent ownership interest in a publicly held company generally is very significant. If Paul had been successful in his attempt to join the board, he may well have been successful in influencing the decisions of the company. Therefore, while his expenditures are not ordinary under most circumstances, in this case, he should be able to easily demonstrate a rational reason for the expense, and if so, he should be able to

take the deduction. The Supreme Court said in *Welch v. Helvering* that the term "ordinary" does not necessarily mean habitual or continuous.

[5] If Paul had been engaged in a trade or business, his educational expense probably would have been deductible since it would be directly related to his business, and he is not pursuing a degree nor do the courses train him for a new and different trade or business. However, § 274(h)(7) takes the guesswork out of this issue for purposes of § 212.

[6] In a divorce, the payor's expenses in determining the amount of alimony payable are not deductible because alimony is deductible to the payor under § 215. Thus, if the payor were able to deduct the legal expenses attributable to the alimony determination, this would provide a double tax benefit, which the Code frowns upon. On the other hand, the payee's expenses incurred in the generation of alimony are deductible because the alimony payments will be included in the payee's gross income under § 71. Thus, the payee's expenses are incurred for the production or collection of income under § 212(1).

[7] Paul will need receipts to verify all expenditures. Verification and allocation are particularly important in the context of the professional fees because the other expenditures are deductible on an all-or-nothing basis, while that one is deductible in part.

6. VARIATIONS ON THE THEME

What result if Paul had spent $20,000 investigating why the company was not doing as well as he thought it should? Also, what if he offered to pay his wife's legal expenses in the divorce? Would either of these items be deductible?

17

MIXED PURPOSE EXPENDITURES

1. OPENING REMARKS

Some expenditures have both a business or profit-oriented character and a personal character, such as meals while traveling for business purposes. In some cases, the personal nature of the expenditure may disallow the deduction altogether. In other cases, the deduction may be limited, or the expenditure may be deductible in its entirety. In general, deductibility depends upon the extent to which the expenditure is business related and the extent to which the expense may be susceptible to manipulation for tax purposes (for instance, the infamous "three martini lunch").

One area in which the deduction of mixed purpose expenditures can arise with complexity is in connection with travel expenses incurred while away from home in pursuit of a trade or business under § 162(a)(2). In *Rosenspan v. U.S.*, 438 F.2d 905 (2d Cir. 1971), the Second Circuit famously held that a traveling salesman who had no residence (the proverbial man without a home) could not be away from home when he was traveling. Therefore, the hapless Mr. Rosenspan could not deduct his travel expenses. The complexity arises when a taxpayer who travels regularly for business purposes maintains a residence in one location and a business in another. The question is where is the taxpayer's "home" for tax purposes? After all, the expenses may not be deducted unless the taxpayer is "away from home." The natural assumption is that home means residence or hearth is home, as the Second Circuit concluded in *Rosenspan*. But the IRS takes the position that "home" for purposes of § 162(a)(2) is the taxpayer's principal place of business. This is not a problem if the taxpayer's residence and business are in the same town. But where the two are some distance apart and the taxpayer commutes to work, the question is when is the taxpayer "away from home" for tax purposes? Also, where the taxpayer maintains two residences and conducts business at both, what deductions, if any, are allowed?

2. HYPOTHETICAL

Quentin Quarles is an associate attorney who works with a large law firm in a metropolitan area. He lives in Smaller City, about 10 miles from the office and commutes to and from work by car each day. In order to avoid going into the office on the weekends, Quentin typically brings work home with him. He has a small room in his house set aside as his office, with its own phone line, fax machine, and computer. He often works in his home office in the evenings and most weekends.

Quentin also is required to travel, and his travel takes two forms: (1) in-town travel between the office and courthouse, and occasionally to the office of other attorneys and, on rare occasions, to the business or residence of clients; and (2) out-of-town travel. Typically, his out-of-town travel expenses are reimbursed by the firm but often his in-town travel is not.

The firm has decided to open an additional office in an area about 200 miles away. Quentin has been traveling between the two locations to help set up this office. The firm has asked him to oversee the establishment of the office, which it estimates should take about six months. Quentin has rented a small, furnished apartment which he lives in during the week. On the weekends, he travels back home to be with his wife.

Quentin's wife, Quynlyn, is a general contractor. She has several ongoing projects, some located in town and some located out of town. She travels between these projects several times per week. Quynlyn has subcontractors who have worked with her for many years and whose expertise she values highly. Twice a year, she takes these subcontractors and their spouses to dinner at a nice restaurant and to a professional ball game. The bill for the dinners last year was $1600, and the tickets for the ball games were around $1000.

Next year, the General Contractors Association is sponsoring a convention/cruise to St. Thomas and St. Croix in the Virgin Islands. Quynlyn has booked a room for herself and Quentin for this trip. They will be gone for a week, and the cost is $4500 for the two of them, which includes the $750 registration fee for the convention.

The Quarleses seek your advice on whether any of their expenses are deductible. Quentin also wants to know if he can obtain a deduction for his home office. Discuss fully.

3. LIST OF READINGS

Internal Revenue Code: §§ 67; 162; 274**;** 280A(c)
Regulations: § 1.162–2(e); 1.162–17; 1.274–2(d)
Rulings: Rev. Rul. 99–7, 1999–1 C.B. 361; Rev. Proc. 2008–72, 2008–50 I.R.B. 1286
Cases: U.S. v. Correll, 389 U.S. 299 (1967); Flowers v. Commissioner, 326 U.S. 465 (1946); Peurifoy v. Commissioner, 358 U.S. 59 (1958); Paolini v. Commissioner, 43 T.C.M. 513 (1982)

4. SAMPLE ESSAY

In order to obtain a deduction for a home office, the office must meet the requirements of § 280A(c)(1). First, the office must be exclusively used on a regular basis. Quentin may be able to establish that his office meets this test, provided that it is not used for anything other than his business activities. Second, the office must be used either as the principal place of the taxpayer's business or as a place to meet with clients, customers, etc., in the normal course of the taxpayer's business. See § 280A(c)(1)(A) and (c)(1)(B). For this purpose, the term "principal place of business" means that there must be "no other fixed location of such trade or business where the taxpayer conducts substantial administrative or management activities of such trade or business." § 280A(c)(1). Quentin cannot meet this test because he has an office at his law firm.

Finally, the use of the office must be for the convenience of the employer. Quentin's use of his home office is for his own convenience and not for the convenience of his employer. Therefore, § 280A(c)(1) will not permit him to take any deductions for his home office.

Quentin incurs several types of travel expenses: (1) expenses in commuting from his home to work and back each day, (2) expenses of travel in town for business purposes, and (3) expenses of traveling out of town for business purposes. He may not deduct his commuting expenses of going from home to office and back every day. This is considered a personal expense that is not deductible, no matter how far the commute. See Reg. § 1.162–2(e) and *Flowers*.

The rules for the deductibility of travel expenses depend on the type of expense at issue. In his in-town travel, Quentin is likely to incur expenses of transportation and meals. Meals may be deducted under two circumstances: (1) where the taxpayer is away from home in pursuit of business for a period of time in which sleep or rest is required, and (2) where the taxpayer dines with business associates or clients and discusses a specific business matter. The first situation is known as the *Correll* "sleep or rest" rule. Under this rule, meals and lodging may be deducted only if the taxpayer is out of town for an extended period of time. Clearly, Quentin may not deduct meals while he is in town because he does not satisfy the *Correll* sleep or rest test. Moreover, his meals in town are regarded as personal, nondeductible expenses. If he has a meal with a client, however, the cost of the meal (his and the client's) may be deductible under § 162, subject to the limitations of § 274. Under § 274(a)(1), the meal must be directly related to or associated with the active conduct of a trade or business. This means that the purpose of the meeting with the client must be more than simply to touch base with the client. In addition, only 50 percent of the cost of the meals is deductible under § 274(n), and the meal cannot be lavish or extravagant under § 274(k). Also, the taxpayer must provide substantiation under § 274(d), which includes not only a receipt for the meal but also a notation of who the taxpayer dined with and what business item(s), in general, were discussed.

Transportation expenses, even while in town, may be deductible provided they are incurred for a business purpose and provided the taxpayer has adequate substantiation of the expenses under § 274(d). Rev. Rul. 99–7 provides guidance on the deductibility of in-town transportation costs. In-town travel between Quentin's office and the court house, and his office and other business locations is deductible as an ordinary, necessary business expense, subject to the substantiation requirement. Rev. Rul. 99–7. The standard federal mileage rate for the business use of an automobile currently is 51 cents per mile. IR-2010-119 (2011 Standard Mileage Rates). The cost of going from the courthouse or other business location in town to his home probably will be considered a commuting cost and not deductible, although that is not entirely clear. If Quentin goes to the courthouse or any other business location on an intermittent but regular basis, it will be considered a regular work location, and he will not be able to deduct the cost of his transportation from that location to his home or vice versa. If, though, the courthouse or other business location qualifies as a "temporary" business location, he can deduct the cost of commuting from his home to that location and back, regardless of the distance. See Rev. Rul. 99–7. Since this expense is not reimbursed, it will be considered a miscellaneous itemized deduction under § 67. This means that it is subject to a floor of 2 percent of Quentin's adjusted gross income and may be taken only as an itemized deduction to the extent Quentin's collective § 162 expenses exceed the floor. Thus, Quentin's ability to deduct these expenses is very limited.

In the routine out-of-town travel, Quentin will incur costs of transportation, meals, and lodging. If he is out of town for an extensive period so that sleep or rest is required, he will be able to deduct the cost of his meals and lodging. In this case, the meals do not have to meet the requirements of § 274(a)(1)(A)(the "directly related to" and "associated with" tests), but they do have to meet the other requirements. The lodging and transportation costs will be deductible in full, subject to the substantiation requirement. Transportation includes the cost of parking at the airport and any cab or bus fares incurred on the trip. Since Quentin is usually reimbursed for these expenses, this transforms the § 162 deduction from a miscellaneous itemized deduction to an above-the-line deduction under § 62(a)(2)(A). Section 274(e)(3) exempts reimbursed expenses from the other limitations of § 274, so Quentin will not have to worry about those limitations. In reality, this is a wash (tantamount to an exclusion) because technically, the amount of the reimbursement constitutes income to Quentin but the above-the-line deduction produces a "wash" of no tax attributable to the reimbursement and no overall tax benefit (i.e., no deduction). The regulations permit the employee to exclude the amount of the reimbursement if the employee is required to account to the employer for the expenses, and the amount of the reimbursement does not exceed the ordinary and necessary expenses incurred by the employee. The employee also is required to state on his return that the total amount of employer reimbursements does not exceed the amount of the ordinary and necessary business expenses incurred by him. See Reg. § 1.162–17(b).

If Quentin should engage in any nonbusiness activities while out of town, his transportation expenses will be deductible in full, provided the trip is primarily related to his trade or business. See Reg. § 1.162–2(b)(1). His other expenses (meals and lodging) will not be deductible on nonbusiness days, unless those nonbusiness days are standby days, such as weekends, when no business is conducted. The primary purpose test is a facts and circumstances determination and generally, the amount of time spent on personal activities versus the amount spent on business activities is the most important factor. See Reg. § 1.162–2(b)(2).

Quentin's travel expenses incurred in traveling to the location of the new office, even while it is being set up, are considered business expenses. Since it is 200 miles from his primary office location, he can satisfy the *Correll* sleep or rest requirement. His expenses will fall into several categories: transportation, meals, lodging, and miscellaneous.

Since he now is considered to have two business locations, his travel expenses between the two locations will be deductible, provided he is traveling away from home for a business purpose. Quentin will be at the new location for a six-month period, thus he is temporarily away from home (see § 162(a), flush language), and his tax home remains either in Smaller City or the metropolitan area where his office is located, depending on the test employed. Under *Flowers*, there are 3 tests: (1) the expense must be a reasonable and necessary travel expense, (2) it must be incurred while away from home (under the hearth-is-home test), and (3) it must be incurred in the pursuit of business and required by the exigencies of the business. Under *Peurifoy*, Quentin retains the requisite ties with his primary place of business in the metropolitan area and thus should be able to deduct his expenses while away from home under § 162(a)(2).

The transportation expenses of traveling between the new location and the metropolitan area will be deductible under § 162; but on the weekends, when he travels back to be with Quynlyn, his expenses are not deductible because he is traveling for a personal reason. If, however, he has a business meeting back at the firm on a Monday morning, he will be able to deduct his weekend transportation expenses equivalent to traveling from the new location back to the metropolitan area. The deductibility of commuting expenses at the temporary work location is unclear. On the one hand, if the taxpayer is temporarily away from home on business long enough to require sleep or rest, all of his transportation expenses should be deductible. On the other hand, the IRS now takes the position that commuting expenses, even while temporarily away from home, are not deductible, and this position has been supported by the tax court in dictum in a memorandum decision. See *Paolini*.

The cost of the apartment is a duplicate expense for Quentin, who is maintaining a residence back in Smaller City, so the rental expense of the apartment should be deductible. Meals also should be deductible (50 percent) while Quentin is temporarily away from home, subject to the limitations discussed above. In *Peurifoy*, the Supreme Court allowed deductions for reasonable expenses incurred while the taxpayer was away from home for a "temporary" rather than an "indefinite" or "indeterminate" period of time. Section 162 adopts the IRS's general rule that a definite period of up to one year is considered temporary. Since Quentin's stay in the new location is not expected to exceed six months, his stay is considered temporary, and he is entitled to deduct his unreimbursed expenses.

Since Quentin is an employee, his unreimbursed business expenses will be considered "miscellaneous itemized deductions" under § 67. Thus, they will be deductible only to the extent they exceed 2 percent of his adjusted gross income. Note that the 50 percent limitation on the deductibility of meals under § 274(n)(1) is applied first.

Quynlyn has several projects, both in town and out of town. Under Rev. Rul. 99–7, she may deduct the costs of transportation in traveling between the projects, whether in town or out. She also may deduct the costs of traveling from her office to the projects and vice versa, and she may be able to deduct the costs of commuting to the out-of-town projects, provided that those projects are temporary, defined under Rev. Rul. 99–7 as irregular or short term (usually a matter of days or weeks). If she regularly has projects out of town, or the ones that she has are longer term, those may no longer be considered temporary, and she may not be able to deduct her commuting costs to and from those projects. If she is self-employed, she has a much better chance than Quentin of successfully maintaining a home office under § 280A(c)(1). If so, then her commuting costs incurred in commuting to and from those projects will be deductible, whether in town or not. See Rev. Rul. 99–7. Otherwise, if she has a separate office, she will be able to deduct her transportation expenses in going from the office to the projects and back, but not the commuting expenses of going from home to office and back.

The dinners and ball games for the subcontractors and their spouses may be considered valid business entertainment expenses, provided they meet the requirements of §§ 162 and 274. The first hurdle is that the expense must be considered an ordinary and necessary business expense under § 162. Quynlyn probably will be able to pass this test because her business depends on her ability to attract skilled subcontractors. Therefore, it is important to her and her business to keep these subcontractors happy. The second test is that of § 274(a)(1)(A), under which the entertainment must be directly related to or associated with the active conduct of the taxpayer's trade or business. Usually this means that a substantial business discussion must occur before, during, or after the dinner and/or ball game, or the taxpayer hopes to obtain new business or to encourage the continuation of an existing business relationship. See Reg. § 1.274–2(d)(2). In this case, the expenses seem to be "associated with" the active conduct of Quynlyn's business because she wants to encourage the continuation of an existing business relationship, and therefore the expenses should be deductible. If so, the deduction also applies to the expenses allocable to the spouses. See Reg. § 1.274–2(d)(2) and (d)(4).

Once the § 274(a) hurdle has been cleared, the next hurdle is § 274(k), which provides that deductions for food and beverages are limited to those amounts that are not "lavish or extravagant." This also means that only the face amount of tickets to entertainment events is potentially deductible. Also, under § 274(k), either the taxpayer or an employee must be present at the meal. Next, the limitation of § 274(n) is applied so that only 50 percent of the remaining amount is deductible. This amount includes the amount of any tax and tip.

In general, expense deductions for conventions on cruise ships generally are disallowed. Section 274(h)(2) provides an exception where the taxpayer meets the reporting requirements, establishes that the meeting is directly related to the active conduct of her trade or business, the ship is registered in the United States, and all ports of call are in the United States or its possessions. If these requirements are met, § 274(h)(2) further limits the deductions to $2000 per individual per calendar year.

U.S. possessions are American Samoa, Guam, Puerto Rico, the Northern Mariana Islands, and the U.S. Virgin Islands. Since St. Thomas and St. Croix are in the U.S. Virgin Islands, Quynlyn should be able to obtain a deduction, provided she meets the other requirements. First, the ship must be registered in the United States; second, she must establish that the convention was directly related to her business (which should not be a problem); third, the substantiation requirements of § 274(h)(5) must be met. These include two signed statements that must be attached to the return: one signed by Quynlyn, listing the scheduled business meetings and the number of hours each day that she spent on business activities; the second signed by an officer of the organization sponsoring the meeting, listing a schedule of business activities each day of the meeting, the number of hours that Quynlyn attended these meetings, and any other information that the regulations may require.

The deductibility of a spouse's expenses on a business trip is very limited. In general, no deduction is allowed unless the spouse would be able to deduct his/her expenses independently under § 162. See § 274(m)(3). Since it does not appear that Quentin would be able to deduct his expenses of the cruise otherwise, the couple must subtract out expenses attributable to Quentin before the application of the $2000 limit.

5. TOOLS FOR SELF-ASSESSMENT

[1] As you can see from this problem, § 162(a)(2) covers much ground. The term "travel expenses" is a generic term that encompasses transportation costs, meals, lodging, and miscellaneous expenses. The best way to approach a mixed purpose § 162 problem is first to separate the various expenses into those incurred while at "home" and those incurred while traveling "away from home." The "at-home" expenses must be separated into commuting expenses and travel from one business location to another. These expenses generally are easier to deal with than the "away-from-home" expenses. The "away-from-home" expenses also must be separated into the various categories: transportation, meals, lodging, and miscellaneous items. Of course, these expenses must be incurred while the taxpayer is away from home, and the issue of the tax "home" arises when the taxpayer (a) has no fixed residence, (b) has more than one residence and more than one business, (c) is temporarily assigned to a new business location, and (d) where a married couple is employed or has a business in two or more locations that are distant from each other. Once the tax home is established, business/travel expenses incurred at other locations are deductible. The fact that an expense is potentially deductible does not mean, however, that the taxpayer will obtain the full benefit, or any benefit, from the expense. Section 274 and § 280A may limit the deductibility of the expense. Finally, one must consider whether the deduction is to be taken above-the-line or below-the-line (e.g., if the taxpayer is an employee, has the employee been reimbursed by the employer?). If it is below-the-line, the expense is a miscellaneous itemized expense under § 67 and can be taken only to the extent that it exceeds 2 percent of the taxpayer's adjusted gross income—another severe limitation.

[2] Applying these principles to the problem, Quentin has routine transportation expenses in commuting to work each day (including parking), in traveling to the courthouse and back to the office, to the office of other attorneys and back, and to the business or residence of clients and back. Quynlyn also incurs expenses in traveling between projects. Both of their transportation expenses must be divided into (1) commuting expenses (from home to work and back), (2) expenses of traveling for business in town, and (3) out of town travel expenses.

[3] Although an argument may be made that expenses incurred in going from one's residence to work and back at the end of the day should be considered a deductible business expense because it is directly related to the production of taxable income, the IRS's argument is that this is a cost that nearly every working person incurs, and while some costs are greater than others, it is largely a matter of personal choice how far one lives from one's place of work. This applies no matter what form the commuting takes, such as bus, train, metro, or car. One exception to this general rule, which is not presented in this hypothetical, is the qualified transportation fringe benefit that can be excluded from gross income under § 132(a)(5). Another exception is found in Rev. Rul. 99–7, which provides that a taxpayer may obtain a deduction for transportation expenses incurred in commuting between home and a temporary work location outside the metropolitan area where the taxpayer

lives and normally works. Unfortunately, Rev. Rul. 99–7 is a very confusing ruling because it is subject to many exceptions, and some of its rules are illogical.

[4] The rationale for the allowance of commuting expenses when the taxpayer is temporarily away from home on business is that there is less personal choice in the matter of where to live in relation to the temporary work site and thus, the taxpayer is likely to incur greater expenses than she normally would in commuting to work within the metropolitan area. A temporary work location is defined as one in which the taxpayer expects to be, and actually is, employed for no longer than a year. However, subsequent cases have held that where the taxpayer regularly works outside the metropolitan area, even though the work locations may vary, no commuting expense deduction is allowed. This may affect Quynlyn, who may not be able to deduct her commuting expenses of going from home to an out-of-town project if she regularly has out-of-town projects. However, Rev. Rul. 99–7 authorizes a deduction for Quentin's commuting expenses when he is at the temporary work location out of town, despite the dictum in the *Paolini* case.

[5] Under Rev. Rul. 99–7, if a taxpayer has a regular work location (whether a home office within § 280A(c)(1) or not), a deduction may be taken for daily commuting expenses of going from home to any temporary work location in the same trade or business, regardless of distance. Obviously, the deductibility of the commuting expense of going from the courthouse to his home will depend on factual circumstances of how often Quentin goes to the courthouse and may depend upon the type of work that he is doing. For instance, if he is a litigator, the courthouse may be considered a regular place of business, even though he is there only intermittently. That would mean that while the commuting expense of going from the office to the courthouse (and vice versa) would be deductible, the expense of going from the courthouse to his home at the end of the day (or from home to the courthouse) would not be.

[6] The other transportation expenses incurred in going from one work location to another should be deductible, subject to substantiation. This applies to both Quentin and Quynlyn. In Quentin's case, if he should fail to submit his claims for reimbursement, hoping to ingratiate himself with his employer, he may not obtain a deduction for the unreimbursed amounts because it would not be considered an "ordinary" expense. In fact, it is extraordinary that an employee who is entitled to reimbursement would not submit a claim. See *Heidt v. Commissioner*, 274 F.2d 25 (7th Cir. 1959). Any amount of reimbursement should technically be included in Quentin's gross income in the year of the reimbursement, and then he should be able to take an above-the-line deduction under § 62(a)(2)(A). The regulations permit Quentin to exclude this amount (which is the practical effect of the inclusion and above-the-line deduction), provided the reimbursement meets certain requirements. See Reg. §§ 1.162–17 and 1.62–2(c)(2) and (c)(4). If the expenses are not reimbursed, the § 67 limitation on the deductibility of "miscellaneous itemized deductions" means, as a practical matter, that the occasional commuting expense will not be deductible for most employees, because it will not exceed the 2 percent floor.

[7] Lodging is not deductible if the taxpayer is not away from home because this also is considered a personal expense. Meals, in general, are not deductible if the taxpayer is not away from home for a business purpose, but business meals with a client or customer may be deductible, subject to the limitations under §§ 162 and 274 (and perhaps § 67). A question the IRS may raise with respect to Quentin's meals at the temporary business location is whether they remain deductible if he buys groceries and prepares the meals himself, as opposed to eating in a restaurant. This question raises two issues: (1) does the term "meals" include groceries and raw materials, as opposed to prepared servings of food; and (2) does the § 162 deduction for meals imply excess expense over that which the taxpayer would otherwise have spent if he had been in his own home?

While the term "meals" in the context of § 119 does seem to imply ready-to-eat servings of food, § 119 is a different provision than § 162. Thus, it appears that Quentin should be able to obtain a deduction under § 162 for the groceries he purchases while temporarily away from home on business. With regard to the second issue, while the overall policy rationale for the allowance of the deduction is that the taxpayer is likely to incur duplicate expenses (in the case of housing) or expenses in excess of those he otherwise would have incurred (in the case of meals), deductibility does not depend solely on duplicate or excess expenses.

[8] The business meals that Quynlyn shares with the subcontractors and their spouses probably will be subject to a further "common sense" requirement in that the expense cannot occur too often with respect to the same subcontractors. If the expense is incurred to encourage the continuing association of these skilled subcontractors, particularly where their spouses are invited as well, by definition, the expense must be "occasional."

[9] The deduction for moving expenses does not apply to Quentin's move to the additional area to oversee the establishment of the new office. First, the deduction applies only to moves made because the taxpayer is commencing work at a new *principal place of work*. It is clear that Quentin's principal place of work remains in the metropolitan area with the law firm. Second, while Quentin meets the distance requirement, he does not meet the time requirement if he is in the additional area only for six months. See § 217(c)(2)(A).

[10] The tone of § 280A is set by its title: "Disallowance of Certain Expenses In Connection With Business Use of Home . . . ." In general, expenses of a home office are disallowed unless the taxpayer can establish that he meets the exceptions under § 280A(c)(1), and Quentin can meet none of them. In general, it is very difficult for an employee to meet the requirements of § 280A(c)(1), unless that person has no other available office space. As an associate attorney, Quentin is considered an employee of the law firm with an office at the firm.

[11] There is an obvious element of abuse and manipulation of the tax system in deducting expenses for conventions on cruise ships because there is such an element of personal activity and pleasure involved. Therefore, the rules here are very strict. For instance, the $2000 limit on expenses has never been increased or indexed for inflation. If it had been, the current limitation

would be more than twice the $2000 limit. This, each year the value of the deduction is lessened. Note that there is a difference between traveling on a cruise ship *as transportation* to a business meeting and a *convention or meeting held on a cruise ship*. In the former, the taxpayer's expenses are limited to twice the federal per diem per day of travel. See § 274(m)(1)(A). This limitation does not apply to conventions held *on* cruise ships because the $2000 limitation overrides the per diem limitation. See § 274(m)(1)(B).

[12] Note also that Quynlyn, as a self-employed taxpayer, will not be subject to the 2 percent floor to which Quentin is subject under § 67. If the Quarleses file a joint tax return (which is probable since that is much more advantageous for married taxpayers), Quynlyn's business expenses will reduce the couple's adjusted gross income and thus will reduce the § 67 floor for Quentin. The trade-off, however, is that Quynlyn's business income will increase their joint gross income and thus will raise the § 67 floor.

6. VARIATIONS ON THE THEME

In the alternative, assume that at the end of the six-month period, the firm requires Quentin to stay on permanently at the new location, and he arranges to rent the apartment on a yearly, rather than a monthly, basis. He continues to go back to Smaller City to see Quynlyn on the weekends and to attend an occasional business meeting at the firm's offices in nearby Metropolitan Area. Does this change any part of your answer above?

18

SALE OF A VACATION/ SECONDARY RESIDENCE

1. OPENING REMARKS

A principal residence qualifies for significant tax benefits, even though the property is used by the taxpayer for personal purposes. The interest on the mortgage on a "qualified residence" is deductible, and as we saw earlier, § 121 allows a certain amount of gain realized on the sale of a principal residence to avoid recognition. The mortgage interest on a vacation or second home also may be deductible, but the sale of such a house that is not the taxpayer's principal residence is not eligible for nonrecognition of gain under § 121 and instead is treated under the usual rules for the sale of property. Thus, if a gain is realized on the sale of a second residence that is not a primary residence, this gain will be recognized. There are, however, some complications that can arise in the sale of such a residence. One is the classification of the property as a primary residence or a secondary residence. This can arise where the taxpayer has two or more residences and spends an equal amount of time in each one. The determination of which location represents the principal residence requires a consideration of all the attendant facts and circumstances. Several issues may arise when the taxpayer decides to sell a residence, whether primary or secondary, but is not successful in finding a buyer until after a considerable period of time has elapsed. For instance, many taxpayers may be forced to purchase replacement property in the interim, before the former residence has sold, and they may decide to rent the old property until a suitable buyer appears, or the taxpayer may list the property for rent and make reasonable efforts to find a suitable renter, but these efforts are not successful. In the alternative, the taxpayer simply may list the house for sale and never make efforts to rent at all. Each of these alternatives raises its own set of tax issues, depending primarily on whether the property has been converted from personal use to property "held for the production of income" and whether there has been a "transaction entered into for profit."

2. HYPOTHETICAL

Roger and Rene Rappaport own a house in Atlanta where they spend the majority of their time. They also have a condominium on the Florida coast where they spend about six weeks out of the year, although last year they spent approximately three months there. They purchased the condominium seven years ago at a cost of $450,000, with a cash down payment of $100,000 and a recourse mortgage of $350,000. During March of last year, they had the condominium appraised and found that the value of the property was $600,000. They decided to sell the condominium, so they put it on the market on April 1, listing it for sale at a price of $650,000. After three months, it had not sold, so the Rappaports decided to list it for sale or rent. After three more months, they were successful in finding a renter who agreed to rent the condominium for $2 000 per month under a month-to-month lease. The renter took possession of the property on November 1 and remained through the following October 31.

In the late spring of year two, a hurricane hit the Florida coast, and as a result, housing prices fell. On December 1 of that year, the Rappaports finally sold the condominium for $400,000.

The Rappaports incurred the following expenses during the current and past year: $12,000 in mortgage interest last year and another $11,000 this year; $4000 in insurance premiums last year and another $4000 this year; property taxes of $4500 in each of the two years; $1500 in maintenance expenses last year and $1000 this year; and $4000 of depreciation last year and $8,000 this year. Discuss what deductions, if any, the Rappaports may take attributable to the condominium in each of these two years. Are there any other facts that you would need to know or assumptions that you would need to make?

3. LIST OF READINGS

Internal Revenue Code of 1986: §§ 62(a)(3), 68, 162, 163, 164, 165, 167, 168, 183, 212, 262, 280A, 469, 1012, 1016, 1211

Regulations: Reg. § 1.163–10T(p)(3)(ii); Reg. § 1.165–9(b); Prop. Reg. § 280A-3(c)

Cases: Bolaris v. Comm'r, 776 F.2d 1428 (9th Cir. 1985); Lowry v. Comm'r,384 F.Supp. 257 (D.N.H. 1974); D.D. Bolton, 77 T.C. 104 (1981), *aff'd.* 694 F.2d 556 (9th Cir. 1982); Grant v. Commissioner, 84 T.C. 809 (1985); William C. Horrmann v. Comm'r, 17 T.C. 903 (1951); Meredith v. Commissioner, 65 T.C. 34 (1976); Frank A. Newcombe, 54 T.C. 1298 (1970); Hulet P. Smith, 26 T.C.M. 149 (1967), *aff'd. per curiam,* 387 F.2d 804 (9th Cir. 1968)

Article: Erck, *And You Thought Moving Was Bad—Try Deducting Depreciation and Maintenance Expenses on Your Unsold Residence,* 26 U. Fla. L. Rev. 587 (1974); Samansky, *Deductions for a Former Residence: Don't Leave Home Without Them,* 16 Hofstra L.Rev. 615 (1988)

4. SAMPLE ESSAY

There are two taxable years at issue for the Rappaports. In the first year, they used the condominium for the first three months for personal purposes and then put it on the market on April 1. During that year, they incurred out-of-pocket expenses for maintenance, insurance, mortgage interest, and real property taxes.

The deductibility of the real property taxes is the easiest of the expense items to address because § 164(a)(1) authorizes the deduction of state, local, and foreign real property taxes, regardless of whether the property is used for personal use, investment use, or business use. Thus, the Rappaports may deduct the real property taxes that they paid on the condominium, regardless of whether the condominium is rented or used for personal purposes. This deduction is an itemized, below-the-line deduction.

The tax treatment of the remaining expense items and the depreciation deduction will depend upon the status of the property. A taxpayer may deduct "qualified residence interest," which is interest paid or accrued during the taxable year on acquisition or home equity indebtedness. See § 163(h)(3). The deduction is not limited to indebtedness on a principal residence but may also include interest paid on a mortgage on a secondary residence, and the definition of "residence" is a broad one. It encompasses condominiums, mobile homes, houseboats, and stock in a cooperative housing corporation. See Reg. § 1.163–10T(p)(3)(ii). The aggregate amount of qualified residence acquisition indebtedness that may be deducted under § 163 is $1 million. See § 163(h)(3)(B)(ii). (Interest is also deductible on up to $100,000 of home equity indebtedness. The deduction is determined in the aggregate, so the total indebtedness on which qualified residence interest is deductible is $1,100,000. See § 163(h)(3)(C)). Any amount of interest attributable to debt that exceeds the $1 million limitation (or $1.1 million limitation) is considered nondeductible personal interest. See § 262. Therefore, we cannot determine whether the Rappaports may deduct the full amount of interest on their mortgage because there are two problems. The first is that the $1 million limitation on the deduction of qualified residence indebtedness is considered in the aggregate. Thus, we need to know whether the Rappaports have a mortgage on their Atlanta house and if so, the amount of that mortgage. Second, if the interest is deductible in full, there is a phase-out of excess itemized deductions for high-income taxpayers, but this phase-out does not apply in taxable years 2010 through 2012. See § 68. So even if the entire $10,000 of mortgage interest is qualified residence interest, the Rappaports may not be able to obtain the full advantage of the deduction, depending on the taxable year in issue and the amount of their income.

A qualified residence is the principal residence of the taxpayer and one other that is used by the taxpayer as a residence. See § 163(h)(4)(A). If the property is not rented at any time during the taxable year, it is treated as a residence during that taxable year. If, however, the taxpayer holds the residence out for rental or resale, or makes repairs to the residence or renovates it with the intention of holding it out for rental or resale, the property is deemed to be rented. See Reg. § 1.163–10T(p)(3)(iii). If the property is rented or considered rented during the taxable year, the taxpayer must use the property for the greater of 14 days or 10% percent of the number of days that it is rented to qualify as a second residence for purposes of § 163. See § 163(h)(4)(A)(i)(II) and § 280A(d)(1). If the property is rented and is not considered a qualified residence, it is considered investment property, and the interest deduction is allowed, subject to the limitation of § 469 or § 163(d).

In this problem, the Rappaports used the condominium for personal purposes during the first three months of the year, put the property on the market for sale during the next seven months, and actually rented the property during the last two months of that year. Since the Rappaports used the condominium in the first year for more than 10 percent of the number of days that it was rented, it will be considered a qualified residence for purposes of § 163. See §§ 163(h)(4)(A) and 280A(d). Thus, the full $12,000 of mortgage interest potentially will be deductible, provided it meets the limitation under § 163 when combined with any indebtedness on their Atlanta primary residence, and subject to the potential phase-out of itemized deductions under § 68.

Maintenance expenses, insurance premiums, and depreciation are not deductible on personal use property. Section 212(2) authorizes a deduction of "ordinary and necessary expenses paid or incurred during the taxable year for the management, conservation, or maintenance of property held for the production of income." Section 212 expenses are those of routine maintenance and repair for rental or investment property that is not being used for personal use. The insurance premiums and maintenance expenses incurred by the Rappaports would fall into this category. In the first year, the issues are whether the Rappaport's property has been converted from personal use property, for which no § 212 deduction is permissible, to property "held for the production of income," and if so, at what point the conversion occurred.

The Rappaports had put the property on the market on April 1, listing it for sale only. Presumably, they listed it for sale or rent on July 1 and it was actually rented on November 1. Clearly, the Rappaports will be able to deduct their expenses for the period that the property was rented, the last two months of year one. From July 1 through October 31, the property had been listed for sale or rent. In *William C. Horrmann*, the Tax Court held that the taxpayer was entitled to take deductions for depreciation and maintenance expenses under § 212(2) because he had made bona fide efforts to rent his property, albeit unsuccessfully, and thus the property was considered "held for the production of income." The Rappaports also made bona fide efforts to rent their property, and these efforts ultimately were successful, so their property should be considered held for the production of income under §§ 167 and 212. This would enable them to deduct their maintenance expenses, insurance premiums, and depreciation for the last half the year (i.e., from July 1 to the end of the year).

The question is whether the Rappaports may obtain deductions for the period from April 1 to July 1 when they had listed their property for sale but not for rent? In contrast to *Hormann*, the taxpayer in *Lowry* ceased using his summer house as a residence and immediately offered it for sale, making no efforts to rent it, but the district court allowed him to deduct his maintenance expenses. The court concluded that the property had been converted into "property held for the production of income" because the taxpayer had demonstrated to the satisfaction of the court that he was holding the property with the expectation of selling it at a profit. But the taxpayer had bona fide reasons for failing to offer the property for rent, and thus there were extenuating circumstances in *Lowry* that are not present in the case of the Rappaports.

In *Hulet P. Smith*, the taxpayer moved out of his old residence, bought a new one, put the old residence up for sale, and sold it after three years. He was successful in taking his maintenance and depreciation deductions, even though he had made no efforts to rent the property during the time it had been on the market. More recent decisions have not been as liberal in allowing deductions where the taxpayer merely abandoned the property as a personal residence, immediately put it up for sale, and made no efforts to rent. The Tax Court in *Meredith* concluded that where a taxpayer is not holding property for rental income, she must show that she is holding the property for postconversion appreciation. The court went to cite *Newcombe* for the proposition that listing property for "immediate sale at or shortly after the time of its abandonment as a residence will ordinarily be strong evidence that a taxpayer is not holding the property for postconversion appreciation in value. Under such circumstances, only a most exceptional situation will permit a finding that the statutory requirement has been satisfied." *Meredith*, at 42–43. While the intent of the taxpayer is the most important consideration, it does not appear that there are any special circumstances that would warrant the deductions for the Rappaports in the first half of the year. If such circumstances are present, the Rappaports will bear the burden of proving them and that their property is being held for the production of income. In determining whether this burden has been met, courts have looked to such factors as (1) the length of time the taxpayers occupied the house as a residence before placing it on the market for sale, (2) whether the taxpayers permanently abandoned any further personal use of the house, (3) the character of the property as recreational or nonrecreational, (4) offers to rent, and (5) offers to sell. *Grant.*

The insurance premiums and maintenance expenses will be deductible for the period in which the property is converted into § 212 property. If we assume that the property was converted into income producing property on July 1, half of the insurance premiums, or $2000, will be deductible. The maintenance expenses are more difficult because unlike insurance, maintenance expenses usually do not arise ratably over the year. Thus, it must be determined when the maintenance expenses arose, whether during the personal use period or during the § 212 period. Only the expenses attributable to the latter period will be deductible. If we assume that half of the expenses arose in the first half of the year and half arose in the second half, then $750 of that expense will be deductible.

If the property was converted into property held for the production of income on July 1, when the property was listed for rent as well as for sale, a depreciation deduction for the period from July 1 through December 31 will be allowed. The $4500 of property taxes will be deductible in full (subject to a potential phase-out of itemized deductions) under § 164.

Thus, the total of the potentially deductible items in year one is:

$12,000—mortgage interest
$750—maintenance expense
$4000—depreciation deduction
$2000—insurance expense
$4500—property taxes
$23, 250 total

Since the property was used as a personal residence during a portion of year one, the Rappaports are subject to the limitations of § 280A in that year. Section 280A applies to limit otherwise allowable deductions where the property is used as a personal residence for the greater of 14 days or 10 percent of the rental time. See § 280A(d). Section 280A(c)(5) provides that the deductions attributable to the rental use shall not exceed the gross rents less the sum of (1) the deductions allocable to the rental use which would have been allowed regardless of the rental (i.e., real estate taxes, and mortgage interest), and (2) the deductions allocable to the rental use that would not have been allowed without that use (i.e., depreciation, insurance and maintenance expenses). Any amount of otherwise deductible expense not allowed as a deduction in the current taxable year can be carried over and used in the succeeding taxable year. See § 280A(c)(5).

The "deductions allocable to the rental use" are the deductions allocable to the actual rental use. But there is a difference of opinion between the IRS and the Tax Court over how to allocate these expenses. The IRS allocates according to rental use versus total use (personal plus rental). See Prop. Reg. § 1.280A-3(c)(1).

In this case, the Rappaports used the property for personal purposes for the first three months of the year and then rented the property for the last two months of that year, so 40 percent (2/5) of the expenses would be allocated to the rental period under the IRS's position. But both the Tax Court and the Ninth Circuit, in *Bolton*, took the position that mortgage interest and real estate taxes accrue ratably, so the expenses should be allocated according to rental use over the entire year. Since the condo was rented for two months in the first year, 31/365 or roughly 1/6 of the expenses would be allocated to the rental use. See Bolton v. Commissioner, 694 F.2d 556 (9th Cir. 1982).

The following table shows the difference in the allowable deductions between the two views:

IRS position	Tax Court position
$4000—gross rental income	$4000—gross rental income
$4800—allocated mortgage interest	$2000—allocated mortgage interest for the two months of rental use
$1800—allocated property taxes	*$750*—allocated property taxes for the two months of rental use
-0-—§ 280A(c)(5) limitation	$1250—§ 280A(c)(5) limitation

Under the IRS position, the allocated mortgage interest and taxes exceed the amount of rental income, so no maintenance, insurance, or depreciation deductions would be allowed in year one, and all allowable expenses attributable to those items would be carried over to the succeeding taxable year. Under the Tax Court's allocation, the Rappaports may take up to $1250 of allowable deductions in year one and the remainder may be carried over to year two.

Under the Tax Court's position, since there is room to take some of these deductions, we must determine what proportionate amount of each of the expenses is deductible under the § 280A limitation. For this, we must turn to § 280A(e). Under this provision, we first allocate the expenses, other than depreciation, according to the number of days the property is *actually* rented compared to the number of days of total use. Unlike § 280A(c)(5), the allocation formula is specified under § 280A(e) so there is no room for interpretation. During the first year, the Rappaports used the property for three months, and it was rented for two months, so 2/5 or 40 percent of the expenses are attributable to the rental. Under this formula, the maintenance expenses otherwise attributable to the rental are $600 and the insurance premiums are $1600, for a total of $2200. Since this amount exceeds the § 280A(c)(5) limitation, $1250 of these expenses will be deductible in year one and the remaining $950 of the expenses, plus the $1600 ($4000 x 2/5) proportionate amount of the depreciation deductions may be carried over to the following taxable year.

Note that § 280A does not limit the deduction of mortgage interest and taxes, which may be taken in full (subject to potential phase-outs of itemized deductions). Thus, in the first year, the Rappaports may take deductions of $17,750 attributable to their vacation/rental property, and they may carry the remaining $2550 over to the succeeding taxable year:

$12,000—mortgage interest
$4500—property taxes
$1250—maintenance and insurance expenses, subject to the § 280A(c)(5) limitation
$0—depreciation because of the § 280A(c)(5) limit
$17,750—total allowable deductions for year one

Note that under the IRS's allocation, none of the maintenance and insurance expenses may be taken in year one, and all of these proportionate amounts (subject to the § 280A(e) limitation) may be carried over to year two.

In the second year, the property is rented from January 1 through October 31 and then sold at a loss on December 1. Since the property is rented for the majority of the year, and there is no personal use in this year, § 280A does not apply. See § 280A(d)(1)(A). However, in year two the Rappaports will have to consider the passive activity loss rules under § 469 and the limitations of § 183 if the activity is not engaged in for profit. If § 280A(c)(5) applies, § 469 does not, because both provisions impose limitations on the taxpayer's ability to deduct otherwise allowable expenses. See § 469(j)(10). The passive loss rules, in general, limit deductions from passive investment activities to income from such activities. Rental activities are considered passive activities. See §§ 469(b)(2) and (b)(4). There is an exception provided for deductions from rental activities in which the taxpayer actively participates in the activity (a more lenient standard than "material participation"). In that case, the taxpayer may take up to $25,000 of the passive deductions against nonpassive income. There is, however, a phase-out of this limitation of 50 percent of the amount by which the taxpayer's adjusted gross income exceeds $100,000. So, a taxpayer with adjusted gross income of $150,000 or more will be limited to taking rental deductions only against rental or passive income. Since we do not know the amount of the Rappaport's adjusted gross income for year two, we do not know whether they are subject to the exception or not. The Rappaport's total deductions for year two are $28,000 ($11,000 interest, $4000 insurance, $4500 taxes, $8000 depreciation, and $1000 maintenance), and their rental income for year two is $20,000. If we assume that the Rappaports are not subject to the phase-out, under § 469(i), they first would net their passive losses against their income from passive activities, so they may offset their $28,500 of passive losses against their $20,000 of rental income. This would produce a net loss of $8500. Since this amount is less than their $25,000 exclusion (provided that they can take the exclusion in full), they could use the $8500 in expenses against nonpassive income, and this would be combined with the $2550 § 280A(c)(5) carryover from year one, so their total net deductions from their rental activity in year two are $11,050. Under the passive loss rules, any unused deductions are allowed in full when the taxpayer's entire interest in the activity is sold in a fully taxable transaction. This amount first will offset any passive income from the rental activity, then any excess will offset any passive income from other passive activities, and then finally, the deductions can be used to offset any other income. So the Rappaports may use their $11,050 deduction to offset other taxable income.

If § 183 applies, not only will the deductions of maintenance expenses and depreciation be limited, but the deduction of interest will be disallowed. The problem for the Rappaports is that they do not use the condo for at least 30 days in year two (i.e., the greater of 14 days or 10 percent of the time the property is rented at a fair rental price under § 280A(d)). Thus, the condo is not considered a qualified residence under § 163(h)(4)(A)(i)(II). If § 183 applies, the rental of the condo will not be considered a valid investment activity so the interest will not be deductible as investment interest. Thus, it will be considered nondeductible personal interest.

It is sometimes difficult to determine whether or not an activity is engaged in for profit. The regulations provide that this determination should be made by reference to "objective standards" considering all relevant facts and circumstances. Reg. § 1.183-2(a). Holding property with the expectation of realizing appreciation in value is considered a for profit activity. Thus, it is unclear whether the Rappaports will be subject to § 183. If so, the $4500 of taxes will first offset the $20,000 of rental income, leaving a balance of $15,500. Next, the deductions not affecting basis (i.e., maintenance and insurance expenses) will offset this amount, leaving $10,500. This is the § 183 limit for depreciation, which exceeds the $9600 of depreciation deductions ($8000 for year two and $1600 carried from year one) so the depreciation may be taken in full, along with the other deductions except interest.

If § 183 does not apply, the interest in year two will be considered investment interest and deductions will not necessarily be limited to gross income from the activity. Under § 163(d), the investment interest would be deductible against net investment income. After the deduction of the other expenses, only $2500 of the net investment income remains ($20,000 rental income less the insurance, taxes, maintenance and depreciation expenses). Therefore, the remainder of the interest can be deducted only if the Rappaports have other investment income against which to offset it, subject to the limitations of § 469.

The Rappaports realize a loss on the sale of their condo at the end of year two. Section 165(c) allows an individual to recognize a loss arising in three situations: (1) in a trade or business, (2) in a transaction entered into for profit, and (3) for a casualty. Where the property is rented and held for the production of income until the time of sale, a loss is allowable. See Reg. § 1.165–9(b)(1). The problem is that the amount of the loss depends upon the fair market value of the property at the time of the conversion. See Reg. § 1.165-9(b)(2). Although we assumed that the property was converted from personal use to property held for the production of income on July 1 of year one, the language of § 165(c)(2) is different from that of §§ 167/168 and 212. While the latter sections require the property to be *held* for the production of income, § 165(c)(2) provides that a loss may be recognized in a *transaction* entered into for profit. On July 1, the Rappaports listed the property for sale or rent but otherwise took no irreversible steps toward converting the property. The Tax Court in *Hormann* stated that merely holding the property for sale or rent without such irreversible steps did not amount to a transaction for purposes of § 165(c)(2). Thus, the transaction in that case would have occurred when the property was rented on November 1 (or before, depending on when the lease agreement was signed). If we further assume that the March appraised value was the fair market value on July 1, the date of the presumed conversion, the Rappaport's property had appreciated in value at that time. That means that their depreciation deductions and the resulting loss on the sale will be determined according to their § 1012 basis, adjusted for the depreciation deductions under § 1016(a)(2). Note that if the property had declined in value at the point of conversion below the amount of the basis, both the depreciation deductions and the deductible loss would be limited because the fair market value of the property, rather than the basis, would be used to determine both. See Reg. § 1.167(g)-1; Reg. § 1.168(i)-4(b); Reg. § 1.165-9(b)(2).

The Rappaports initially purchased the condo for $450,000 and converted it from personal use property to "property held for the production of income" in year one. Also, the property was rented in year one and sold at the end of year two. Since the property was converted to income producing property, the Rappaports were entitled to take depreciation deductions (subject to the mid-month convention in the year of the conversion and in the year of the sale). See § 168(d). The depreciation deductions will reduce their basis by the amount of the deductions they have taken. See § 1016. Since their depreciation deductions were limited under § 280A, they were able to take only $9600 in depreciation deductions in the two years in which their property had been converted. Thus, their adjusted basis is $440,400, and when they sell the condo for $400,000, they will realize a loss of $40,400. Since the property was rented, the loss will be deductible under § 165(c)(2) as a loss incurred in a transaction entered into for profit. This loss will be deductible above the line under § 62(a)(3),but it will be a capital loss subject to the capital loss limitations of § 1211. Thus, the Rappaports will be able to recognize the loss to the extent of any other capital gains, plus an additional $3000 which may be taken against ordinary income. See § 1211(b)(1).

If the sale is an arm's length transaction with an unrelated third party, the loss deduction will be allowed. But if the property is sold to a related party, the loss will be disallowed under § 267.

5. TOOLS FOR SELF-ASSESSMENT

[1] As this problem illustrates, the sale of a vacation home can have complicated tax consequences. These same consequences apply to the sale of a primary residence that sits on the market for a considerable period of time and eventually is rented or held for sale or rent. Particularly when dealing with mixed use property, there are limitations that apply to the deductions. Therefore, the analysis will involve the preliminary determination of whether the deductions are authorized and then another determination of what amount of authorized expense deduction may be taken. In a problem of this type, it is essential to approach the transactions in chronological order.

[2] The potentially deductible items differ in several respects. First, depreciation, insurance, property taxes, and interest are attributable to an entire taxable year and accrue ratably during the year. Maintenance expenses are attributable to specific items that may arise at different times during the taxable year. Since the status of the property may vary during the year (i.e., personal residence versus investment or rental property), it is important to allocate the expenses to the proper period. Second, qualified residence

interest and real property taxes are deductible regardless of whether or not the property is used as a personal residence. Thus, these items are not subject to the additional limitations of §§ 163 and 280A (except for the § 163(h)(3)(B) $1 million limit and the phase-out of itemized deductions).

[3] Section 280A imposes two limitations on the deductibility of expenses attributable to the rental of a personal residence. Although the model answer first addressed the § 280A(c)(5) limitation, which is the overall limitation, it is equally permissible to first address the § 280A(e) limitation. Section 280A(e) imposes a limitation on the actual amount of deductible expenses attributable to the rental use. The § 280A(c)(5) limitation is an overall limitation on the amount of otherwise allowable deductions that may be taken in a given year, after the § 280A(e) limitation has been applied. Note that any excess expense (other than those attributable to taxes, interest, and casualty losses) remaining after the § 280A(e) limitation has been applied may not be taken at all. In contrast, any excess expense remaining after the § 280A(c)(5) limitation has been applied may be carried over to succeeding taxable years.

[4] Note that if the § 280A(c)(5) limit had been higher in year one (i.e., if the rental income had been greater), the Proposed Regulations provide that the deductions are taken in order of (1) the allocable portion of amounts otherwise deductible (e.g., mortgage interest and real property taxes), (2) the allocable amounts otherwise allowable as deductions by reason of the rental use of the property (other than those that would result in an adjustment to the basis of the property), and (3) the allocable portion of the amount otherwise allowed as deductions by reason of the rental use of the property which would result in an adjustment to the basis of the property (e.g., depreciation).

[5] This problem also illustrates that property may be considered in different ways for different purposes. For instance, even though the condominium is considered converted to property held for the production of income as of July 1 of year one for purposes of the deduction of maintenance expenses and depreciation under §§ 212 and 167/168, § 163 considers the property a personal residence in year one for purposes of the deduction of mortgage interest on a qualified residence.

[6] There are various assumptions that can be made about the maintenance expense. If the assumption is that this expense arose entirely after the property had been converted, then the entire maintenance expense legitimately could be deducted. Thus, it is important to consider when the expense arose, but any rational attribution should be correct in this problem.

[7] Under § 280A(d)(4), there is relief for taxpayers who use their property for personal purposes and then convert it either to rental property or to property held for the production of income. In that case, if the personal use occurs before or after a qualified rental period (defined as a 12 consecutive month period or less if the property is sold at the end of the rental period, during which the property is rented or held for rental at a fair rental price), the use is not considered personal use and thus does not count against the taxpayer in determining the amount of deductions to which the taxpayer is entitled. However, this provision applies only to principal residences and

does not apply to secondary or vacation residences, so it is not available to the Rappaports.

[8] The limitations on the deductions for the rental use of the property are myriad and complex. Perhaps the best way to deal with these is to first apply the § 280A(d) use as a residence test (personal use for the greater of 14 days or 10 percent of the rental time). If the personal use falls with § 280A(d) then § 280A applies and none of the other limitations apply. If the personal use does not fall with § 280A(d), then § 280A does not apply but § 183 may apply if the activity is not engaged in for profit. Under § 183, no interest is allowed and the other deductions are limited to the income from the activity. If neither §§ 183 nor 280A apply, §§ 163(d) and 469 may apply, although these provisions are mutually exclusive. See § 163(d)(3)(B)(ii).

[9] Sections 280A and 469 also are mutually exclusive provisions that work in similar ways to limit the amount of the deductions that a taxpayer may take under certain circumstances. Section 280A applies when a qualified residence is converted into property held for the production of income where there is some personal use of the property during the taxable year. Section 469 applies if § 280A does not.

[10] The determination of whether there is a transaction entered into for profit must be made because while the sale itself is considered a transaction, it results in a loss. Thus it cannot be considered a transaction entered into for profit.

[11] Losses on the sale of mixed use property often are difficult to characterize. The Tax Court appeared to take the position early on that if the property was rented, the taxpayer was considered to be in the rental business. See, e.g., Leland Hazard, 7 T.C. 372 (1946), *acq.*, 1946–2 C.B. 3; Stephen P. Wasnok v. Comm'r, 30 T.C.M.39 (1971). Later, it appeared to retreat from that position. See, e.g., Curphey v. Commissioner, 73 T.C. 766 (1980) (the court stated that the ownership and rental of real property does not, as a matter of law, constitute a trade or business). The issue ultimately is one of fact in which the scope of the ownership and management activities is an important consideration. In Rogers v. United States, 69 F.Supp. 8 (D. Conn.1946), the court stated that the trade or business test requires activity that is continuous, systematic, and, at least in view of the number of properties managed, substantially extensive. In Grier v. United States, 120 F.Supp. 395 (D.Conn.1954), *aff'd,* 218 F.2d 603 (2d Cir.1955), the Second Circuit determined that a residential rental home inherited by the taxpayer was a capital asset because it appeared to be more in the nature of property held for investment than property used in a trade or business. When the house was inherited, it had been rented to a long-time tenant, and the taxpayer continued to rent to this tenant. The court noted that although the rental activities were of long duration, they were minimal in nature. There was no activity to rent and re-rent the property, and no employees were regularly engaged for maintenance or repair.

In this hypothetical, the Rappaports' activities also are unlikely to give rise to a trade or business. Thus, the answer assumes the characterization of the loss as an investment loss rather than a business loss.

6. VARIATIONS ON THE THEME

What deductions, if any, would the Rappaports have been entitled to if they had never offered the condominium for rent but had held it solely for sale during the two years in question? What result if the appraised value of the condominium in March of year one had been $430,000?

19

ACCOUNTING METHODS

CASH RECEIPTS/DISBURSEMENTS AND ACCRUAL

1. OPENING REMARKS

Taxpayers must use an acceptable method of tax accounting in compiling their financial transactions for the taxable year and in calculating their tax liability. An acceptable accounting method is one that clearly reflects income. According to the regulations, "a method of accounting which reflects the consistent application of generally accepted accounting principles in a particular trade or business in accordance with accepted conditions or practices in that trade or business will ordinarily be regarded as clearly reflecting income, provided all items of gross income and expense are treated consistently from year to year." Reg. § 1.446–1(a)(2).

There are two general methods of accounting—the cash receipts and disbursement method and the accrual method—although the tax Code may prescribe specific accounting treatment for certain transactions. The cash method typically is used by individual taxpayers, and under this method, the taxpayer includes an item in income (whether in cash, property, or services) when it is actually or constructively received. A deduction is allowed under this method when an otherwise deductible item is paid. The accrual method typically is used by businesses, and in some cases, a business may be required to use the accrual method. Under this method, an item is included in income when the right to receive it arises. A deduction is allowed when all events have occurred that establish the liability to make the payment, and the amount can be determined with reasonable accuracy. But the deduction may not be taken before economic performance has occurred.

Methods of tax accounting are important, not only because they provide consistency in reporting income and deductions, but also because the accounting method may affect the amount of the tax liability owed for a particular year. Once an accounting method is adopted, it may be changed only with the consent of the Commissioner. See § 446(e). In order to obtain consent, the taxpayer must show that the purpose of the change of accounting method is to avoid a distortion of income, and generally, there must be a business purpose for making the change.

2. HYPOTHETICAL

Samantha Smythson is a single, calendar year taxpayer. She is a best-selling author and is under contract to write a book for a national publisher. The publisher has agreed to pay Samantha an advance royalty of $20,000. Although the publisher is willing to pay this amount immediately, Samantha has requested that the publisher wait until the following year to pay the advance royalty because she does not need the money this year. The publisher agreed, and this was written into Samantha's contract. Samantha gave a talk at a banquet shortly after Christmas and was to be paid $2500. On December 31, her agent called to say that the organizer had the check ready for her and that she could either pick it up at his office, a distance of 75 miles, or he could mail it to her. Samantha opted for the latter, and she received the check on January 4 of the following year.

In the same year, Samantha won $200,000 in the state lottery. She was given the option of receiving either an annuity of $22,000 for 10 years or a lump sum, one-time payment of $200,000 immediately. Samantha opted for the annuity, which she will begin to receive next year.

Samantha incurred unreimbursed travel expenses in December in connection in with the promotion of one of her earlier books. She paid these expenses with a credit card and did not receive the credit card bill until January, when she paid it. In working on her current book, Samantha traveled to Miami, Florida, because Miami is the setting of her story. She planned to spend a week staying at the Fontainebleau Hotel in February at a cost of $4000. The hotel required a deposit for her stay, so she sent a check for the required amount of $1500 in December. This check cleared her bank in December.

Samantha also has some continuing expenses for supplies that she uses in her work: printer paper, ink, notebooks, and other miscellaneous office supplies. She normally purchases these items about every two months. A local office supplies store offered to give her a significant discount if she would purchase her supplies exclusively from them on a standing order basis, billed three months in advance. On December 1 of the current year, Samantha paid $200 for three months of supplies.

Compare and contrast the inclusion or deduction of these various items under (1) the cash receipts and disbursement method and (2) the accrual method of accounting.

3. LIST OF READINGS

Internal Revenue Code: §§ 74; 446; 451; 461

Regulations: § 1.162–3; § 1.446–1(c); § 1.451–2(a); § 1.461–1(a)

Rulings: Rev. Rul. 79–229, 1979–2 C.B. 210; Rev. Rul. 78–38, 1978–1 C.B. 67; Rev. Rul. 68–126, 1968–1 C.B. 194; Rev. Rul. 60–31, 1960–1 C.B. 174; Rev. Rul. 54–465, 1954–2 C.B. 93

Cases: INDOPCO, Inc. v. Commissioner, 503 U.S. 79 (1992); Baxter v. Commissioner, 816 F.2d 493 (9th Cir. 1987); Commissioner v. Boyleston Market Ass'n, 131 F.2d 966 (1st Cir. 1942); Zaninovich v. Commissioner, 616 F.2d 429 (9th Cir. 1980); Charles F. Kahler v. Commissioner, 18 T.C. 31 (1952); Vander Poel Francis & Co., Inc. v. Commissioner, 8 T.C. 407 (1947)

Articles: Jensen, *The Deduction of Future Liabilities by Accrual Method Taxpayers: Premature Accruals, the All Events Test, and Economic Performance,* 37 Fla. L. Rev. 443 (1985)

4. SAMPLE ESSAY

Under § 446, taxable income must be computed according to the method of accounting in which the taxpayer regularly computes income in keeping her books. Permissible methods of accounting include the cash receipts and disbursement method and the accrual method, although some taxpayers may use a combination of these methods.

Cash Receipts and Disbursements: Under the cash receipts and disbursements method, all items of gross income (whether in the form of cash, property, or services) must be included in the taxable year in which they are actually or constructively received. Reg. § 1.446–1(c)(1)(i).

Reg. § 1.451–2(a) provides that "[i]ncome although not actually reduced to a taxpayer's possession is constructively received by him in the taxable year during which it is credited to his account, set apart for him, or otherwise made available so that he may draw upon it at any time, or so that he could have drawn upon it during the taxable year if notice of intention to withdraw had been given." It further provides that "income is not constructively received if the taxpayer's control of its receipt is subject to substantial limitations or restrictions."

In Rev. Rul. 60–31, the IRS addressed several factual situations in determining whether the doctrine of constructive receipt applied. While Samantha's situation is not quite the same as that of the ruling, it is close to the situation in example three, in which an author contracted to defer royalties before they were earned. The ruling clarifies that an effective deferral of income may occur for tax purposes if the agreement to defer is made before the services are rendered and is part of an enforceable contract. This applies even though the payor is ready, willing, and able to pay the advance royalty at the time the agreement is made.

A check is considered the equivalent of cash, provided that it is honored when presented, and is includable in income when it is actually or constructively received, even if it is received at the end of the year after the banks have closed. See *Charles F. Kahler*. The question here is whether Samantha is in constructive receipt of the check on December 31 of year one when her agent offers her the check, or whether the actual receipt of the check on January 4 controls.

This question does not have a clear answer. The IRS has said in Rev. Rul. 68–126 that where the check is available for the taxpayer to pick up in year one and the taxpayer elects instead to have the check mailed so that it arrives in year two, constructive receipt applies, and the taxpayer must include the payment in year one. This ruling did not address the effect of restrictions on actual receipt. In *Baxter*, however, the Ninth Circuit disagreed with the government's position and noted that the application of constructive receipt is a question of fact and substantial restrictions, if present, should be taken into account. In *Baxter*, the court held that constructive receipt did not apply to include income where the taxpayer was required to drive a distance of 80 miles round-trip on a nonbusiness day to collect the check. Thus, this was a substantial restriction that prevented the application of constructive receipt. Here, Samantha will be required to drive 150 miles round-trip to collect her check, so under the view of the Ninth Circuit in *Baxter*, she will be not be required to include this amount until year two when she actually receives the check. Under the IRS's view, however, constructive receipt applies, and Samantha will be required to include the $2500 in year one.

Another issue is whether Samantha's agent was able to receive the check on her behalf. If so, since he is her agent, receipt by the agent may be considered receipt by Samantha if the agent is authorized to act for her and to receive checks on her behalf. Thus, Samantha may not be able to avoid the application of the doctrine of constructive receipt if the agent was authorized to act on her behalf. In that case, the check would be included in Samantha's gross income in year one.

Prizes and awards are includable in income under § 74(a) unless certain narrow requirements listed in §74(b) are met. Those requirements are not met in this problem because lottery winnings can never be excluded from gross income under §74, even if the recipient should transfer the winnings to a governmental unit or organization. This is because the lottery prize is not made in recognition of religious, charitable, scientific, educational, artistic, literary, or civic achievement. Moreover, the recipient usually must purchase a lottery ticket to win, so § 74(b)(1) (the recipient must be selected without any action on his part to enter the contest or proceeding) is not met. Thus, Samantha will be taxed on her lottery winnings. Therefore, the question is: when will she be taxed? Normally, Samantha's election of the annuity option for receipt of her lottery winnings would require her to include the present value of the lump sum payment in income in the year of the election. But this was a trap for the unwary and unsophisticated taxpayer, so Congress changed this rule in 1998 with the enactment of § 451(h). This provision applies to disregard the lump sum option for tax purposes for a qualified prize. If applicable, it would mean that the IRS must disregard the fact that Samantha had an option to receive a lump sum payment and instead must tax her only as she receives each payment under the annuity.

A qualified prize for purposes of § 451(h) is a prize or award received "as part of a contest, lottery, jackpot, game or similar arrangement," which neither relates to past services nor requires the recipient to render substantial future services. In addition, the annuity must be payable over at least a 10-year period. See § 451(h)(2)(B). Samantha appears to meet these requirements. Her only other hurdle is whether she meets the requirements of a "qualified prize option." Section 451(h)(2)(A) provides that the individual must have the option of receiving a single, lump sum payment, and the option must be exercisable by the recipient no later than 60 days after the prize is won. Provided the terms of the prize specify this, and provided Samantha has made her election within 60 days of winning the prize, she should be home free under § 451(h). This means that she will include the payments in her gross income as she receives them over the 10-year period.

The remainder of the hypothetical deals with deductions rather than inclusions. The general rule is that a cash method taxpayer is entitled to a deduction when a deductible item is paid. There is no doctrine of constructive payment. See *Vander Poel Francis & Co.*

If Samantha otherwise is able to deduct her travel expenses (see §§ 162 and 274), she can deduct this amount in year one, when she charges it to her credit card. According to Rev. Rul. 78–38, the use of a third-party credit card creates a debt to the third party that is the equivalent of the use of borrowed funds to pay a deductible expense. Thus, the legal obligation to pay the third party (i.e., the credit card company) is tantamount to payment of the deductible expense.

The office supplies order involves a prepayment for supplies that will not be used until year two. The *Boyleston Market* and *INDOPCO* cases prohibit the deduction of prepaid expenses by a cash method taxpayer where the prepayment creates "an asset having a useful life which extends substantially beyond the close of the taxable year." Reg. § 1.461–1(a)(1). Generally, these cases are regarded as prohibiting the deduction of prepayments for supplies that will be used gradually over an extended period of time that extends beyond the taxable year. In *Zaninovich*, the Ninth Circuit permitted the deduction of a prepayment of rent for a 12-month period that straddled two taxable years. Since the rental period did not extend substantially beyond the close of the taxable year, no allocation of the prepayment was required. In Samantha's case, although she pays in December of year one for supplies that she will not use until year two, she appears to use those supplies within a two-month period. Under her new arrangement, she may be using these supplies within a three-month period. However, she should be able to deduct her payment because she has a valid business reason for the prepayment. Over time, her income will not be distorted by the prepayment, and she consumes the supplies within a relatively short period of time. Further, the regulations under § 162 permit a deduction in the year of the purchase for "incidental materials and supplies" that are not part of inventory or recorded as consumed, provided the treatment of the item is a clear reflection of income. See Reg. § 1.162–3.

The $4000 payment for her stay in the Fontainebleau Hotel first must pass muster under §§ 162 and 274. This expense will be deductible if it is considered a reasonable expense and meets the limitations of § 274. As far as the timing of the deduction, in Rev. Rul. 79–229, the IRS permitted a deduction for an advance payment, provided it met three requirements: (1) the payment must be a purchase and not a deposit, (2) it must serve a business purpose, and (3) it must not materially distort income. Samantha will not be able to deduct her deposit in year one because it is a refundable deposit. In year two, when she stays at the hotel, if the expenses otherwise are deductible under §§ 162 and 274, she will be able to deduct her full hotel expenditures at that time.

Accrual: Assuming that Samantha used the accrual method of tax accounting, she must include items in income when "all the events have occurred which fix the right to receive such income and the amount thereof can be determined with reasonable accuracy." § 446(c)(2); Reg. § 1.446–1(c)(1)(ii). Under the accrual method, constructive receipt does not matter.

Samantha's right to receive the advance royalty does not arise until she signs the contract. At that time, the contract provides that the royalty will be payable the following year, so under the accrual method of accounting, Samantha will include the $20,000 in the following year when she actually receives the royalty payment. Thus, the cash method and the accrual method will produce the same result with respect to the royalty payment.

Samantha will have to include the $2500 for the talk in year one because all events have occurred that fix her right to receive the income; she has given the talk, i.e., performed the services requested. The fact that she does not receive actual payment until year two will not matter in this case. Thus, the cash method and the accrual method produce different results in this situation.

Section 451(h), discussed above, applies only to cash method taxpayers. An accrual method taxpayer must accrue the present value of the lump sum payment because at the time the taxpayer exercised the option to receive the annuity, she could have received the lump sum amount. All events have occurred to fix her right to receive this prize, and the amount can be determined with reasonable accuracy. Thus, there is no statutory protection for an accrual method taxpayer as there is under § 451(h) for a cash method taxpayer. Samantha will have to accrue the present value of the lump sum amount and include this in her gross income in the year in which she wins the prize. There is, obviously, much more favorable tax treatment in this case for the cash method taxpayer than there is for the accrual method taxpayer.

Deductions under the accrual method are not linked to payment but to whether "all events have occurred which determine the fact of the liability and the amount thereof can be determined with reasonable accuracy." Reg. § 1.461–1(a)(2). Section 461(h) provides that economic performance must occur before the "all events" test is met. In keeping with the "clear reflection of income," a prepayment of a deductible expense that creates "an asset having a useful life which extends substantially beyond the close of the taxable year" may be deducted proportionately only for the taxable year in which it is incurred.

In the case of services or property, economic performance occurs as the services or property is received. The December travel expenses that Samantha pays with her credit card should be deductible, subject to the constraints of §§ 162 and 274, mentioned above. Both the all events and economic performance tests have been met, so she should be able to deduct the expense in year one, even though she does not pay the credit card bill until year two.

The $1500 deposit that Samantha makes to the hotel in year one ordinarily would not be deductible under the accrual method because economic performance has not occurred. Since she is buying a service when she rents a hotel room, economic performance ordinarily occurs as the service is performed, so as with the cash method, she ordinarily would be able to deduct the full amount only in year two, when she stays at the hotel. However, the regulations allow an exception to economic performance in which the services or property are treated as received when the taxpayer pays for them, provided they are reasonably expected to be performed or delivered within three and a half months after payment is made. See Reg. § 1.461–4(d)(6)(ii). Since Samantha will receive the hotel services in February of year two, which is within three and a half months of payment, she can deduct her $1500 deposit when she pays it in December.

Economic performance with respect to the advance payment for her office supplies would occur normally when the office supplies are furnished to Samantha. See Reg. §1.461–4(d)(6). Thus, if she receives the supplies when she pays for them, she may accrue the deduction in year one. Otherwise, if she does not receive the supplies until year two, she would have to accrue the deduction then. However, 461(h)(3) provides an exception for certain recurring items. If this exception is met, the taxpayer may accrue the item in the year in which the all events test is met, even though economic performance has not yet occurred. In order to fall under § 461(h)(3), the following requirements must be met: (1) the all events test must be met; (2) economic performance must occur within a reasonable period of time (but no later than 8 1/2 months after the close of the taxable year; (3) the item must be recurring in nature, and the taxpayer must consistently treat this type of item as incurred in the taxable year in which the all events test is met; (4) the item is either (i) not material or (ii) accrual of the item in the year in which the all events test is met results in a better matching of the item with the income to which it relates than would accruing in the item in the year in which economic performance occurs. Reg. § 1.461–5. In addition, an item is material if it is considered material for financial accounting purposes. In this case, Samantha's payment of $300 for her office supplies probably is immaterial to her.

Since Samantha has agreed to the company's terms, the fact of the liability has been determined, and the amount is fixed. Thus, the all events test appears to be met. Economic performance occurs within a two- to three-month period, well within the 8 ½-month time frame. Thus, the item is recurring and provided that Samantha consistently treats it as incurred at the same general time each year, it should not result in a distortion of income. Thus, she should be able to accrue this deduction in year one.

5. TOOLS FOR SELF-ASSESSMENT

[1] As the old saying goes, "time is money," so timing issues are very important to both the government and taxpayers. The government is particularly concerned about accounting methods used by taxpayers because these methods determine the timing of inclusions or deductions. The cash method generally is easier to apply than the accrual method.

[2] Note that § 409A applies to many deferred items under nonstatutory deferred compensation arrangements, such as those of Rev. Rul. 60–31. If § 409A applies, the income will become immediately taxable, plus the taxpayer must pay interest on the deferred amount, along with a 20 percent penalty. As a result, § 409A provides an additional hurdle that the taxpayer must clear in order to successfully defer income without an immediate tax consequence. For this purpose, deferred compensation includes "any legally binding right to payments earned in one tax year that could be paid in a subsequent tax year." Reg. § 1.409A-1(b)(1). In Samantha's case, she has no legally enforceable right to an advance royalty until the publisher agrees to that term in the contract. When Samantha requests a deferral of the advance royalty, she is not deferring a right that she has at that moment. Instead, the right arises only when she signs the contract. Since that right arises at the same time as the deferral, § 409A should not apply in this problem, and Samantha should be able to validly defer the receipt of her royalty payments if she chooses.

[3] The IRS's inclusion of the payment for the talk Samantha gave shortly after Christmas is reflected in Rev. Rul. 68–126, which stands for the proposition that if a check is made available to a taxpayer, even though there are some restrictions on the taxpayer's ability to obtain the check, it is the constructive receipt of a cash equivalent. Although Rev. Rul. 68–126 is an older ruling, the IRS cited it with approval in a private letter ruling issued in 1996. See PLR 9651020. But Rev. Rul. 68–126 has very few facts from which to determine how easy it was for the taxpayer in the ruling to receive the check in advance of its being mailed. For this reason, the Ninth Circuit's decision in *Baxter* is a better reasoned decision than that of the revenue ruling. In advising Samantha about whether to include this amount or not, she should be able to rely on the *Baxter* case because of the significant restriction that she faced in obtaining actual receipt of the check and the fact that the ruling is not clear on the underlying facts. This, of course, depends upon the constructive receipt issue of whether the agent was able to receive the check on her behalf being resolved in her favor.

[4] Section 451(h), enacted in 1998, alleviates a hardship for many recipients of prizes and awards. Prior to this provision, if a recipient elected to receive an

annuity instead of a lump sum payment, the recipient was taxed on the present value of the lump sum anyway. Thus, a cash method taxpayer was placed on an accrual method under this view, to the great detriment of the taxpayer. This result could be avoided only if the recipient was able to make the election to receive the annuity prior to winning the prize. Since most people who buy lottery tickets never "hit it big," there would be little use in making such a declaration, and it would be an onerous requirement to have to do this every time one purchased a lottery ticket.

[5] Note that a promissory note is not considered a "payment," so a cash method taxpayer would not be able to obtain a deduction when her promissory note was delivered to the recipient. By the same token, a credit card payment in a two-party credit card transaction is considered the same as a promissory note or promise to pay. So, if Samantha had deductible expenses that she charged on a store credit card, she would not be able to deduct that amount until she paid the credit card bill. A third-party credit card charge, such as Visa or American Express, is considered payment when the charge is made because the charge creates an enforceable obligation between the taxpayer and the credit card company.

[6] The economic performance test has the effect of putting an accrual method taxpayer on the cash method because it may change the result under the all events test since the all events test is not treated as met any earlier than when economic performance occurs. When the liability arises because of a service contract or a contract to supply goods, economic performance occurs as the services are performed or goods are provided. There are two exceptions to economic performance: (1) the 3 1/2-month rule under Reg. § 1.461–4(d)(6)(ii) provides that a taxpayer may treat services or property as provided when the taxpayer makes payment if the taxpayer can reasonably expect the services or property to be provided within 3 1/2 months after the date of payment, and (2) the "recurring item exception" of § 461(h)(3) provides that a liability is treated as incurred if the four requirements under § 461(h)(3) are met. The first exception contemplates a one-time or occasional liability, while the recurring item exception contemplates recurring items.

6. VARIATIONS ON THE THEME

Would your answer change under either method if Samantha held more than 50 percent of the stock of the office supply company, and the company was an accrual method taxpayer? What result if the check that she received after her talk was postdated January 15? What result if the office supplies were a one-time order?

20

CLAIM OF RIGHT AND TAX BENEFIT DOCTRINES

1. OPENING REMARKS

If a taxpayer receives an amount of income that she subsequently is required to return, either because the amount was paid by mistake or because there is a controversy as to whether she is entitled to the amount, the taxpayer generally is required to include this amount in income in the year of the receipt, if it was received under a claim of right. If the taxpayer is forced to repay the amount, the taxpayer should be entitled to a deduction because at that point it is clear that the earlier inclusion of the full amount was erroneous. The question then is whether the taxpayer is entitled to a deduction when the amount is returned or repaid, or whether the taxpayer should be entitled to a refund with respect to the overpayment in the prior year, provided that year remains open.

In *U.S. v. Lewis*, 340 U.S. 590 (1951), the taxpayer was an employee who in 1944 received an erroneously computed bonus that was larger than the amount he was entitled to receive. Later, the error was discovered, and Mr. Lewis was required to repay the erroneous amount in 1946. His marginal tax rate in 1946 was lower than it had been in 1944, and he argued that if he was required to deduct the amount in 1946, he would not be made whole because he would have paid a tax on the income in 1944 at a much higher rate. Also, if the taxpayer could open up the 1944 taxable year and claim a refund with respect to that year, he would have been entitled to receive interest on that amount, so he would have benefited more from a refund from the earlier year than from a deduction in the current year.

The Supreme Court denied Mr. Lewis's request, though, reasoning that it would not depart from the claim of right doctrine, which authorized only a current deduction, simply because it was more advantageous to Mr. Lewis. The Court further reasoned that in other cases, the current deduction might be more advantageous to the taxpayer. Thus, it was the luck of the draw!

In 1954, Congress reacted to the *Lewis* result by enacting § 1341 to provide relief to taxpayers who found themselves in similar situations to that of Mr. Lewis.

2. HYPOTHETICAL

Thomas Trainor is the CEO of WidgeCo., a company that produces widgets. He is a married, calendar year, cash method taxpayer. Five years ago, he hired a new engineer to design a better widget. The engineer succeeded, which gave WidgeCo. a significant competitive edge in the marketplace. Because the company had thrived under Thomas's leadership, the board of directors voted three years ago to give him a bonus based on a percentage of the company's profits. In that year, the bonus was $1.5 million.

When the board voted on this bonus, the company's tax attorney advised it to add a clause to the resolution that would require Thomas to return any portion of this or any future bonuses determined by the IRS to constitute unreasonable compensation and thereby nondeductible to the company. Last year, WidgeCo. was audited, and the IRS challenged $800,000 of Thomas's bonus. This year, the Tax Court agreed with the IRS. WidgeCo. has now asked Thomas to return this portion of his bonus. What effect, if any, will that have on Thomas's tax liability?

Also, last year, Thomas filed a timely income tax return on which he itemized his deductions. He received a state income tax refund last year and wants to know if that refund is taxable for federal purposes.

3. LIST OF READINGS

Internal Revenue Code: §§ 55; 56(b); 68; 111; 164; 1341

Regulations: Reg. § 1.1341–1(a)(2)

Cases: North American Oil Consolidated v. Burnet, 286 U.S. 417 (1932); U.S. v. Skelly Oil Co., 394 U.S. 678 (1969); Van Cleave v. U.S., 718 F.2d 193 (6th Cir. 1983); Cinergy Corp. v. U.S., 55 Fed.Cl. 489 (2003)

Rulings: Rev. Rul. 68–153, 1968–1 C.B. 371

Article: Willis, *The Tax Benefit Rule: A Different View and A Unified Theory of Error Correction*," 42 Fla. L. Rev. 575 (1990)

4. SAMPLE ESSAY

The tax benefit doctrine requires the inclusion in income of a recovery of any item that produced a tax benefit in an earlier year. This doctrine has been codified in § 111, which provides that the recovery of any amount deducted in a prior year is not includable if it did not reduce the amount of the tax liability. Thus, the recovery of an item that was deducted in a prior year must be included in the taxpayer's gross income to the extent that it produced a tax benefit in the earlier year.

In Thomas's case, he was able to itemize his deductions, so theoretically, he was able to take advantage of the deduction for state income taxes under § 164(a)(3). However, there are two considerations that may have affected the amount of Thomas's deduction. First is the phase-out of itemized deductions for higher income taxpayers under § 68, which provides for a reduction of up to 80 percent of these deductions. The second is the alternative minimum tax under § 55. In determining this additional tax, certain deductions must be added back into gross income. One of these is the deduction for state taxes. See § 56(b)(1)(A). Thus, the benefit that Thomas received from his deduction of state income taxes probably was significantly reduced, and this should be taken into account in determining the amount of the inclusion, if any.

The return of the bonus raises the issue of the claim of right doctrine, and these facts are very similar to those of *Van Cleave*. Although it was not clear at the time Thomas received the bonus that he would be allowed to retain it, it was clear that he had control over this income for the entire taxable year. The claim of right doctrine requires him to ignore any contingency at this point and to include the entire amount of the bonus in gross income in the year that he receives it. See *North American Oil Consolidated*. In the year of the repayment, § 1341 applies to alleviate the result in *Lewis* by providing that the tax liability in the year of the repayment is the lesser of (1) the tax for the year computed after deducting the repayment or (2) the decrease in tax from the earlier year if the repayment had not been included in that year. Thus, § 1341 gives the taxpayer the advantage that Lewis sought: a consideration of the tax liability in both years (the year of the inclusion and the year of the return of the item) and the opportunity to use the one that is more beneficial. Section 1341 is a very pro-taxpayer provision, and for that reason, it is very strictly construed.

Section 1341 applies only if three conditions are met: (1) an item was included in gross income in a prior taxable year because it appeared that the taxpayer had an unrestricted right to the item, (2) a deduction is allowable in the current taxable year because it was established after the prior year that the taxpayer did not have an unrestricted right to the item or portion of the item, and (3) the deduction exceeds $3000. § 1341(a). Section 1341 is designed to restore the taxpayer to the position she would have been in if she had never received the item in question.

The problem for Thomas is that the IRS tends to read § 1341 very narrowly. It could argue that § 1341 applies only where it appears that the taxpayer has an unrestricted right to the item. Reg. § 1.1341–1(a)(2) provides that § 1341(a)(1) applies if it appears "from all the facts available in the year of inclusion that the taxpayer had an unrestricted right to such item." In Thomas's case, the IRS might argue that he did not have an unrestricted right to the full amount of the bonus because there was a chance that the IRS would declare a portion of the bonus unreasonable under § 162 (which authorizes the deduction of *reasonable* salaries). The government raised this issue and lost in *Van Cleave*.

The IRS provided some clarification of the term "appearance" in Rev. Rul. 68–153. In that ruling, the government interpreted the word "appeared" to mean "a semblance of an unrestricted right in the year received as distinguished from an unchallengeable right (which is more than an "apparent" right) and absolutely no right at all (which is less than an "apparent" right)." The important point is what the taxpayer reasonably believed, based on facts available at the end of the year of receipt. Under section 1341(a)(2) of the Code, it must be established in the subsequent year that in the year of inclusion the taxpayer did not, in fact or in law, have an unrestricted right to the amount in question.

In this case, Thomas's right to the bonus is unrestricted except for the contingency in the board's resolution. Provided that Thomas knew about the resolution, which he more than likely did, or about which he was at least on constructive notice, in the IRS's view this should serve as an apparent right, as opposed to an absolute right.

Under § 1341(a)(2), a deduction must be allowable for the current taxable year because it is established after the year of inclusion that the taxpayer did not have an unrestricted right to the item in question. Section 1341 is not a deduction authorizing provision; it merely allows alternative treatment of an otherwise deductible item. Therefore, the taxpayer must have an authorizing provision that allows him to deduct the repaid amount. Usually, this provision will be either § 162 or § 165. But if there is no authorizing provision, § 1341 does not apply.

5. TOOLS FOR SELF-ASSESSMENT

[1] The tax benefit rule is easier to discuss than the claim of right doctrine, so perhaps it is best to start with the tax benefit rule, although it not

necessary that your answer be organized in this way. As a practical matter, the IRS has a worksheet in the Form 1040 packet to help the taxpayer calculate the amount of the inclusion attributable to a state tax refund.

[2] Claim of right issues can arise in several contexts: an erroneously calculated payment, an erroneous payment, and a payment under a contingency such as that in *North American Oil*. The nit picking in which the IRS engages under § 1341 is a function of the fact that it is a very pro-taxpayer provision. If §1341 applies, the taxpayer always wins because it provides the best of both worlds. Section 1341 is very important to the taxpayer if the tax rates in the two years in question (i.e., the year of inclusion and the year of repayment) differ.

[3] The IRS has argued, with some success, that § 1341 should not apply if the taxpayer has an *actual* right, as opposed to an *apparent* right to the income. If there is an actual right to the income at the time of the receipt, then *Glenshaw Glass* applies to include the item in income, and if it is subsequently required to be returned, the taxpayer is limited to the *Lewis* situation of deducting the returned amount in the year of the return. See *Cinergy Corp. v. U.S.*, 55 Fed.Cl. 489 (2003).

[4] In Rev. Rul. 68–153, the IRS addressed each of the three situations with respect to what "appeared" meant. The first situation, in which the taxpayer has a "semblance" of an unrestricted right, is the classic situation in which § 1341 applies. An example of this is a salesperson who earns a commission in one taxable year and is required to return it in a later taxable year because the customer fails to pay the employer for the goods. The *Van Cleave* case is another example of this situation. The second example is where the taxpayer receives an item of income under an unchallengeable right, such as the payment of liquidated damages under a contract. The third type is where the taxpayer has no right to the income at all, such as in the case of an embezzlement. It is only in the case of the first situation that § 1341 applies.

[5] The second requirement, that it must be established after the close of the taxable year of receipt that the taxpayer did not have an unrestricted right to all or part of the item, is not met if the taxpayer voluntarily returns all or a portion of the item.

[6] Note that there may be some mechanical problems in the application of § 1341. These are addressed in Willis, "The Tax Benefit Rule: A Different View and A Unified Theory of Error Correction," 42 Fla. L. Rev. 575 (1990).

6. VARIATIONS ON THE THEME

Assume, in the alternative, that Thomas was a salesperson who was required to return his commission after a customer returned merchandise purchased through him. Would this change your answer?

21 CAPITAL GAINS AND LOSSES

1. OPENING REMARKS

A capital gain or loss arises on the sale or exchange of a capital asset. The term "capital asset" is broadly defined under § 1221 to include all property with eight exceptions, most of the exceptions pertaining to property used, produced, received, or held by a taxpayer's trade or business (e.g., stock in trade or other property of a kind that would properly be included in inventory; property used in a trade or business subject to depreciation, and real property used in a trade or business; notes; or accounts receivable acquired in the ordinary course of a trade or business).

The definition of capital asset has been broadened and refined in three judicial decisions. In the first, *Corn Products Refining Co. v. Commissioner*, 350 U.S. 46 (1955), the U.S. Supreme Court held that the sale of corn futures (contracts to purchase fixed amounts of corn at fixed prices on a future date) by a manufacturer of corn syrup and related products, who had purchased the futures to ensure a source of corn at a fixed price, generated an ordinary gain instead of a capital gain because the futures were an "integral part" of the taxpayer's business. Thus, the taxpayer was holding the futures for a business purpose rather than an investment purpose. The second case was *Arkansas Best Corp. v. Commissioner*, 485 U.S. 212 (1988), in which a holding company acquired stock in a commercial bank as an investment. When the bank began to experience financial difficulties, the holding company contributed substantial amounts of capital and received additional shares in return. When the holding company later sold these shares at a loss, it claimed an ordinary loss deduction. The Supreme Court held that the entire loss was a capital loss. The taxpayer had acquired the stock as an investment: it was not a broker or dealer in securities. And the shares, unlike the futures in *Corn Products,* could not be considered part of the taxpayer's inventory. The third decision was *Commissioner v. Bagley & Sewell Co.*, 221 F.2d 944 (2d Cir. 1955). The taxpayer in that case entered into a contract to manufacture equipment for a foreign government. The taxpayer was required under the contract to deposit U.S. bonds as security to guarantee its performance under the contract. Later, the taxpayer sold the bonds at a loss and attempted to deduct an ordinary loss. The Second Circuit allowed the ordinary loss because the taxpayer had not purchased the bonds as an investment. Instead, it had been required to purchase the bonds as part of the conduct of its business. Thus, the bonds did not constitute a capital asset to the taxpayer. These cases all illustrate that capital asset status is determined not by the property itself but by the taxpayer's purpose in purchasing or holding the property.

When a capital gain or loss is realized, it is divided into either long-term or short-term gains or losses. A long-term gain arises from the sale or exchange of a capital asset that has been held longer than 12 months. This is referred to as the "holding period." Long-term capital gains are taxed at lower rates than ordinary income. This favorable treatment is referred to as a "tax preference," and the general policy rationale behind it is (1) to prevent a "bunching" of income in one taxable year attributable to appreciation that has accrued over several to many taxable years (much of which may be due to inflation); and (2) to encourage investment, although this rationale has been much debated. The trade-off is that the deductibility of capital losses is limited for individual taxpayers. In general, capital losses can be deducted against capital gains, plus an additional $3000 against ordinary income in a single taxable year. Any excess losses (i.e., net capital losses, defined under § 1222(10) as the excess of capital losses over the amount that may be deducted currently under § 1211) may be carried over to the succeeding taxable year under § 1212(b). These losses retain their character as long term or short term.

The computation of preferential capital gains and deductible capital losses involves a netting of long-term and short-term capital gains and losses. The tax preference for capital gains, the limitation on capital losses, the different rates that apply to different types of capital assets, and the fact that Congress has changed the capital gains rates several times over the past several decades (and may do so again soon) have all contributed greatly to the complexity of the tax Code.

2. HYPOTHETICAL

Umberto Ulrich is a partner in a large law firm in a metropolitan area. His salary in 2010 was $350,000. His wife is an interior designer who earned $85,000 from her business in 2010. The Ulriches sold stock in six publicly held companies during 2010. Their realized gains and losses were:

Company	When Purchased	Number of Shares	Total Purchase Price	Total Sales Price
ABC Co.	6 yrs. ago	100	$3500	$8000
DEF Co.	3 yrs. Ago	100	$6000	$4500
GHI Co	6 months ago	100	$2500	$1000
JKL Co.	8 months ago	100	$2000	$2800
MNO Co.	2 yrs. ago	100	$5000	$8000
PQR Co.	2 yrs. ago	100	$4500	$3000

In 2009, the Ulriches purchased 100 shares of stock in the UVW Company for $3000 and 100 shares in the XYZ Company for $2000. At the end of 2010, the UVW stock is worth $3300 and the XYZ stock is worth $1600. In addition, the Ulriches sold a three-acre tract of undeveloped land for $37,000. They had purchased this property for $16,000 over 10 years ago, and they had been holding it as an investment. Finally, in 2010, Umberto sold a portion of his coin collection that he had begun 15 years ago. All of the coins sold had been held at least five years. He had paid $1500, collectively, for the coins and sold them for $10,000.

If the Ulriches have no other items of income or loss during 2010, discuss their tax consequences. (Ignore issues of the effect of the standard deduction and personal exemptions on the Ulriches' tax liability).

3. LIST OF READINGS

Internal Revenue Code: §§ 1(h); 408(m); 1202; 1221, 1222

Articles: Mayhall, *Capital Gains Taxation—The First One Hundred Years,* 41 L. L. Rev. 81 (1980); *Johnson, Fixing Capital Gains At the Core,* 2009 Tax Notes Today 240–11 (Nov. 30, 2009).

4. SAMPLE ESSAY

If the Ulriches have no other income during 2010, their gross income will consist of their combined salaries of $430,000 plus their net capital gains. Since neither of the Ulriches is a broker or dealer in securities, land, or coins, their sales of these items held for investment generate capital gains and losses. Net capital gains are taxed at lower rates than ordinary income. See § 1(h). Section 1222(11) defines a net capital gain (NCG) as "the excess of the net long-term capital gain for the taxable year over the net short-term capital loss for such year." Sections 1222(1) and 1222(2) define short-term capital gains and losses as gains or losses "from the sale or exchange of capital assets held for not more than one year." Similarly, §§ 1222(3) and 1222(4) define long-term capital gains and losses as gains and losses "from the sale or exchange of capital assets held for more than one year."

A net long-term capital gain (NLTCG) is defined under § 1222(7) as "the excess of long-term capital gains for the taxable year over the long-term capital losses for such year." A net short-term capital loss (NSTCL) is defined under § 1222(6) as "the excess of short-term capital losses for the taxable year over the short-term capital gains for such year."

The coins generate a long-term capital gain of $8500 ($10,000 less $1500); the land generates a long-term capital gain of $11,000 ($37,000 less $16,000); and the stock sales generate a long-term capital gain of $7500, a long-term capital loss of $3000, a short-term capital gain of $800, and a short-term capital loss of $1500.

Total long-term capital gains from all transactions during 2010 are $37,000.
Total long-term capital losses from all transactions during 2010 are $3000.
Total short-term capital gains from all transactions during 2010 are $800.
Total short-term capital losses from all transactions during 2010 are $1500.
The netting process produces a NLTCG of $34,000 ($37,000 less $3,000) and a NSTCL of $700 ($1,500 less $800). Thus, there is a NCG of $33,300 ($34,000 less $700).

But not all NCGs are equal. Capital gains are taxed at rates of 15 percent, 25 percent or 28 percent through 2012, depending on the type of asset involved. The highest rate (28 percent) applies to the sale of collectibles (e.g., art, gems, coins, antiques, etc., defined under § 408(m)) and certain small business stock under § 1202. §1(h)(4). The 25 percent rate applies to unrecaptured § 1250 gain on the sale or other disposition of certain depreciable real property. The lowest, 15 percent rate, applies to an "adjusted net capital gain." Adjusted NCG is NCG reduced by §1202 gain and the gain from the sale of collectibles and §1250 property. § 1(h)(3). For lower bracket taxpayers (i.e., those whose ordinary income tax bracket is below 25 percent), the rate on adjusted NCGs is 5 percent, although for taxable years 2008–2012, there is no tax on adjusted NCGs for taxpayers in this bracket. After December 31, 2012, up to six different rates will apply to long-term capital gains: 28 percent for collectible gain and certain gain on qualified small business stock, 25 percent on unrecaptured § 1250 gain, 20 percent on other gain (10 percent on other gain where the regular rate is 15 percent or lower), 18 percent on qualified five year gain (eight percent for taxpayers in the 10 or 15 percent brackets).

In this hypothetical, none of the Ulriches' gain is § 1202 gain or gain from the sale of § 1250 property (since land is not a depreciable asset). They do have gain from the sale of a collectible, however, and that gain will be taxed at 28 percent. Thus, they will have a tax liability of $2380 on the gain from the sale of the coin collection.

The remainder of their NCG, or $24,800, is an "adjusted net capital gain," subject to the more favorable rate of 15 percent. See § 1(h)(1)(C). Their tax liability on this amount is $3720, and their total capital gains tax for 2010 will be $6100 ($2380 from the sale of the coins + $3720 from the adjusted net capital gain). This amount will be added to the tax at ordinary income rates on their combined salaries.

5. TOOLS FOR SELF-ASSESSMENT

[1] Generally, in a capital gain or loss problem, there are two threshold issues to be addressed. The first issue is whether the asset in question is a capital asset. In this case, that is not a problem because the Ulriches purchased the properties for investment and are not holding any of them for use in their trade or business. The second issue is that there must be a sale or exchange, and that requirement is met in this problem as well. Note that only realized gains and losses will affect taxable income, so the two blocks of stock purchased by the Ulriches in 2009 and not sold will have no effect on their tax liability until they sell this stock.

[2] The next step is to determine whether the Ulriches have an overall gain or loss from their various capital transactions during the 2010 taxable year. The stock sales produce a collective gain of $3,800, and the other two transactions also produce a gain, so it is evident that they will be reporting a gain from the sale of capital assets. The various gains and losses then must be separated according to holding period and netted against each other. The netting process is clearer to visualize if expressed as a formula:

NCG = NLTCG (LTCG less LTCL) less NSTCL (STCL less STCG)

[3] Three things are evident from this formula: (1) that the favorable capital gain rates apply only to long-term capital gains, (2) capital losses may be taken to the extent of capital gains, and (3) net short-term capital gains (NSTCG) have absolutely no effect on NCGs and thus do not get the benefit of the favorable rates. Thus, short-term capital gains are taxed at ordinary income rates.

[4] The netting process is required because of the difference in tax treatment between long-term and short-term capital gains. If capital gains exceed

capital losses, we are not too concerned about the character (long term or short term) of the losses. We are only concerned about the character of the gains. But if the losses should exceed the gains, then we should be concerned about the character of the losses, because long-term capital losses are treated differently than short-term capital losses.

[5] Once the net amount has been determined, the next step is to determine how that amount is taxed. Capital gains are taxed at various rates depending upon the holding period and the type of asset being sold or exchanged. Section 1(h) requires that we go back and separate out the net gain from each type of asset subject to the 5 percent, 15 percent, 25 percent, or 28 percent rates. Note that the 5 percent rate is zero through 2012 (from 2008 to 2012), and the 15 percent rate will rise to 20 percent in 2013. For taxable years beginning in 2001 and ending on or before May 6, 2003, a lower rate of 18 percent instead of 20 percent (8 percent for those taxpayers in the 10 percent or 15 percent rate brackets) applied to the sale of capital assets held for more than five years. This special provision was repealed in 2003, but it will reappear in taxable years beginning after December 31, 2012, unless Congress provides otherwise.

6. VARIATIONS ON THE THEME

Assume, instead, that the Ulriches' gains (both long term and short term) are losses, and their losses are gains (in other words, their bases and sales prices are reversed for each asset sold). What result now?

DEPRECIATION

22

1. OPENING REMARKS

Depreciation is a tax accounting concept in which a taxpayer is entitled to a current deduction for the progressive exhaustion of property used in a trade or business or held for investment. There are two authorizing provisions for depreciation deductions: (1) §167 is the basic provision that spreads the deduction over the asset's useful life and considers any residual salvage value that may remain at the end of that useful life; while (2) § 168, enacted in 1981 and modified in 1986, is an accelerated cost recovery system (ACRS) that does not necessarily reflect the economic decline of the property. ACRS provides a shorter write-off than the actual useful life (and thus larger current deductions). It initially was enacted during the Reagan administration to encourage investment in equipment and to stimulate the economy. The Tax Reform Act of 1986 modified the ACRS to provide a slower recovery of the cost. This system is generally referred to as modified ACRS or MACRS.

The amount of the yearly deduction is determined by several factors. The first factor is the cost or other basis of the property. Thus, a taxpayer does not have to purchase property in order to be able to depreciate it. On the other hand, if the property is purchased, a depreciation deduction is allowed for mortgaged property, provided the mortgage is included in the basis. The older depreciation rules provided that the asset could not be depreciated below the salvage value. This is the residual value that is likely to remain at the end of the asset's useful life. The ACRS rules, however, disregard salvage value and allow a recovery of the entire basis of the asset. The second factor is the applicable depreciation method, which determines the amount of depreciation deductions that may be taken annually. The standard method is straight line, in which the cost of the property is divided by its useful life/recovery period, and a ratable deduction is taken each year. The other is an accelerated, declining balance method (either 200 percent or 150 percent declining balance) in which greater deductions are taken in the earlier years of the property's useful life/recovery period with tapering deductions in the later years. The third factor is the applicable recovery period or useful life of the property. Theoretically, this is the period over which the property will be used in the business or held for the production of income. Because this period can be speculative, Congress has attempted to alleviate uncertainty and disagreements between Treasury and taxpayers by issuing guidelines for certain assets to help determine the useful life and by establishing class lives. The ACRS provides shorter recovery periods than under the former rules, which affects the amount of depreciation that may be taken in a given year. The fourth factor is the applicable convention. Conventions are fictions that treat property as being placed in service during a set point within the year rather than on the actual date that it was placed in service. This fiction applies to the disposition of the property as well or to the final year that the deduction is allowed. Different conventions apply to personal property and real property.

Only property that falls within the permissible categories that will wear out or become obsolete may be depreciated. Thus, unimproved land may not be depreciated. The permissible categories are (1) property used in the trade or business or (2) property held for the production of income. Since inventory and property held for sale to customers do not fit within these categories, they are not eligible for depreciation.

Section 168(g) provides an alternative depreciation that generally is slower than ACRS. This system is mandatory for some types of property and for others, it can be elected. If elected, the election is irrevocable and for personal property, the election applies to all property within the class, while for real property, the election applies on a property-by-property basis. For nonresidential real property, there currently is not much difference between ACRS and alternative depreciation because both require straight line depreciation, and the recovery period under the ACRS is 39 years, while § 168(g) uses a 40-year recovery period.

Since depreciation deductions are based on cost recovery, as the deductions are taken the basis in the property must be reduced each year by the greater of the depreciation "allowed or allowable" under § 1016(a)(2). The amount of depreciation allowable is determined under the straight line method. If the taxpayer takes less depreciation than the amount allowable, the basis will be reduced by the amount allowable, nonetheless. Thus, failure to take at least straight line depreciation will not benefit the taxpayer. On the other hand, if the taxpayer takes greater deductions than "allowable," the basis is reduced by the amount "allowed." This is a "heads I win, tails you lose" provision for the government.

When the property is sold or otherwise disposed of, the taxpayer must realize a gain to the extent that any amount realized on the sale or disposition exceeds the adjusted basis of the property. The character of this gain is addressed in Problem XXIV.

2. HYPOTHETICAL

Victor VanKamp is an attorney who had practiced with the same law firm for 10 years. Several years ago, Victor decided to leave the firm and open his own practice. He purchased an office building on August 15 of year one for $900,000, of which $120,000 was attributable to the underlying land and the remaining $780,000 was attributable to the building. Victor paid $100,000 in cash and financed the remaining $800,000 through a nonrecourse mortgage obtained from a commercial lender.

The building had three separate offices, and Victor immediately moved into one and began to advertise for tenants for the remaining two offices. He was successful in finding one tenant on the following December 1 but it was not until July of the following year (year two) that he was able to rent the remaining office. At the end of five years, the property had increased in value to $955,000.

A year after moving into his office, Victor purchased a painting by Salvadore Dali at an auction for $15,000. He hung this painting in his office, and at the same time, he installed a new burglar alarm system in the office for $4000. Victor also has to make regular trips to the courthouse and to other business locations. He uses his personal automobile for this purpose. He purchased a new BMW automobile last year for $50,000, and he estimates that he uses it about 50 percent of the time for business purposes. Victor also purchased a $5000 computer system for his office this year.

Victor's practice has been successful, and he would like to maximize his depreciation deductions to the fullest extent possible. He seeks your advice about what assets he may depreciate and what amount of deductions he may take.

3. LISTS OF READINGS

Internal Revenue Code: §§ 167; 168; 179; 280F; 1012; 1016
Regulations: Reg.§ § 1.167(a)-10; 1.168–1
Rulings: Rev. Rul. 68–232, 1968–1 C.B. 79; TAM 8501009, Sept. 28, 1984.
Cases: review Crane v. Commissioner, 331 U.S. 1 (1947); Simon v. Commissioner, 68 F.3d 41 (2d Cir. 1995) *nonacq*; Consumers Power Co. v. Commissioner, 89 T.C. 710 (1987)

4. SAMPLE ESSAY

Section 168(a) authorizes an accelerated depreciation deduction for any tangible property used in a trade or business or held for the production of income. §§ 168(a); 167(a). The first question to be addressed is whether the property is depreciable property. Depreciable property is property that wears out and has a determinable life that exceeds one year. Land is not a depreciable asset because it does not wear out, even though the use of the land may have a determinable life. The building, however, is depreciable because it eventually will wear out, and it has a determinable life that exceeds a year. Victor immediately begins to use one of the offices in his business, and he immediately advertises the other offices for rent. Eventually, he is successful in renting both of these spaces. Therefore, he is in the business of renting commercial property, and the office building is considered depreciable property (i.e., property used in a trade or business). Victor will be entitled to take the deduction in the year in which the property is placed in service. See Reg. §§ 1.167(a)-10(b); 1.168–1(a). This will be in the year during which the property is purchased and ready for its assigned use, even though the last office is not actually rented until the following year. See *Consumers Power Co.*

The next step is to determine the amount of the deduction that may be taken on the building. Since Victor pays $780,000 for the building, he has a § 1012 basis in the building of $780,000. Even though the mortgage on the property is nonrecourse and Victor has no personal liability, as long as it is included in the cost basis of the building, it makes no difference that it is a nonrecourse mortgage. See *Crane*. Next, the applicable depreciation method must be determined under § 168(b). Since Victor's property is nonresidential real property, it is not eligible for an accelerated depreciation method and instead must be depreciated under the straight line method. See § 168(b)(3)(A). The recovery period of this property is 39 years under §168(c). Thus, the amount of the depreciation deduction will be $20,000 (rounded) per year except in the first and last years when the mid-month convention will apply. See § 168(d)(2). This convention treats all property placed in service during any month of the taxable year as placed in service at the mid-point of the month. See § 168(d)(4)(B). The first year that he owns the building, Victor will be able to deduct only $7500 (rounded) because he is treated as having placed the property in service in the middle of August. Thus, he is entitled to 4 1/2 months of depreciation deductions. At the end of each taxable year, his basis in the building will be adjusted for the depreciation deductions that were taken. See § 1016(a)(2). So at the end of the first taxable year, Victor will have to adjust his basis in the building to $772,500. Each year, until he sells or abandons the building, he will adjust his basis in a similar manner to reflect the depreciation deductions that he has taken.

The painting is not a depreciable asset because it does not suffer wear and tear, nor does it have a limited and ascertainable useful life. See *Simon v. Commissioner*. Since it is a collectible painting, it will increase in value and thus will not be depreciable. See Rev. Rul. 68–232. The burglar alarm system is considered part of the structural component of the building, so it will be depreciable over the building's 39-year recovery period. See TAM 8501009. The computer system is considered personal property that would be depreciable over a five-year recovery period. See § 168(e). However, § 179(a) allows an additional deduction as an expense in the year in which § 179 property is placed in service. Section 179 property is tangible personal property used in a trade or business. The maximum amount of the deduction depends upon the year in which the property is placed in service. For property placed in service in taxable years 2006 and 2007, the dollar limitation was $25,000; for taxable years 2008 and 2009, the limitation was $250,000; for taxable years 2010 and 2011, the limitation is $500,000; and in taxable year 2012, the limitation returns to $25,000. Thus, if Victor wants to maximize his deductions, he can elect to expense the computer in the year in which he purchases and uses it in his business. A §179 deduction can be taken only to the extent of business income, although any excess deduction may be carried over to the following taxable year. If Victor chooses to elect § 179 and to deduct the entire cost of the computer in the year of the purchase, he must reduce his basis by this amount, and thus he may not obtain any further depreciation deductions for the computer.

An automobile used in a trade or business qualifies for several types of deductions: an expense deduction under § 179, bonus depreciation under § 168(k), and ACRS depreciation as five year property under § 168(a). However, an automobile that qualifies for these deductions is also "listed property" under § 280F(d)(4)(A)(ii), and as such, it is subject to restrictions on deductibility. Since Victor uses this car 50 percent of the time for business purposes, his business use of the car is 50 percent and thus he normally would be entitled to half the deductions he otherwise would have been able to take if the car had been used entirely for business purposes. Under § 280F, however, if listed property is not "predominantly" used in the trade or business, it is subject to further limitations. For instance, since the predominant use test is not met here, Victor may not obtain the benefit of a § 179 expense deduction for the automobile. In addition, he may not take advantage of bonus or special depreciation, regardless of the year in which he places the car in service. Thus, the deductions that Victor otherwise would have been able to take are severely limited.

Since Victor uses the car only 50 percent of the time for business purposes, his basis for depreciation is $25,000 (50 percent of the $50,000 cost of the car). In addition, he is limited to the alternative depreciation system under § 168(g). This means that he may use only straight line depreciation over a five-year recovery period (see § 168(g)(3)(D)) subject to the § 280F(a) dollar limitation. If we assume that Victor uses the mid-quarter convention under § 168(d)(3) (which in turn assumes that all property placed in service, or disposed of, during any quarter of a taxable year was placed in service or disposed of at the mid-point of that quarter) and that he placed the car in service during the first quarter, his depreciation deduction in the first year of service would have been $4375 if this had not been listed property. Since the car is listed property, Victor's depreciation deduction is limited to $1280 (50 percent of $2560). In year two, his deduction is limited to $2050 (50 percent of $4100), year three would be $1225, and from year four on, the deduction would be limited to $738. Victor then may continue to take depreciation deductions for the life of the car, reducing his basis in the car by the amount of deductions taken. See § 1016(a)(2).

5. TOOLS FOR SELF-ASSESSMENT

[1] Victor has several different types of assets to consider, and the rules for each asset are different. It is best to begin with his largest asset, the building, although this is not imperative.

[2] The fact that Victor's property has increased in value does not affect the amount of depreciation deductions that may be taken. Depreciation, even under § 167, was never intended to reflect an accurate economic indication of the exhaustion of an asset. Instead, it always has been a system of cost allocation. Thus, economic depreciation may not coincide with tax depreciation. For instance, even though real property may appreciate in value, a depreciation deduction nevertheless is allowed if the property is depreciable (see *Simon*). By the same token, since depreciation is based on the cost basis of the building, the increase in value of the building does not have an effect on the cost basis and thus has no effect on the depreciation deductions.

[3] Since Victor's building is depreciable under the straight line method of depreciation, he will be able to deduct a ratable portion of the cost basis of the building over the 39-year recovery period. The recovery period determines the length of time over which the deductions may be taken and that, in turn, will determine the amount of the deduction that may be taken in any given year. The basis in the land remains $120,000 because the depreciation deductions do not affect the basis of the land since land is not a depreciable asset. Therefore, the basis in the land will not change unless there are capital improvements made to it.

[4] The mid-month convention means that regardless of when during the month of August that Victor purchased his property, it will be treated as purchased (and placed in service) during the middle of the month. Thus, in the year of the purchase, when the building is placed in service, Victor will be able to take 4 1/2 months of depreciation deductions.

[5] Section 1016(a)(2) provides that the basis shall be adjusted by the amount of depreciation deductions "allowed" in computing taxable income "but not less than the amount allowable . . . ." Thus, if Victor does not take the full amount of straight line depreciation in any given taxable year, his basis will be reduced by that amount anyway. On the other hand, if he takes more than the amount of deductions that are allowed, his basis will be reduced by that amount.

[6] The artwork will not be depreciable because it cannot pass the threshold test found in § 167 that a depreciable asset is one that is likely to suffer

exhaustion, wear, tear, and obsolescence. Rev. Rul. 68–232. The Second Circuit in *Simon* noted pithily in dictum, "Nor is valuable artwork purchased as office ornamentation apt to suffer anything more damaging than occasional criticism from the tutored or untutored . . .," (68 F.3d at 47), yet the court held that the violin bow at issue was depreciable to the taxpayers because it was subject to exhaustion, wear, and tear as a musical instrument even though it would appreciate in value over time as a collector's item. Thus, even though the bow did not have an ascertainable useful life, it was considered five-year property under the ACRS. The government objected to this result and issued a nonacquiescence in *Simon*. See AOD 1996–09 and 1996–29 I.R.B. 4 (Jul. 15, 1996).

[7] The computer equipment is not considered listed property because it is used exclusively at a regular business establishment. See § 280F(d)(4)(B). Since the automobile is listed property, Victor must keep records to establish the business versus personal use of the car. This is a stringent requirement for the depreciation deduction.

[8] Although the normal recovery period under ACRS for an automobile is five years, under § 280F, it takes far longer to depreciate a car because there is a ceiling on the amount of depreciation deductions that may be taken in any given year. (Note that while § 280F provides a limitation on the depreciation of *luxury* automobiles, in reality the limitation applies to non-luxury automobiles as well). Since the predominant business use test is not met (i.e., since the car does not receive greater than 50 percent business use), Victor may not take advantage of either § 179 or the special 50 percent bonus depreciation available in taxable years 2008 through 2012. See § 168(k). A further misfortune for Victor is that since his business use of the automobile initially is not greater than 50 percent, he may not increase his deductions if his later business use should rise above 50 percent. See § 280F(b)(1).

6. VARIATIONS ON THE THEME

What result if Victor used the automobile 70 percent for business purposes in the first three years of his business, and then his business use fell to 50 percent in the following years?

23

CHARACTERIZATION OF GAIN AND LOSS IN THE SALE OF BUSINESS PROPERTY

1. OPENING REMARKS

Gains and losses are characterized as ordinary or capital, and this characterization is important because it determines the ultimate amount of tax liability owed since capital gains are taxed at more favorable rates than ordinary income. The trade-off is that ordinary losses generally are more favorable than capital losses. As we saw in Problem XXI, a capital gain or loss is realized on the sale or other disposition of a capital asset. The term "capital asset" is broadly defined to include any property held by the taxpayer, with eight specified exceptions. See § 1221. Section 1221(a)(1) excludes as capital assets inventory, stock in trade, or property held primarily for sale to customers in the ordinary course of business. Section 1221(a)(2) excludes property used in the trade or business subject to an allowance for depreciation, or real property used in the trade or business. Section 1221(a)(4) excludes accounts or notes receivable, and § 1221(a)(8) excludes supplies used or consumed in the ordinary course of the taxpayer's trade or business. Excluded from the list of exceptions, and therefore considered a capital asset, is an intangible property right such as goodwill.

Although depreciable property used in the taxpayer's trade or business is excluded from the definition of a capital asset, it is subject to several other characterization provisions. Sections 1245 and 1250 recharacterize as ordinary income the depreciation deductions taken previously up to the amount of gain realized. This is referred to as "recapture." The previous depreciation deductions offset ordinary income, so if gain is realized on the sale or other disposition of the asset, all or a portion of that gain is characterized as ordinary income. Section 1231 may recharacterize any remaining gain as capital (sometimes referred to as "quasi-capital gain"). Section 1231 is a taxpayer-favorable provision that may transform an ordinary gain into a long-term capital gain or a long-term capital loss into a more favorable ordinary loss. Simplistically stated, if losses from § 1231 property exceed gains, all gains and losses are characterized as ordinary. If gains exceed losses, then all gains and losses are long-term capital gains. Section 1231 also includes gains and losses from involuntary conversions of property used in the trade or business, or any capital asset held for investment or in connection with a trade or business that has been held by the taxpayer for more than one year. Inventory or property held primarily for sale to customers in the course of the taxpayer's trade or business is excluded from § 1231. Thus, sales of this type of property will generate ordinary income and are not subject to any of the recharacterization provisions.

2. HYPOTHETICAL

Wade Williams, a cash method taxpayer, sold his widget business, a sole proprietorship, and realized the following amounts from the following assets:

Asset	Amount Realized	Adjusted Basis
Receivables	$55,000	$-0-
Supplies	$15,000	$-0-
Inventory	$70,000	$55,000
Equipment	$70,000	$35,000(with $25,000 of depreciation deductions taken)
Building	$650,000	$490,000 (with $60,000 of depreciation deductions taken)
Land	$200,000	$150,000
Goodwill	$100,000	$-0-
NoncompeteAgreement	$ 25,000	$-0-

Wade had purchased the building and land five years ago and had depreciated the building under the straight line method of depreciation. The equipment had been purchased three years ago, and the supplies had been purchased last year and had been deducted. Wade agreed not to compete in the same business and in the same geographical area for a period of 10 years.

In addition, in the same taxable year of the sale, the State requisitioned some property that Wade had purchased for investment five years ago for $50,000 and that was worth $40,000 at the time of the condemnation. Wade received $40,000 from the State for this property.

If these are Wade's only transactions for this taxable year, what is the amount and character of his gain/loss? Assume that the goodwill was not eligible for amortization under § 197 because it was entirely generated by Wade's business. Assume further that Wade has had no previous sales of § 1231 property in the past five years.

3. LIST OF READINGS

Internal Revenue Code: §§ 1(h); 1060(a); 1221; 1231; 1245; 1250

Cases: Williams v. McGowan, 152 F.2d 570 (2d Cir. 1945); Rodney B. Horton, 13 T.C. 143 (1949)

4. SAMPLE ESSAY

For tax purposes, the sale of a business is considered a sale of the separate assets rather than a sale of the business as a whole, because the character of those assets may vary, producing different tax consequences. See *Williams v. McGowan.* So, the sale of Wade's business is not considered a sale of the entire business for $1,185,000 (the total amount realized on the sale) but rather a sale of the individual assets of the business.

Wade realizes $55,000 on the sale of the accounts receivable. Accounts receivable are neither capital assets (because they are excluded under § 1221(a)(4)) nor

§ 1231 property (see § 1231(b)(1)), so they generate ordinary income. Thus, Wade must recognize $55,000 of ordinary gain on the sale of the accounts receivable. The $15,000 amount realized for the supplies results in $15,000 of ordinary gain recognition for Wade for the same reason (i.e., the supplies are neither a capital asset (§ 1221(a)(8)) nor a § 1231 asset). In addition, the supplies had been deducted, so under the tax benefit doctrine, the recovery attributable to them will generate ordinary income because their deduction offset ordinary income. Inventory also is neither a capital asset (§ 1221(a)(1)) nor § 1231 property (excluded under § 1231(b)(1)(A)), so it too generates an ordinary gain of $15,000.

The equipment is depreciable property, and Wade has taken $25,000 of depreciation deductions in the three years that he has held the equipment. These deductions have reduced his basis to $35,000, so he realizes a gain of $35,000 on the sale of the equipment ($70,000 amount realized less his $35,000 adjusted basis). Unlike the other assets to this point, the equipment is § 1231 property because it is depreciable property used in Wade's trade or business. See § 1231(b)(1). Also, since the equipment is depreciable personal property, it is subject to depreciation recapture under §1245. See §1245(a)(3)(A). Sections 1245 and 1250 override § 1231, so the § 1245 gain must be determined before the § 1231 gain.

Section 1245(a)(1) treats as ordinary income the gain realized on the sale to the extent that the lesser of the recomputed basis or the amount realized exceeds the adjusted basis of the property. The recomputed basis is the adjusted basis with the depreciation deductions added back in. See § 1245(a)(2)(A). The recomputed basis in this case is $60,000 ($35,000 adjusted basis plus the $25,000 of previously taken depreciation deductions), and this basis exceeds the adjusted basis by $25,000, the amount of depreciation deductions taken. Thus, $25,000 of the $35,000 gain must be recharacterized (or recaptured) under § 1245 as ordinary gain. The remaining $10,000 of gain is §1231 gain and must be considered with all other § 1231 transactions for the taxable year. Thus, its character cannot be determined until it has been compared to the other § 1231 gains and losses for that taxable year.

The sale of the building produces a gain of $160,000 ($650,000 amount realized less $490,000 adjusted basis). Since the building is depreciable property, it also is subject to two characterization provisions: § 1250 and § 1231. Section 1250 operates slightly differently than § 1245. Section 1250 recaptures as ordinary gain the depreciation deductions that exceed straight line depreciation. Since the building has been depreciated under the straight line method of depreciation, there is no recapture under § 1250. Thus, the $160,000 gain is entirely § 1231 gain.

The land is not depreciable, but it is § 1231 property because it is held in connection with the business and does not fall within any of the four exceptions under § 1231(b). Thus, the $50,000 gain from the sale of the land ($200,000 amount realized less $150,000 basis) is § 1231 gain.

The sale of goodwill produces a $100,000 gain that is a straight capital gain (or net capital gain) because it is not § 1231 property but rather a capital asset under §1221. If we assume that the goodwill has a holding period of more than a year, the character of this gain is a long-term capital gain. The covenant not to compete generates ordinary income because it is considered a payment for future services, even though the payment is for nonperformance. See *Rodney B. Horton*.

Thus, it is not § 1231 property. The $10,000 loss from the condemnation of the investment property falls under § 1231(a)(3)(A)(ii) and will be considered a long-term capital loss.

There are three §1231 gains in the sale of this business: $10,000 from the sale of the equipment, $50,000 from the sale of the land, and $160,000 from the sale of the building. There is one §1231 loss of $10,000 recognized during the year on the condemnation of the investment property. Since the § 1231 gains exceed the losses, all the gains and the loss are long-term capital in nature. See § 1231(a)(1).

At the end of the taxable year, Wade recognizes $55,000 of ordinary income from the accounts receivable; $15,000 of ordinary income on the supplies; $15,000 of ordinary income on the inventory; $25,000 of ordinary income recapture under § 1245 from the sale of the equipment and $10,000 of long-term capital gain from the remaining gain from the sale of the equipment under § 1231; $160,000 of long-term capital gain on the sale of the building; $50,000 of long-term capital gain on the sale of the land; $100,000 long-term capital gain on the sale of the goodwill; $25,000 ordinary income from the agreement not to compete; and $10,000 long-term capital loss on the condemnation of the investment property. This is a total of $135,000 of ordinary income and $310,000 of net long-term capital gain.

The capital gains must be separated further because § 1(h) taxes the gains differently. While § 1250 does not require any recapture of the depreciation deductions taken on the building, §§ 1(h)(3) and (h)(6) tax "unrecaptured § 1250 gain" (the depreciation deductions previously taken that were not subject to recapture because they did not exceed straight line depreciation) at a rate of 25 percent while the remainder of the long-term capital gain on the sale of the building will be taxed at a rate of 15 percent as net capital gain. See § 1(h)(3). Thus, on the sale of the building, Wade will be taxed on $60,000 of § 1231 gain from the building at a rate of 25 percent and the remaining $100,000 of § 1231 gain will be taxed at a rate of 15 percent.

5. TOOLS FOR SELF-ASSESSMENT

[1] Section 1060(a) requires the consideration for the sale of the business to be allocated among the assets as provided by § 338(b)(5). Section 338(b)(5) authorizes the Treasury to promulgate regulations allocating the consideration among the various assets. Those regulations are beyond the scope of this problem, so for our purposes we will assume that the purchase price has been allocated among the assets in accordance with the regulations.

[2] There are two ways to approach this problem. One is to address the various assets in the order given. The other is to separate the assets according to those that fall under § 1231 and those that do not. None of the characterization provisions affect the ultimate amount of gain or loss realized, but they do affect the amount of the ultimate tax liability. Note that this problem involves three separate characterizations: (1) § 1231 for the sale or involuntary conversion of § 1231 property, (2) recapture of earlier depreciation deductions under § 1245 and §1250, and (3) a netting and recharacterization under § 1(h) to determine the tax rate.

[3] Since Wade is a cash method taxpayer, he has not been taxed on his receivables, therefore, they have a zero basis. Although he has paid for the

supplies, they were deducted as an ordinary and necessary business expense under § 162 when they were purchased so they also have a zero basis to reflect Wade's earlier tax benefit. Thus, the amount of the earlier deduction must be "recaptured." A recapture may be regarded as a tax "payment" for the earlier benefit taken by the taxpayer. Since the earlier deduction offset and reduced ordinary income, the "payment" for that benefit must be an inclusion of ordinary income.

[4] While inventory would seem to be an ordinary and necessary business expense that would generate a deduction under § 162, the regulations provide that the cost of inventory offsets the sales price of the inventory when it is sold. See Reg. § 1.61–3(a). Thus, gross income for a taxpayer engaged in the merchandising, manufacturing, or mining business is total sales less the cost of goods sold, plus any other income realized during the taxable year. Cost of goods sold is determined by the cost of inventory on hand at the beginning of the taxable year (opening inventory), plus inventory purchases during the taxable year less cost of inventory on hand at the close of the taxable year (closing inventory). The closing cost of inventory on hand reflects not only the sale of inventory during the taxable year but also losses due to casualty, theft, shrinkage, subnormal goods, etc. These losses will reduce the closing inventory value and thus will increase the cost of goods sold. This, in turn, will decrease the total gross income recognized.

[5] In determining the depreciation recapture on the sale of the equipment, the recomputed basis is the adjusted basis, adjusted upward to reflect either the actual depreciation deductions taken on the property or, if less, the amount of deductions allowable on the property. See § 1245(a)(2)(A) and (B). Unlike § 1016, which reduces the taxpayer's basis by the amount of depreciation deductions "allowed or allowable," whichever is greater, § 1245 allows the taxpayer to establish that the amount allowed (i.e., actually taken) was less than the amount allowable. See § 1245(a)(2)(B). This is because § 1245 is a mechanism to ensure that the taxpayer "pays" for the earlier deductions taken that did not reflect the economic depreciation in the property. Thus, § 1245 is a tax benefit mechanism that recharacterizes as ordinary income the gain realized on the sale or other disposition of the asset to the extent of the depreciation deductions actually taken. The amount of the recapture is limited to the realized gain.

Section 1250 is not as aggressive as § 1245. Section 1245 recaptures all depreciation deductions taken to the extent of the gain realized, whereas § 1250 recaptures only depreciation deductions to the extent accelerated depreciation exceeds straight line depreciation. The trade-off is that the "unrecaptured §1250 gain" is subject to a higher tax rate than net capital gain under § 1(h). But this rate is less than the ordinary income rate.

[6] After analyzing the individual assets to determine what type of gain or loss they generate, the next step is to determine the gains and losses under § 1231. In applying § 1231, the gains and losses cannot be netted because they may be treated differently under § 1(h). Section 1231(a)(4)(C) creates what is called a "subhotchpot" for involuntary conversions of § 1231 property. If losses from involuntary conversions exceed gains, the gains and losses are not characterized under § 1231 and instead retain their character as ordinary

gains and losses. If the gains exceed the losses, then they go into the "main hotchpot" under § 1231(a)(3)(A) and are characterized according to whether overall § 1231 gains exceed losses. If so, all gains and losses are long-term capital; if not, all gains and losses are ordinary. Since the subhotchpot gains will affect the main hotchpot characterization, all subhotchpot gains and losses must be considered before those in the main hotchpot. Involuntary conversions in the § 1231(a)(4)(C) subhotchpot include only casualty losses from fire, storm, shipwreck, or theft, etc. Involuntary conversions from requisitions or condemnations are not included in this category. Instead, they fall under the main hotchpot. See § 1231(a)(4)(B). Since the gains exceed the losses under the main hotchpot in this problem, the condemnation loss is characterized as a long-term capital loss rather than an ordinary loss.

[7] Prior to the enactment of § 197 in 1993, goodwill was not amortizable, and when sold, it generated capital gains (in excess of the basis). A covenant not to compete was an ordinary asset that was amortizable over the life of the agreement, typically three to five years, and it generated ordinary income upon sale. After the enactment of § 197, goodwill became an amortizable intangible asset, provided it is not self-created, and both goodwill and a noncompete agreement are amortizable over a 15-year period. Upon sale of the goodwill, all or a portion of the gain will be recaptured as ordinary income to reflect the amortization.

Since the interests of the buyer and the seller were diverse prior to the enactment of § 197 (the seller was interested in allocating a greater portion of the sales price to goodwill while the buyer was interested in allocating a greater portion of the price to the noncompete agreement), the IRS had no reason to challenge the allocation. After the enactment of § 197, the 15-year recovery period will not be as attractive to the buyer as the 5-year recovery period of equipment. The seller also will not be particularly interested in allocating much of the sales price to a noncompete agreement because in addition to generating ordinary income, it is subject to self-employment tax. Therefore, since the enactment of § 197, the IRS has been more inclined to scrutinize the allocation of the purchase price between noncompete agreements and equipment.

[8] Since the problem states that Wade has had no previous sales of § 1231 property in the past five years, the recapture provision of § 1231(c) does not come into play to recharacterize a portion of the long-term capital gain under § 1231(a) into ordinary gain.

6. VARIATIONS ON THE THEME

What is the purchaser's basis in these assets, and will the purchaser be able to obtain any tax benefit from any of the assets? In the alternative, what result if the investment property had consisted of $10,000 of land and $50,000 attributable to a small office building that Wade had held for rental to third parties, and this building had been totally destroyed in a tornado with no insurance recovery?

INSTALLMENT SALES

24

1. OPENING REMARKS

An installment sale is a disposition of property in which at least one payment is to be received after the close of the taxable year in which the disposition occurs. Section 453 governs the treatment of gains from installment sales and applies automatically unless the taxpayer opts out. The effect of § 453 is to place all taxpayers on the cash method of accounting with respect to the disposition. In general, § 453 spreads the basis out over the payment period, and as each payment is made in each taxable year, a proportionate amount of the basis offsets the payment to produce a gain to the taxpayer. Section 453 does this through a ratio of gross profit (total amount of the selling price less the adjusted basis in the property) to total contract price. The resulting amount is expressed as a percentage, and this percentage is applied to each payment to determine the taxable portion. Section 453 may not be used for losses, and the character of the gain is the same as the character of the underlying property. Section 453 is purely a timing device because the amount and character of the gain do not change, only the timing of the inclusion. So instead of immediate recognition of gain upon sale, the gain instead is deferred and will not be recognized in full until the final payment is received. Another way to state this is that § 453 puts all taxpayers on the cash method of accounting, regardless of their actual accounting method.

Occasionally, a taxpayer may sell or otherwise dispose of the installment notes before receiving full payment. If so, the taxpayer will realize a gain or loss to the extent of the difference between the basis of the obligation and the amount realized on a sale or exchange, or the fair market value of the obligation if the disposition of the notes is not through a sale or exchange. See § 453B(a). The taxpayer's basis in these notes is the face amount of the note less the amount that would be reportable as income if the note were satisfied in full. See § 453B(b).

If the disposition of property is to a related party, special rules apply to prevent abuse of the tax system. The installment method can be used for such dispositions, unless the property is depreciable. If it is depreciable, the installment method is not available. If the property is not depreciable, the seller may use § 453 to defer the gain, but if the related party sells the property within two years of the first disposition, the second disposition will trigger gain recognition by the first seller under § 453(e). An exception to this rule is where the property consists of marketable securities. In that case, there is no two-year time limit unless the taxpayer can establish to the satisfaction of the IRS that the two transactions did not have as one of their principal purposes the avoidance of federal income tax. See §§ 453(e)(2) and (e)(7).

Interest is not dealt with directly under § 453, except for certain dispositions of property by dealers. If interest is adequate and properly stated, it is included when paid. Thus, it is not a part of the § 453 calculation of gross profit but is separately included as paid. If interest is not stated or is not adequate, it becomes much more complicated because it then will be imputed, which will have consequences to both the buyer and the seller.

2. HYPOTHETICAL

Some years ago, Malcolm Xavier, a veterinarian and a cash method taxpayer, purchased a small office building on a half acre of land for his practice. He paid $250,000 for the building and $50,000 for the land, at the time paying $50,000 in cash and financing the remainder with a nonrecourse mortgage. Earlier this year, he sold the property, subject to the mortgage (now $200,000), to an unrelated third party for $450,000, of which $375,000 was attributable to the building and $75,000 was attributable to the land. The buyer paid Malcolm $50,000 in cash at the time of the sale and agreed to pay an additional $50,000 each year for the next four years with market rate interest to be paid each year on the unpaid balance. Malcolm had taken depreciation deductions of $60,000 on the building attributable to straight line depreciation.

After two years, Malcolm sold the remaining two notes for $95,000, their fair market value, to an unrelated third party. Discuss his tax consequences on the initial sale of the property and on the subsequent sale of the notes.

3. LIST OF READINGS

Internal Revenue Code: §§ 1(h); 453; 1001; 1016; 1231; 1250
Regulations: §§ 15A.453–1; 1.453–12
Cases: Review Crane v. Commissioner, 331 U.S. 1 (1947)

4. SAMPLE ESSAY

When Malcolm sells his property, he realizes a gain of $210,000 on the sale. His basis in the building was $250,000 when he purchased it, and he has taken $60,000 of depreciation deductions on it. Thus, his adjusted basis in the building is $190,000. See § 1016(a)(2). His total basis in the property is $240,000 ($190,000 adjusted basis in the building plus the $50,000 cost basis of the land). His amount realized on the sale under § 1001(b) is $450,000 (see *Crane*). Thus, he realized a gain of $210,000 on the sale ($450,000 amount realized less $240,000 adjusted basis). See § 1001(a).

If at least one payment of the purchase price is to be received after the close of the taxable year of the disposition, the sale is an installment sale under § 453(b)(1), and the provisions of § 453 apply automatically, allowing the taxpayer to spread the gain over the contract payment period. Since Malcolm meets this requirement, he must calculate the gross profit percentage that will apply to each payment to determine the amount on which he will be taxed. Section 453(c) calculates this percentage based on the ratio of gross profit to total contract price. Malcolm's gross profit is $210,000 (the amount of gain realized on the sale) and the total contract price is $450,000, which normally would result in a gross profit percentage of 42 percent. The regulations provide, however, that where property is sold subject to a mortgage under the principles of *Crane*, the mortgage relief is not treated as a payment in the year of the sale to the extent that the relief does not exceed the seller's adjusted basis in the property. See Reg. §§ 15A.453–1(b)(2)(iv) and 15A.453–1(b)(3)(I). To the extent that the mortgage liability exceeds the adjusted basis, the excess is treated as a payment in the year of the sale. Since the mortgage liability of $200,000 does not exceed Malcolm's basis of $240,000, there is no constructive payment in the year of the sale.

However, the total contract price under § 453(c) is adjusted downward by the amount of the mortgage relief that does not exceed Malcolm's basis. Thus, the total contract price is reduced by the $200,000 amount of the mortgage relief. This produces a new ratio of $210,000 gross profit/$250,000 total contract price or 84 percent. Thus, 84 percent of each payment that Malcolm receives will be taxable. In year one, when he receives the first payment of $50,000, he will be taxed on $42,000. Thereafter, he will include $42,000 in income as each payment is made under the notes.

Section 453 authorizes a deferral of the realized gain, but it does not address the character of the gain, because the character is determined by the underlying asset. In this case, Malcolm sells land and a depreciable building, both of which are § 1231 assets. Depreciation recapture is not subject to deferral under § 453 and must be recognized in the year of the disposition. But in this case there is no recapture because the building has been depreciated under the straight line method. See § 1250. If the sale of this property is Malcolm's only § 1231 transaction in that year, the entire gain on both the land and the building would be characterized as long-term capital gain. The payments of interest are not covered under § 453, so they must be recognized either when paid or under the imputed interest rules. In this case, the stated interest is adequate so it will be recognized as ordinary income when paid and will not be considered in the § 453 calculations.

Although there is no recapture on this property, Malcolm is subject to differential capital gains rates to reflect the depreciation that he has taken on the building. Under § 1(h), $80,000 of his gain will be taxed at a rate of 25 percent (§ 1(h)(1)(D)) as unrecaptured § 1250 gain, while the remaining gain will be taxed at a 15 percent rate as an adjusted net capital gain (§ 1(h)(1)(C)). The regulations require the full amount of the 25 percent gain to be recognized prior to recognition of the 15 percent gain. See Reg. § 1.453–12(a). Thus, in the year of the sale, Malcolm will recognize a long-term capital gain of $42,000 that will be taxed at a 25 percent rate. The following year, when he receives another $50,000 payment, $18,000 of this payment will be taxed at a 25 percent rate while the remainder, $24,000, will be taxed at a 15 percent rate. As he receives the next three payments under the contract, the entire $126,000 of gain will be long-term capital gain taxed at a 15 percent rate.

But Malcolm sells the two remaining notes in year three. The tax consequences then are governed by § 453B. Since there is no longer a liquidity problem because Malcolm now has the case in hand, he will be taxed immediately on his gain, determined under § 453B(a). His amount realized on the sale is the selling price of $95,000 less his basis in the obligation. Section 453B(b) provides that the basis in the obligation is the face amount of the obligation ($50,000) less the amount that Malcolm would have had to include in income if the obligation were paid in full. Since he would have had to include 84 percent of the face amount ($42,000) if the obligations were paid in full, his total basis in the notes is $16,000 ($8000 x 2), and thus he must include $79,000 ($95,000 less $16,000) in gross income in the year of the sale. The character of the gain is determined by the character of the underlying property because § 453B does not change the amount or character of the gain, only the timing of the recognition. Thus, the $79,000 realized gain is recognized as a long-term capital gain, taxable at a 15 percent rate. § 453B(a).

5. TOOLS FOR SELF-ASSESSMENT

[1] This transaction is what is known as a "seller financed" transaction or mortgage. In any § 453 problem, the first step is to calculate the amount of the taxpayer's gain realized and recognized on the sale.

[2] The amount of the outstanding mortgage that the buyer agrees to pay will reduce the cash paid to the seller, so the buyer will pay Malcolm $250,000 in cash over the four-year period and also will take the property subject to the $200,000 outstanding mortgage. Since Malcolm included the amount of the mortgage in his basis and had been taking depreciation deductions calculated from that basis, the principals of *Crane* require that the mortgage relief be included in the amount realized, even though the mortgage is nonrecourse. So Malcolm's amount realized on the sale is $450,000, which produces a realized gain of $210,000 ($450,000 amount realized less his adjusted basis of $240,000).

[3] The second step is to determine the timing of the gain recognition. Prior to 1980, § 453 was an opt-in provision, but in 1980, Congress amended the provision to provide for its automatic application. Thus, if a taxpayer wishes to avoid the application of § 453, she must make an election to opt out. See § 453(d)(1). Without § 453, Malcolm would have to recognize his entire realized gain in the year of the sale. Since he does not receive the entire sales price in that year, he may not have the cash with which to pay the tax liability, and this could cause liquidity problems for him. It was in recognition of this problem that Congress enacted § 453. Another part of the rationale behind § 453 is that the seller's tax situation may change from year to year, and this may affect the treatment of the gain. For instance, the taxpayer may be in a different tax bracket in a subsequent year.

[4] The relief of the mortgage liability generally would be considered a payment in the year of the sale because there would be no opportunity otherwise under the installment sale rules to tax this amount. However, the liquidity problem would arise again because Malcolm would not have received a payment of that amount in the year of the sale. Thus, the regulations allow him to exclude gain recognition up to the adjusted basis in the property being sold. The effect of the adjustment to the total contract price is to exclude the amount of the *Crane* realization up to the adjusted basis of the property and to compensate for this exclusion by treating a greater portion of the cash payments as gain under § 453. This is demonstrated in the problem, because Malcolm's gross profit percentage, without the adjustment, is 42 percent while after the adjustment the percentage is 84 percent.

[5] If Malcolm were to receive all payments under the notes, he would receive total payments of $250,000 ($50,000 in the year of the sale and $50,000 per year for the next four years), plus the $200,000 mortgage relief, for a total of $450,000, which is in accordance with the contract of sale. His realized gain on this sale was $210,000 and under § 453, he recognizes $42,000 in the year of the sale with the same amount recognized in each of the following four years as the payments are made on the notes. His entire recognized gain over

this period is $210,000. As noted earlier, § 453 does not affect the total amount of the gain recognized, but it determines the timing of the recognition. In general, it spreads the recognized gain over the period in which payments are made under the sales contract.

[6] When Malcolm sells the remaining three notes for $95,000, he realizes a gain of $79,000 on the sale. This makes sense, because he already has realized and recognized a gain of approximately $126,000 from the initial cash payment plus the payments on the first two notes. His initial realized gain on the sale of the property was $210,000. Thus, he will have recognized $205,000 of this gain ($126,000 recognized on the down payment and the notes plus $79,000 recognized on sale of the notes). The remaining $5000 is attributable to the discounted sales price of the notes to reflect the time value of money. Malcolm is not taxed on this amount since he does not receive it. Thus, the economics of the transaction make sense, and the numbers have not changed under § 453; the only thing that has changed is the timing of the gain recognition.

6. VARIATIONS ON THE THEME

What result if the buyer had been Malcolm's son instead of an unrelated third party, and the son then resold the property before the payment on the next note was due?

25

NONRECOGNITION TRANSACTIONS

LIKE-KIND EXCHANGES AND INVOLUNTARY CONVERSIONS

1. OPENING REMARKS

Section 1001(c) provides that gain or loss on the sale or exchange of property shall be recognized unless otherwise provided. There are numerous nonrecognition provisions under the Code that apply to specific transactions, such as the nonrecognition of gain on the sale of a principal residence (discussed in Problem IV), the transfer of property between spouses incident to a divorce (discussed in Problem V), and the nonrecognition of gain or loss on a wash sale of stock or securities (discussed in Problem XXVI). There are, however, two general categories of nonrecognition transactions that are used frequently: like-kind exchanges and involuntary conversions.

The term "nonrecognition" is misleading because the taxpayer usually does not permanently escape recognition of the gain on a transaction. Instead, the gain is merely deferred. This is achieved through a substituted basis, so the taxpayer takes the same basis in the new property that she had in the old property, with some adjustments. Thus, the taxpayer recognizes the gain or loss when the new property is later sold or disposed of in a taxable transaction.

Section 1031 provides nonrecognition of gain or loss on the exchange of like-kind property held for investment or used in a trade or business. The policy rationale behind this provision is twofold: (1) to encourage investment in new property in the hope of stimulating the economy and increasing the tax base, and (2) there has been no significant change in the taxpayer's economic investment if property held for investment or used in the taxpayer's trade or business is exchanged for property of like kind. Many business transactions today are structured as like-kind exchanges, and some are very complex: for example, sophisticated transactions that involve multiple parties and property that has yet to be acquired. In order to have a successful like-kind exchange, the taxpayer must meet four requirements: (1) the properties must be qualifying properties; (2) the properties exchanged must be "like kind"; (3) there must be an exchange, as opposed to a sale; and (4) the taxpayer must meet the holding period requirements. If nonqualifying property, such as cash, is received in the transaction, it is called "boot," and it triggers a gain recognition. Boot, whether it is given or received, requires a basis adjustment.

Section 1033 allows a nonrecognition of gain on an involuntary conversion of property. The policy rationale behind this provision is obvious: this is not an appropriate event to trigger a tax liability because the taxpayer has suffered a conversion of property over which she had no control. Section 1033 applies in very specific situations. First, the triggering events are destruction of the property (in whole or in part), theft, seizure, or requisition, condemnation or threat thereof. Second, the property must be converted into property "similar or related in service or use to the property so converted." If cash is received, § 1033 does not apply unless the taxpayer purchases qualifying property within a two-year period.

2. HYPOTHETICAL

Yancey Young is a cash method, calendar year taxpayer who is not a dealer in real estate. Ten years ago, he purchased as an investment a 100-acre tract of undeveloped land in a rural area for $250,000. Yancey paid $100,000 in cash from his own funds for this property and financed the remainder of the purchase price through a nonrecourse mortgage. This purchase turned out to be a good investment because eight years later the property had appreciated in value to $800,000. At that time, Yancey was approached by a large manufacturing corporation that was interested in acquiring his property. Yancey was not interested in incurring a large tax liability, but he was interested in continuing to hold investment property, so he proposed a swap of his property for other investment property.

Since the company did not own suitable property for a swap, Yancey proposed that he locate acceptable property that the company would purchase, and the swap could be made. Four months later, he located suitable property near an urban area consisting of a half acre of land with an office building on it. The value of the property was $1 million, with the land being worth $500,000 and the building worth $500,000. One month after Yancey notified them, the company purchased this property with a cash down payment of $800,000 and an assumable mortgage of $200,000.

One month after the purchase, Yancey and the company exchanged properties. Yancey's property was subject to an outstanding mortgage of $100,000. In the transaction, each party assumed the mortgage of the other. In addition, Yancey gave the company $50,000 in cash plus $50,000 of stock that he owned in another company. Yancey's basis in this stock was $55,000.

Yancey held the new property for four years, making no significant improvements to it in the meantime. He took approximately $25,000 of depreciation deductions on the building during that period under the straight line method of depreciation. Just after the end of the fourth year, the office building was destroyed by fire. Yancey collected $650,000, the value of the building, from his insurance company and immediately began to rebuild the building. The construction was completed seven months later (in year five) at a cost of $500,000. Discuss Yancey's tax consequences as a result of these transactions.

3. LIST OF READINGS

Internal Revenue Code: §§ 1012; 1016(a)(1);1031; 1033, 1223; 1231; 1250(a)
Regulations: §§ 1.1002–1(d); 1.1031(a)-1; 1.1031(d)-1; 1.1031(d)-2
Rulings: Rev. Rul. 77–297, 1977–2 C.B. 304
Cases: Bloomington Coca-Cola Bottling Co v Commissioner, 189 F.2d 14 (7th Cir. 1951); Commissioner v. Crichton, 122 F.2d 181 (5th Cir. 1941); International Freighting Co. v. U.S., 135 F.2d 310 (2d Cir. 1943); Peabody Natural Resources Co. v. Comm'r, 126 T.C. 261 (2006); Review Crane v

Commissioner, 331 U.S. 1 (1947); and Philadelphia Park Amusement Co v. U.S., 126 F.Supp. 184 (Ct. Cl. 1954)

4. SAMPLE ESSAY

Section 1031(a) provides that no gain or loss is recognized if property held for productive use in a trade or business, or for investment, is exchanged solely for property of a like kind to be held either for productive use in a trade or business or for investment. Section 1031(a) can be distilled into three requirements for nonrecognition treatment: (1) the property must be held for productive use in a trade or business, or for investment; (2) the property must be like kind; and (3) the transaction must constitute an exchange and not a sale.

The Manufacturing Company's tax consequences: The property exchanged by the company does not meet the first or second requirements for nonrecognition treatment. The company had not previously held the property for investment or for use in its trade or business. Instead, it had purchased the property for the purpose of the exchange. Therefore, the transaction does not constitute a tax-free exchange for the company. But the manufacturing company probably does not care because it has held its property such a short time that it will realize no gain or loss on the exchange anyway. Its amount realized on the exchange is $1 million ($800,000 value of Yancey's property + $100,000 cash and stock received + $100,000 net mortgage relief) less its $1 million cost basis in the property, which produces no gain/loss realized in the transaction.

Since the transaction is not a § 1031 transaction for the company, its basis in the property it receives is determined under the general principals of § 1012. Thus, it will have a basis of $800,000 in the undeveloped property that it receives and a $50,000 basis in the stock, determined under § 1012, *Philadelphia Park* and *Crane*. The company's holding period in the undeveloped land begins to run on the date that the land is received by the company.

Yancey's tax consequences on the exchange: Since Yancey held his property for investment and will also hold the new property for investment, he easily meets the first requirement under § 1031(a). The second requirement is that the properties must be "like kind." The term "like kind" has a broad meaning when real estate is exchanged. See *Peabody Natural Resources and Crichton*. The regulations provide that the term "like kind" refers to the nature and character of the property, not to its grade or quality. See Reg. § 1.1031(a)-(1)(b). While the regulation goes on to provide that "one kind or class of property may not . . . be exchanged for property of a different kind or class," it also clarifies that improved land may be swapped for unimproved land because this "relates only to the grade and quality of the property and not to its kind or class." *Id.* Similarly, property held for investment may be swapped for property held for productive use in a trade or business. See Reg. § 1.1031(a)-1.

The fact that the manufacturing company is not eligible to use § 1031 does not prevent Yancey from taking advantage of § 1031. However, § 1031(b) excludes certain types of properties from § 1031(a). Stocks, bonds, notes, and property held primarily for sale are included in this subsection (and thus are excluded from § 1031(a)). Since Yancey is not a dealer in real estate, the parcels of real estate that are exchanged in the transaction are not disqualified from nonrecognition treatment under § 1031(b). The stock that Yancey gives the company does not qualify, however (see § 1031(a)(2)(B)) and by definition, neither does the cash, because the exchange of property for cash constitutes a taxable sale.

This brings us to the third requirement under § 1031(a), that the transaction must be an exchange and not a sale. The regulations provide that an exchange is a reciprocal transfer of property, as distinguished from a transfer of property for monetary consideration. Reg. § 1.1002–1(d). Although some cash and nonqualifying property (called "boot") is exchanged in this transaction, it does not disqualify the transaction as a whole from being considered a like-kind exchange. See *Bloomington Coca-Cola Bottling Co.* However, § 1031(b) provides that any gain realized on the exchange must be recognized to the extent of the fair market value of any boot received in the transaction.

The exchange between Yancey and the manufacturing company is an example of a "three-cornered" or "three-party" exchange. It is similar to the transaction in Rev. Rul. 77–297, except that the third party is not involved in the actual exchange because the company purchases the property from the third party then exchanges it for Yancey's property.

Yancey realizes a gain of $550,000 as a result of the exchange, none of which will be recognized because the transaction falls entirely within § 1031(a) for him. His amount realized on the transaction is $1.1 million (the $1 million fair market value of the property he received plus the $100,000 nonrecourse indebtedness of which he is relieved under *Crane*), less his basis of $250,000 plus $100,000 in cash and stock that he transfers, plus the $200,000 liability he assumes equals gain realized of $550,000. Normally, the $100,000 relief of his nonrecourse mortgage indebtedness would be treated as cash boot, requiring him to recognize that amount. See Reg. § 1.1031(d)-2 (assumption of liabilities of the taxpayer by the other party to the exchange is treated as money received by the taxpayer). But the regulations permit him to net the liabilities. See Reg. § 1.1031(d)-2, Example 2(c). Since Yancey assumed a greater liability than he gave up, he has no recognition attributable to the mortgage relief, and since he received only qualifying property in the exchange, none of his realized gain is recognized under § 1031(a).

The transfer of the stock, though, is not considered part of the like-kind exchange because stock is not qualifying property under § 1031(a). Thus, the transfer of the stock is treated as a sale (see *International Freighting*), so $50,000 of the property is treated as payment for the $50,000 of stock. Since Yancey's basis of $55,000 exceeds this deemed amount realized by $5000, he realizes and recognizes a $5000 loss. Since he appears to be holding the stock as an investment, his loss will be characterized as a long-term capital loss.

Yancey's basis in his new property is determined under § 1031(d). It is the same as the basis in the old property (a substituted basis), less cash received on the exchange, increased by any gain recognized and decreased by any loss recognized. Any liability of the taxpayer assumed by another party to the exchange is considered the same as money received in the exchange. Yancey's basis in his new property is $445,000: his old basis of $250,000, decreased by the $100,000 of mortgage relief from his old property, increased by $200,000 of the mortgage assumption on the new property, increased by the $50,000 of cash that he paid on the exchange and the $50,000 of stock, and decreased by the $5000 of recognized loss on the exchange. Since his new property consists of both land and a building, the regulations provide that the basis is to be allocated between the properties according to their fair market value. See Reg § 1.1031(d)-1(c). If the building and land are of equal value, the basis will be divided equally between them ($222,500 each).

Yancey's holding period in his old property will tack onto the holding period of his new property. See § 1223(1). Thus, if he were to immediately sell the new property, it will be considered to have been held long term for purposes of capital gains.

Yancey's tax consequences of the involuntary conversion: Since Yancey's new property consists of an office building, he is eligible to take depreciation deductions on this building, and in fact, he took approximately $25,000 of deductions during the four-year period in which he owned the building. These deductions reduce his basis in the building to $197,500 ($222,500 basis in the building after the exchange less $25,000 depreciation deductions) and result in an overall basis in the property of $420,000 under § 1016(a)(1) ($222,500 basis of the land under § 1031(d) plus $197,500 basis of the building).

When the building is destroyed by fire, Yancey receives $650,000 from his insurance company to compensate him for the loss of the building. This produces a realized gain of $452,500 on the building ($650,000 less $197,500). Section 1033 provides that no gain shall be recognized if property is involuntarily converted (as a result of destruction in whole or in part, theft, seizure or requisition, or condemnation or threat or imminence thereof) into property similar or related in service or use to the property so converted. See § 1033(a). While the term "similar or related in service or use" is not as broad (even with respect to real estate) as the term "like kind" under § 1031, it is clear that a replacement office building will qualify for Yancey, even if the new building is smaller than the converted property, provided Yancey's use of the building does not change significantly. There is also a two-year replacement period in which Yancey must rebuild in order to take advantage of § 1033. This period runs from the date Yancey receives the insurance money. Since he rebuilds within this period, this requirement is met.

However, § 1033(a)(2)(A) provides that gain realized on an involuntary conversion of property shall be recognized to the extent that the amount realized on the conversion exceeds the cost of the replacement property. Since the insurance proceeds of $650,000 exceed the cost of the new building by $150,000, Yancey must recognize $150,000 of his realized gain. The remaining gain of $302,500 will not be recognized, provided Yancey elects to exclude this amount under § 1033(a)(2)(A).

The character of the $150,000 gain is determined by the character of the underlying property. There is no depreciation recapture because the property was § 1250 property, and Yancey depreciated this property under the straight line method. Thus, there was no "additional depreciation" to recapture under §1250(a)(1)(A). Since there is no depreciation recapture, the full amount of the gain is § 1231 main hotchpot gain. If this is Yancey's only § 1231 gain for the year, it will be characterized under § 1231 as a long-term capital gain. (See Problem XXIII.)

Yancey's basis in the new building is $197,500, determined under § 1033(b)(2). Under this subsection, the basis in the new property is its cost ($500,000) reduced by the amount of gain not recognized on the conversion ($302,500). Thus, the gain inherent in the old building is preserved in the new building until the point of a later sale or other taxable disposition. Yancey may continue to depreciate the building using the new basis.

5. TOOLS FOR SELF-ASSESSMENT

[1] Since the tax consequences of the manufacturing company are not as complex those of Yancey, the essay begins with the consequences to the manufacturing company. This is not essential, however.

[2] The most difficult concept for most students in a problem involving an exchange of properties (whether taxable or nontaxable) is keeping track of the gain or loss realized in the exchange and then determining the basis in the new property, particularly where mortgages are exchanged. In determining the gain or loss realized, one must start with the basic principals of § 1001, under which the amount realized is the amount of cash received and the fair market value of any property received in the exchange. Under *Crane*, the undiminished value of the property received is considered an amount realized. "Property" for this purpose also includes the amount of nonrecourse mortgage liability relief. The basis in this leg of the transaction (i.e., the initial calculation of gain or loss realized on the exchange) is fixed by the previous transaction in which the property was acquired. So, the old basis offsets the amount realized on the exchange. If any cash is paid on the exchange, this amount also will offset the amount realized, as will the amount of any mortgage liability assumed or taken subject to on the exchange. So the amount of cash paid and any mortgage liability assumed or taken subject to on the transaction will be considered a cost of the transaction.

[3] The basis in the new property held by the manufacturing company after the exchange is determined under § 1012 because the transaction is a taxable exchange to the company, even though it owed no tax on the exchange because its amount realized was equal to its cost basis. Since it is a taxable exchange, the principal of *Philadelphia Park* applies to interpret § 1012 so the "cost" basis of the new property (both the land and the stock) is its fair market value at the time of the exchange. This makes sense because the company acquired property worth $800,000 ($700,000 equity value of the land plus $50,000 of cash and $50,000 of stock) and it transferred property with an equity value of $800,000. Thus, the equities on both sides of the transaction are equal, and all of the tax consequences have been realized for the manufacturing company. If the company were to immediately sell the stock and land for their fair market values, it would have no further tax consequences.

[4] Since this hypothetical involves a simultaneous exchange of properties, the parties do not have to worry about § 1031(a)(3), which provides that in a three-cornered exchange, the property to be received in the exchange must be identified within 45 days of the transfer of property by the prospective recipient. This section also provides that the taxpayer must receive the new property within the earlier of (1) 180 days after the transfer of the property or (2) by the due date (including extensions) of the tax return for the year of the transfer.

[5] After Yancey's realized gain or loss is calculated, the next step is to determine whether any of the realized gain will be recognized. Note that Yancey's basis in the new property cannot be determined until this step has been completed because any recognized gain or loss will affect the basis of the new property.

Recognition will depend upon whether Yancey received any disqualifying property in the exchange or whether the liabilities of which he was relieved were greater than the liabilities he assumed or took subject to. Since he did not receive any disqualifying property (such as cash or stock), and the liabilities that he assumed were greater than those of which he was relieved, he is not required to recognize any of his $550,000 gain realized.

[6] Students often assume that the loss realized on the transfer of the stock will not be recognized because of § 1031(c), which disallows the recognition of losses. However, upon closer reading, this provision applies only where nonqualifying property is received in the exchange. Since Yancey transfers the stock, § 1031(c) does not apply to him, and he will be able to recognize his realized loss. The transfer of the stock is treated as a sale to the extent of its fair market value. See *International Freighting*.

[7] The next step is to determine Yancey's basis in the new property. His basis of $445,000 makes sense because he initially had a gain potential of $550,000 in his old property ($800,000 value less his $250,000 § 1012 basis). When he swaps this property for the new property worth $1 million, he acquires property worth $200,000 more than his old property, but the new property is subject to a $200,000 mortgage. The equities of the properties are not equal, though, because the equity in the new property is $800,000 ($1 million less the $200,000 mortgage) while the equity in his old property is only $700,000 ($800,000 value less the $100,000 mortgage), so Yancey must "sweeten the pot" by paying an additional $100,000 in cash and stock to the company in order to equalize the equities.

[8] Since Yancey's basis in the new property immediately after the exchange is $445,000, if he were to sell this property immediately for its fair market value, he would realize a gain of $555,000 on the sale. If he had sold his old property instead of exchanging it, he would have realized a gain of $550,000 on the sale. The difference is attributable to the $5000 loss recognition on his stock. Thus, his unrealized gain from the old property is preserved in the new property. This illustrates that § 1031 is not a permanent nonrecognition provision but rather a deferral provision because Yancey will realize and recognize his gain at a later point when he sells the new property.

[9] However, Yancey does not sell the property. Instead, he suffers a loss through a fire that completely destroys the office building. This brings him under § 1033 because the destruction of the building is considered an involuntary conversion. In determining whether he will have a tax consequence as a result of this conversion, special attention must be paid to the terminology under § 1033(a)(2)(A), particularly to the distinction between the terms "amount realized" and "gain." These terms have very different meanings under § 1001. The amount realized on the involuntary conversion is the amount of insurance proceeds that Yancey received. The gain realized is the amount realized reduced by the adjusted basis of the converted property.

[10] Note also that § 1033(g) provides a special "like-kind" rule for real property that has been involuntarily converted by "seizure, requisition, or condemnation, or threat or imminence thereof." Since Yancey's property

was destroyed by fire, the special rule is not available, although Yancey should not have a problem under the "similar or related in service or use" test, provided his use of the building does not change significantly.

[11] Since the converted property is an office building, this falls under § 1250. (In general, any depreciable property that does not fall under § 1245 falls under § 1250; most depreciable real property falls under § 1250.) Section 168 currently applies the straight line method of depreciation to nonresidential real property and residential rental property. See § 168(b)(3). Thus, with this type of property, there generally will be no depreciation recapture to worry about, unless the taxpayer has held the property for less than a year.

[12] As you can see from this answer, if Yancey were to immediately sell the property, the unrecognized gain then would be recognized, demonstrating that §1033, as well as § 1031, is a deferral provision instead of a true exclusionary provision.

6. VARIATIONS ON THE THEME

Assume that the manufacturing company wanted Yancey's land immediately and did not want to wait around for him to identify replacement property. The parties agreed to a transaction in which Yancey transferred his property to the company on April 1 of year one, and the company established an escrow account in which it placed $800,000, an amount equal to the value of Yancey's land. Under the agreement, when Yancey locates suitable replacement property, the company will use the money in the escrow account to purchase the property. If Yancey fails to locate such property within two years, he will be entitled to receive the money in the escrow account. On September 1, Yancey located the property with the office building on it, and the parties effected the purchase and transfer of the property on November 10 of year one. What tax consequences to Yancey?

26 NONRECOGNITION TRANSACTIONS

WASH SALES OF STOCK AND SECURITIES

1. OPENING REMARKS

If a taxpayer has realized a sizeable capital gain from the sale of investment property and is holding stock for investment that has declined in value (not hard to find in today's economic environment), she could sell the stock and use the loss to offset the capital gain. So far, no problem. But if the taxpayer does not want to give up her control of the stock (maybe she thinks it will increase in value in the future), and she repurchases stock in the same company within a 30-day period before or after the sale, § 1091 applies to disallow the loss recognition. The policy rationale behind this provision is that the taxpayer has realized no economic loss because her investment has not changed in form. She was holding shares in the same company before the sale and after it. Thus, the sale has no economic substance. It is a transaction effected purely for tax purposes; therefore, it will not be recognized for purposes of allowing her to take a loss deduction.

Section 1091 is mechanical in its application; even without a tax avoidance motive, a taxpayer's losses will be disallowed if within the requisite 30-day time frame (actually a 61-day time frame since the measuring point is 30 days before the sale and 30 days after the sale), the taxpayer buys and sells substantially identical securities. If the purchase and the sale involve securities issued by different corporations, the securities are not substantially identical. If the securities are issued by one corporation, they may be substantially identical if they have substantially the same voting, liquidation, and dividend rights.

2. HYPOTHETICAL

Zachery Zachman purchased 100 shares of stock in the XYZ Corporation as an investment on June 6 of year one for $10,000. On January 31 of year three, when the stock was worth $4500, Zachery decided to sell. On March 1 of year three, the stock rose slightly in value, and Zachery decided to repurchase, so he bought another 100 shares of XYZ stock for $4800. On August 7 of year four, he sold the XYZ stock for $7500. What are the tax consequences to Zachery as a result of these transactions?

3. LIST OF READINGS

Internal Revenue Code: §§ 1012; 1091; 1223(3)

4. SAMPLE ESSAY

Zachery acquired his original shares by purchase, so his basis in those shares under § 1012 is his cost of $10,000. On the sale, he realizes a loss of $5500 ($10,000

§ 1012 basis less $4500 amount realized). Since he was holding this stock as an investment and has held it longer than a year, this loss will be a long-term capital loss. When Zachery repurchases XYZ stock, this purchase occurs within 30 days of his initial sale. Section 1091(a) disallows the loss recognition on the sale of the XYZ shares because Zachery has purchased "substantially identical" shares within 30 days of his sale. Note that the requisite time period is 30 days, not one month. Since Zachery's repurchase occurs within 30 days of his sale, § 1091 applies even though the sale and repurchase occur more than a month apart.

Under § 1091(d), Zachery's basis in his newly acquired XYZ stock is determined by taking the basis of his old stock ($10,000) and increasing it by the excess cost of the replacement stock over the selling price of the old stock ($300) or decreasing it by the excess of the selling price of the old stock over the cost of the replacement stock ($-0-). Thus, his basis in the new XYZ shares will be $10,300 instead of $4800. When he later sells the XYZ stock, he will realize and recognize a loss of $2800 ($10,300 basis less $7500 amount realized).

Zachery's holding period in the new shares under § 1091 as of the date of the purchase will be 22 months and 11 days because the holding period of the old shares tacks onto the replacement shares. This is authorized under § 1223(3) because of the substituted basis.

5. TOOLS FOR SELF-ASSESSMENT

[1] As we saw with §§ 1031 and 1033, nonrecognition provisions often are deferral provisions, and the same is true of § 1091. The loss potential in the shares is preserved in the new basis so Zachery may take his loss, but not within the 30-day period of his sale. Thus, § 1091 is a timing provision that defers the loss recognition to the point of later sale of the newly acquired shares. When Zachery sells his shares the following year, he will be able to realize and recognize his loss at that time.

[2] The basis in the repurchased shares makes sense because it embodies Zachery's total expenditures ($10,000 on the original purchase and $4800 on the repurchase) less his total receipts ($4500), thereby neutralizing the transaction from a tax perspective and preserving the losses in the new basis.

[3] The rationale of § 1091 is that there has been no meaningful change in the underlying investment, so the transaction should be completely tax neutral. Thus, it makes sense that the holding period of the old shares should tack onto the holding period of the new shares. Note that the holding period applies only for purposes of characterization of the realized gain or loss and not for purposes of avoiding the application of § 1091.

6. VARIATIONS ON THE THEME

What result if Zachery had sold the original shares of XYZ stock for $10,500 on April 17 of year three then repurchased 100 shares of the same stock on May 10 of year three for $9800?

27

LOSS TRANSACTIONS BETWEEN RELATED PARTIES

1. OPENING REMARKS

Taxpayers must be careful about transactions between related parties. Sometimes these transactions may have advantageous tax consequences (such as tax-free transfers between spouses or former spouses under § 1041), but if the property being transferred will generate a loss or other deduction, the transfer to a related party may be a tax trap for the unwary taxpayer. The problem with such transactions is that taxpayers tend to manipulate the realization rules to reduce their tax consequences. In a transfer of property between related parties, the underlying rationale is that there has not been a sufficient relinquishment of control of the property to allow the tax benefit. There are several tax provisions that address this problem. Section 267 applies to disallow a loss on the sale or exchange of property to a related party and to preserve the loss potential in the property until a subsequent sale by the related party. It is at that point that the normal realization and recognition rules apply. If the property is depreciable, § 1239 provides that the entire gain realized on the transfer to the related party must be characterized as ordinary income. This prevents the transfer of low-basis property to a related party where the purchaser takes depreciation deductions against ordinary income and the seller gets capital gain treatment. In addition, § 453 installment sale treatment is not available for the gain on depreciable property transferred between related parties.

Related parties for this purpose are not only family members but also entities in which the transferor has a sufficient interest. The attribution rules apply to attribute to the taxpayer stock owned by certain family members and certain entities in which the taxpayer has an interest. So, if the taxpayer does not have a sufficient ownership interest by virtue of her actual stock ownership, she may be deemed to have such an interest because of the stock ownership of others.

2. HYPOTHETICAL

Abby Baucus acquired 10 acres of real property upon the death of her father seven years ago. Her father had purchased the property 10 years before his death for $55,000, but at the time of his death, the property had a fair market value of $50,000. At present, it is worth $35,000, and Abby sells the property to her son, Chad, for $35,000. Chad held the property for six months before selling it to an unrelated third party for $38,000.

Abby also is a shareholder in the Widget Corporation. She owns 15 percent of Widget Co.'s shares, and her other son, David, owns 25 percent of the shares. David's wife owns another 15 percent of these shares, and the BC partnership owns another 30 percent. Abby is a 50 percent partner in this partnership, and her partner, Emmet Coatsworth, owns the other 50 percent. Abby recently has sold to Widget Co. an office building on an acre of land that she owned. She had acquired this property by gift from her father before his death. Her basis in the property (a carryover basis from her father under § 1015) was $200,000 for the building and $25,000 for the land. She had taken straight line depreciation deductions of $25,000 on the building when she sold the property to the Widget Co. for $300,000, of which $265,000 was attributable to the building, and the remaining $35,000 was attributable to the land. Widget paid nothing on the property in the year of the sale but it transferred to Abby six notes, payable over six years, for $50,000 each plus interest.

Discuss the tax consequences of these transactions to all parties.

3. LIST OF READINGS

Internal Revenue Code: §§ 102; 267; 453(g); 1012; 1014; 1016; 1239
Regulations: § 1.267(d)-1(c); § 1.1239–1(a)
Rulings: Rev. Rul. 69–339, 1969–1 C.B. 203
Cases: United States v. Parker, 367 F.2d 402 (5th Cir. 1967)

4. SAMPLE ESSAY

When Abby first acquired the 10 acres of real property, it was through transfer from a related party by reason of death. The property had declined in value from the time Abby's father initially had purchased this property. Abby realized $50,000 upon receipt of the property but was not required to recognize any of this amount because § 102 excludes from the recipient's income the value of gifts, bequests, devises, and inheritances. Abby's basis in this property is determined under § 1014 and is a date-of-death value basis. Since the property has declined in value, her basis will be a stepped-down fair market value basis of $50,000 under § 1014.

When Abby sells the property to Chad, she realizes $35,000 on the sale. After offsetting her basis of $50,000, she realizes a loss of $15,000, which normally would be a long-term capital loss. However, § 267(a)(1) disallows losses between family members. See §§ 267(b)(1) and (c)(4). Thus, Abby will not be able to recognize her realized loss.

Chad purchased the property in a straight sale. Thus, his basis is a § 1012 cost basis of $35,000, the amount that he paid for the property. See Reg. § 1.267(d)-1(c)(3). When he later sells this property for $38,000, he realizes a gain of $3000 ($38,000 amount realized less his cost basis of $35,000). Section 267(d) provides that gain from the sale or exchange of property acquired from a related party is not recognized to the extent of the loss disallowed to the transferor under § 267(a)(1). Since Abby had a $15,000 loss realized on the sale to Chad that she was not able to recognize, Chad will have no gain recognized until his realized gain exceeds Abby's disallowed loss. Thus, Chad's realized gain of $3000 is not recognized.

Chad's sale to the third party is a straight sale to an unrelated party, so § 267 does not apply. Thus, the third party's basis in the newly acquired property is $38,000, a straight cost basis determined under § 1012. This party's holding period begins to run from the point of the sale.

In the second transaction, Abby sells depreciable property to the Widget Co. She realizes $100,000 on this transaction ($300,000 amount realized less her total adjusted basis of $200,000 in the building and the land). Under normal circumstances, she would recognize nothing in the year of the sale because she has received no payment in that year, and she has taken straight line depreciation deductions on the building. When she receives the payments under the notes, she would recognize her $100,000 of gain under § 453 over the six-year period as the notes are paid. This gain would be a § 1231 gain.

However, the sale is to a "related party" under § 1239 because the Widget Co. is considered a "controlled entity." Section 1239(c)(1) defines a controlled entity as "a corporation more than 50% of the value of the outstanding stock of which is owned (directly or indirectly) by or for such person." Since the definition refers to "value," this means more than the number of shares or the voting power of the stock. Thus, a shareholder who owns less than 50 percent of the shares may own more than 50 percent of the value of the stock because of a control premium on the shares. On the other hand, if there are restrictions on the stock, a shareholder may own less in value of shares than are reflected by the percentage ownership. See *Parker* and Rev. Rul. 69–339.

Section 1239(c)(2) provides that in determining ownership, the attribution rules under § 267 apply. Section 267 attributes stock owned by members of the taxpayer's family under § 267(c)(2), defined under § 267(c)(4) as siblings, spouses, ancestors, and lineal descendants. Thus, the stock owned by David, Abby's son, will be attributed to Abby. While David's wife's shares will be attributed to him, they will not be reattributed to Abby because § 267(c)(5) prevents such double attribution. Since the BC partnership owns 30 percent of the shares, Abby is deemed to own half of those shares or 15 percent under § 267(c)(1) ("Stock owned, directly or indirectly, by or for a partnership shall be considered as being owned proportionately by or for its partners"). The stock of Emmet, Abby's partner, ordinarily would be attributed to her under § 267(c)(3) but not under § 1239. See § 1239(c)(2).

Abby directly owns 15 percent of the shares of Widget Co. and indirectly owns 40 percent (25 percent from David under § 267(c)(2) and (c)(4), and 15 percent or half of the BC partnership's shares under § 267(c)(1)). Thus, she owns actually and constructively 55 percent of the stock of the Widget Co. If there are no restrictions on the shares that would bring the total value below 50 percent, then § 1239 applies because the sale to Widget Co. is considered a sale to a controlled entity.

Section 1239 will recharacterize the gain recognized on the sale as ordinary income instead of § 1231 gain. However, § 1239 applies only to sales or exchanges of depreciable property to a controlled entity. The building is the only piece of depreciable property that Abby sells to Widget Co. The land is not a depreciable asset, so it is not within the reach of § 1239. Thus, the $10,000 of gain from the land remains § 1231 gain. The $90,000 gain from the building, which normally would have been § 1231 gain, is now ordinary income under § 1239.

Also under normal rules, this blow would have been softened somewhat by the application of § 453, which allows qualifying taxpayers to spread the profit from a sale over the period of payments to be received from the sale. Under § 453, a proportionate amount of the profit is included in income as each payment is made, in a ratio of gross profit to total contract price. See § 453(c). This would have allowed Abby to spread the income inclusion over the six years in which payments are to be received. However, because the sale is to a "related party" within the meaning of § 1239, § 453(g) denies installment sale treatment to Abby. Thus, she will have to include all payments from the building (i.e., the depreciable property) in income in the year of the sale. In the year of the sale, Abby realizes $100,000, of which $10,000 (attributable to the land) will be a § 1231 gain, eligible for § 453 treatment, while the remaining $90,000 (attributable to the building) will be ordinary income. Section 1239 recharacterizes *all* gain as ordinary income, not just the amount of any "additional depreciation" under § 1250. Abby must recognize the entire $90,000 in the year of the sale, even though she receives no payments from the sale in that year. Section 453(g) further provides that Widget Co. may not increase its basis in the purchased property until Abby includes the gain recognition in her gross income.

Section 453(g)(2) provides that if the parties can demonstrate that the transaction did not have as one of its principal purposes the avoidance of federal income tax, the harsh effects of § 453(g) can be avoided.

The $90,000 of income that Abby recognizes in the year of the sale will increase her basis in the property for purposes of § 453. Thus, her basis becomes $290,000 ($175,000 adjusted basis in the building + $25,000 basis of the land + $90,000 tax cost basis). Her gross profit will be the amount realized ($300,000) on the sale less her basis ($290,000) or $10,000. Her gross profit ratio is $10,000/$300,000. As she receives each payment of $50,000 in each of the next six years, she will include $1,667 in income as a § 1231 gain. The remaining $48,333 will be a tax-free recovery of her basis. Any interest that she receives will be included separately in income.

5. TOOLS FOR SELF-ASSESSMENT

[1] Tax consequences encompass realization, recognition, basis, gain, loss, and character of the gain or loss. Students often assume that the term means simply the gain or loss recognized on the transaction. Do not fall into his trap because if you see such a question on an exam, the answer should encompass all of the tax consequences, not simply the gain or loss!

[2] In transactions between related parties, the tax Code may treat these parties as one economic unit. Abby's father originally purchased the property for $55,000, but at his death it had declined in value to $50,000. The date-of-death valuation becomes Abby's basis, and the $5000 loss potential in the property will not be realized except that the value of the gross estate will be less than it would have been if the property had not declined in value. Thus, the economic unit would have benefited if Abby's father had sold the property prior to his death and realized and recognized the loss. He also could have transferred the property to Abby as an inter vivos gift, but the special rule under § 1015 for property that has declined in value may not have produced any better results for Abby than acquiring the property after her father's death.

[3] This is not a good tax result for Abby and Chad. The property initially had a loss potential of $15,000, of which only $3000 will be recognized by them (the economic unit). Thus, $12,000 of loss potential again vanishes because of § 267. Abby will be in for a nasty surprise if she anticipated taking a $15,000 loss on the sale to Chad. She will lose this benefit simply because she sold to the wrong party for purposes of § 267. A much better result would have been for her to sell the property to an unrelated third party and

to transfer the cash to Chad. In this way, Abby would have been able to recognize the full tax loss potential in the property, and Chad would have ended up with the cash, which he ultimately got anyway. Of course, if the parties were fully aware of the tax consequences, and Chad really wanted this particular property, then all is well. But that does not appear to be the case, because Chad quickly sold the property to a third party and reduced his holding to cash.

[4] If Chad had been required to recognize a gain (i.e., if his realized gain exceeded $15,000), it would have been a short-term capital gain. Because his basis is determined under § 1012, he does not get the benefit of Abby's holding period. See Reg. § 1.267(d)-1(c)(3).

[5] Abby's terrible tax result on the sale of the depreciable property to the Widget Co. would occur regardless of whether the property had been depreciable by her. Section 1239 applies if the property is depreciable by the related party/transferee. Note that while § 1239(a) applies to the transfer between related parties of property subject to an allowance for depreciation under § 167, the regulations clarify that § 1239 applies in the case of property subject to depreciation under §§ 168 and 169. See Reg. § 1.1239–1(a).

6. VARIATIONS ON THE THEME

What result if Chad instead sold the property to the unrelated third party after two years for $55,000? Would it change the result if the Widget Company intended to demolish the office building and to hold the land for investment? Would it change the result if the property that Abby had sold to Widget Co. was her personal residence?

28

TRANSFERS OF PROPERTY FOR SERVICES

1. OPENING REMARKS

A common means of compensating upper-level employees is through stock options in the employer company. These options give the employees the right to purchase stock in the employer company at a stated price, regardless of whether the stock is selling at a higher price at the time the options are exercised. This provides an incentive for the employees to work to ensure the success of the company so that the stock will be worth more when the options are exercised. It also preserves the cash flow of the company because the stock option bonuses are noncash compensation. If a taxpayer performs services for a third party and is compensated in property, rather than in cash, § 83 includes the value of the property, less any amount the employee paid for the property, as compensation income.

While § 83 is an inclusionary provision, it is also a timing and characterization provision because it determines when the amount is included in income, the character of the inclusion, and the basis of the property. In general, property that is subject to a substantial risk of forfeiture at the time of the transfer is treated as owned by the employer/transferor, and no income is realized by the employee. When there is no longer any substantial risk of forfeiture or when the property is transferable, the fair market value of the stock, less any amount the employee paid for the stock, is includable in the employee's gross income. Section 83 also provides some flexibility to the recipient because it allows the recipient to elect under § 83(b) to currently include the value of property received, rather than to defer the inclusion until the point where the property is substantially vested. The advantage of such an election is that if the property appreciates substantially in value between the time the employee receives it and the time the restrictions lapse, the employee will be taxed on the lower value and can control the recognition of further gain by deciding when to sell the property. However, a § 83(b) election is a gamble because if the property should decline in value, the employee will be over taxed. Another risk is that if the property should be forfeited, there is no deductible loss for the amount previously included in income. The taxpayer may make a § 83(b) election even though the taxpayer pays full market value for the property. See *Alves v. Commissioner*, 734 F.2d 478 (9th Cir. 1984); Reg. § 1.83–2.

The employer is entitled to a deduction under § 162 in the year in which the employee includes the value of the stock in income. After the inclusion in income under § 83, the compensation phase ends and the investment phase begins. Thus, the holding period begins and if the taxpayer should sell the stock at a gain, the gain will be a capital gain.

2. HYPOTHETICAL

Candice Davis is a single, cash method, calendar year taxpayer. She is the general manager of the ABC Company, a small widget-producing company. Four years ago, the company gave Candice 50 stock options, with no readily ascertainable market value, under a nonqualified stock option plan that entitled her to purchase 10 shares per option at the stock's then-current fair market value of $15 per share. The options provide that they are exercisable only by Candice and are not transferable except by death. Although the options can be exercised at any time, the retention of the stock is conditioned on Candice's working with ABC Co. for five years from the grant of the option.

Candice exercises 20 of the options immediately, acquiring 200 shares of ABC stock at $15 per share. Three years later, she exercises 10 more options when the value of the ABC stock is $25 per share. At the end of year five, when the restrictions lapse, ABC stock is worth $40 per share. In year six, Candice exercises the remaining 20 options when the ABC stock is worth $45 per share. In year seven, Candice sells all of her stock for $27,500.

What tax consequences to Candice in each of these years, and what tax consequences, if any, to ABC Co.? What result if Candice makes a § 83(b) election in the years in which she receives the stock?

3. LIST OF READINGS

Internal Revenue Code: § 83
Regulations: § 1.83–1(a); 1.83–3; 1.83–4; 1.83–6
Cases: Venture Funding, Ltd. v. Commissioner, 110 T.C. 236 (1998)

4. SAMPLE ESSAY

Section 83 provides that if property is transferred to any person in connection with a performance of services, the service provider has gross income in an amount equal to the excess of the property's fair market value over the amount paid for the property, determined when the property is substantially vested (i.e., when the property either is transferable or is not subject to a substantial risk of forfeiture). Property, for purposes of § 83, includes real and personal property other than cash or an unfunded, unsecured promise to pay. See Reg. § 1.83–3(e). The regulations provide that a transfer of property occurs when the taxpayer acquires a beneficial ownership interest in the property. See Reg. § 1.83–3(a)(1). However, the regulations also clarify that the grant of an option to purchase property does not constitute a transfer of such property. See Reg. § 1.83–3(a)(2). Since the options that were granted to Candice do not have a readily ascertainable value, § 83 does not apply to them. See § 83(e)(3). Thus, the grant of the options is not a taxable event.

The exercise of the options, though, is a taxable event under § 83(a) if the property either is transferable or is not subject to a substantial risk of forfeiture. Under § 83(c)(1), property is subject to a substantial risk of forfeiture if the recipient's rights to full enjoyment are conditioned upon the future performance of substantial services. In this problem, Candice must continue to work for ABC Co. until the end of the five-year period in order retain the stock, so the restrictions are substantial. This delays the taxable event under § 83(a) until either the restrictions lapse, or the stock is sold in an arm's length transaction, whichever occurs earlier.

When Candice immediately exercises her options, acquiring 200 shares of ABC stock, she realizes no income at that point because the amount that she pays for the stock ($3000) is equal to its fair market value at the time of the exercise, and the stock is subject to a substantial risk of forfeiture. When she exercises the next 10 options, she receives 100 shares of stock valued at $2500, for which she pays $1500. Now she realizes $1000 in the year in which she receives the stock ($2500 value of stock less the amount she pays for it, $1500). But the stock is still subject to a substantial risk of forfeiture, so there is no recognition under § 83(a). Note that until the restrictions lapse, the company is considered the owner of the stock, and any dividends payable on this stock that are received by Candice will be considered additional compensation to her. See Reg. § 1.83–1(a)(1). When the restrictions lapse, Candice will be considered the owner of the stock, and the dividends will be considered true dividends, which are taxed at a lower rate than compensation.

At the end of year five, the restrictions lapse, and Candice is still working for the company, so the stock now vests. Under § 83(a), she must include the excess of the fair market value of the property at the end of year five when the restrictions lapse ($40/share times 300 shares = $12,000) less the amount she paid for the shares ($3000 for the first 200 shares and $1500 for the next 100 shares = $4500). Thus, she has an inclusion at the end of year five of $7500. This amount must be included under § 61(a)(1) as compensation income, which is ordinary income. The ABC Co., as her employer, takes a deduction of $7500 at that time under § 162. See § 83(h). The Tax Court has held that if the taxpayer does not include this amount in income on her tax return, the employer does not get to take the deduction. See *Venture Funding Ltd.*

Also at the end of year five, the compensation phase has come to an end with respect to these 300 shares, and the investment phase begins at this point. Thus, Candice's holding period in these 300 shares begins to run at the end of year five when the restrictions lapse. At that time, she is holding 300 shares of ABC stock for which she has paid $4500 ($3000 for the first 200 shares and $1500 for the next 100 shares). In addition, she has included $7500 in income under § 83(a). This amount will be added to her basis in the shares to give her a total basis in the 300 shares of $12,000. See Reg. § 1.83–4(b)(1).

In year six, when Candice exercises the remaining 20 options, this exercise occurs after the restrictions have lapsed. Thus, she receives 200 shares when she exercises these options, and there is an immediate taxable event. These shares are valued at $9000 ($45/share), but she pays $3000 for them. Thus, she has $6000 of compensation income, includable in year six when she exercises the options. Her holding period begins to run at the point of exercise, and her basis in these 200 shares is $9000, their fair market value at the point of exercise (attributable to the $3000 that she paid for the shares plus the $6000 on which she is taxed).

In year seven, Candice sells all of her 500 shares for $27,500. At this time, her collective basis in these shares is $21,000 ($12,000 for the first 300 shares and $9000 for the last 200 shares). She thus realizes a gain of $6500, all of which will constitute a long-term capital gain, provided that she has held the final 200 shares for at least a year, which is not obvious from the problem.

If Candice had made a § 83(b) election, she would have had an income inclusion at the point of exercise of the options, regardless of whether or not there was a substantial risk of forfeiture. Later, when the restrictions lapsed, there would have been no further tax consequences. In year one, when Candice exercised the first 20 options, she would have had no income inclusion when she received the 200 shares because she paid fair market value for those shares. She would have had a basis in those shares of $3000, the amount that she paid. In the second exercise in year three, of the 10 options, she would have had an income inclusion of $1000 (100 shares at $25/share = $2500 less $1500 option price) at that time. Her basis in those shares would have been $2500 (the $1500 that she paid, plus the $1000 that she included in income). In the final exercise of the 20 options in year six, Candice would have had an inclusion of $6000 ($9000 value of stock less $3000 amount paid). Her basis in these shares would have been $9000 (amount paid plus amount included in income). Her total basis in the 500 shares would have been $14,500, and her gain realized and recognized on the sale in year seven would have been $13,000—a long-term capital gain—provided she met the one-year holding period for the last 200 shares.

5. TOOLS FOR SELF-ASSESSMENT

[1] Section 83 probably is most commonly used in connection with the transfer of stock or options to employees, but it applies to any property (i.e., noncash) transfer in connection with the performance of services. Section 83 is both a timing and a characterization provision. Once it applies, the income is included under § 61(a)(1) as compensation. The same applies to the employer's deduction. Section 162 is the authorizing provision, while § 83(h) merely tells the employer when to take the deduction and how much to take. Note that the employer's deduction is tied to the employee's inclusion. See Reg. § 1.83–6 and *Venture Funding, Ltd.*

[2] There are three events to be concerned about in this problem: (1) the grant of the options, (2) the exercise of the options, and (3) the sale of the stock. The grant of the options with no readily ascertainable fair market value is not a taxable event. While a § 83(b) election may be made even though the property has no value at the point of transfer, the property must be § 83 property. If the option has no readily ascertainable market value, it is not § 83 property so Candice may not make a § 83(b) election upon receipt of the options. Thus, § 83 will apply only upon *exercise* of the options and transfer of the stock.

[3] When § 83(a) applies to include the value of property in income, the compensation phase of the transaction ends, and the investment phase begins. Thus, the first part of the transaction generates ordinary income as compensation, while the second phase, which applies after the application of § 83(a), generates a capital gain.

[4] A taxpayer in Candice's situation should consider making a § 83(b) election on the exercise of the first 20 options because she pays fair market value for those shares. Thus, she has nothing to lose and everything to gain. If the value of the shares rises, she will be able to defer her tax liability until she sells the shares. If the value of the shares should fall, she then would be able to recognize a loss when she later sells the shares, but otherwise she would not have included anything in income upon making the election because she paid fair market value for those shares. If she were to forfeit the stock by leaving the employment of ABC Co. before the end of the five-year period, she would not be any worse off because she would have had no income

inclusion upon exercise. Also, she can make a § 83(b) election for the exercise of the first 20 options and no election for the exercise of the remaining options since the exercise occurs in different taxable years.

[5] In comparing the § 83(b) election to straight § 83(a), under both provisions, Candice will recognize the same amount of income, $20,000. The difference, though, is in the timing and character of the income. The § 83(b) election requires Candice to accelerate the recognition of $1000 of gain in year three because § 83(a) otherwise requires no income recognition until year five. But under § 83(a), Candice must recognize $13,500 of ordinary income as compensation in years five and six. The § 83(b) election requires her to recognize only $7000 in ordinary income. In the year of the sale, she will realize and recognize $6500 of long-term capital gain under the § 83(a) approach, while she would recognize $13,000 of long-term capital gain by having made a § 83(b) election earlier. Thus, the § 83(b) election will pay off over time because the tax on the appreciation in the first 300 shares is deferred until year seven when Candice finally sells the shares, and she will have increased her recognition of capital gains over ordinary income. So, Candice would be very well advised to make the § 83(b) election for all the exercises of her options.

6. VARIATIONS ON THE THEME

What result (with and without the § 83(b) election) if Candice terminates her employment before the end of the five-year vesting period?

29

INCOME IN RESPECT OF A DECEDENT

1. OPENING REMARKS

When a taxpayer dies, the estate will have to pay an income tax on items of income attributable to the decedent that have not been taxed previously. Likewise, the estate also may deduct items that are allowed under the Code. This is a simple principal to state, but it can be difficult to apply because often there are issues of timing (i.e., in which taxable year does the item of inclusion or deduction occur), characterization (i.e., whether the items are capital or ordinary), and determination of who is the proper taxpayer to include or deduct the items.

Any items of income or deduction not previously taxed or deducted by the decedent must be included on the income tax return for the taxable year that ends on the date of the decedent's death (usually referred to as a "short" taxable year). Items of income or deduction that arise after that period are addressed under § 691 as "income in respect of a decedent (IRD)." If the items do not fall within the decedent's final taxable year, they will be taxed to the person or entity that acquires the right to receive the amount from the decedent. Similarly, the person or entity will be able to deduct items in respect of a decedent when such items are paid. The character of the income or deduction is the same as it would have been in the hands of the decedent.

Under normal circumstances, when an estate includes an item in income and pays an income tax on it, the value of the gross estate is decreased by the amount of the tax paid and this, in turn, decreases the amount of any estate tax that would be owed on the gross estate. So any income tax owed by the estate would lower the estate tax bill. In order to address the overpayment of the estate tax that would arise under § 691(a), the recipient of IRD may obtain an income tax deduction under § 691(c) for any estate tax attributable to the inclusion of the IRD.

2. HYPOTHETICAL

Evan Fellers was an attorney who was killed in an automobile accident last year. Evan was a cash method, calendar year taxpayer. His surviving spouse, Gayle, is his only heir. His executor has determined that Evan has the following assets as of January 1 of the current year:

(1) two accounts receivable: one for $25,000 and one $15,000. These receivables will be collected by the estate.
(2) two bonds, both of which were purchased by Evan about 10 years ago. One is a Series EE bond that will be due later in the year in the amount of $15,000 principal with $2500 accrued interest, and the other is a $15,000 tax-exempt bond that has accrued interest of $2000 payable this year.

(3) Before he died, Evan discovered that his office manager had embezzled $40,000 from him. Gayle is bringing suit for the recovery of this amount.
(4) Evan and Gayle also owned a joint bank account with accrued interest (in the current year) of $350. Gayle collected this interest.
(5) Evan had entered into a contract to sell some property that he had owned for the past 10 years. This property consisted of one acre of land with a rental residence on it. Evan initially had purchased the property for $65,000 and had taken straight line depreciation deductions of $15,000 on it. The contract price for the property was $165,000, to be paid in equal installments over a three-year period. The buyer is demanding that the sale go forward as agreed.
(6) Shortly after his death, a case on which Evan had been working was decided by the court in his client's favor for $100,000. Under the agreement with the client, Evan was entitled to a contingent fee of 30 percent.

The executor has determined that the estate has the following liabilities:

(a) Evan owed the bank $16,000 in payment for advances from a line of credit.
(b) He also owed $4000 in property taxes on his office building.

Assuming all of the items of income are received in the current taxable year, and the estate pays the liabilities in the current taxable year, which, if any, of these items constitute IRD?

3. LIST OF READINGS

Internal Revenue Code: §§ 691; 1014
Regulations: § 1.691(a)-1

4. SAMPLE ESSAY

IRD does not include any income items that may have been included either before or immediately after Evan's death. (1) Since Evan is a cash method taxpayer and has not yet collected any of the receivables, none of these amounts would have been included during his lifetime, and thus they constitute IRD. See Reg. § 1.691(a)-1(b)(1). If the estate collects the receivables, they will be includable in the income of the estate. The character of this income will the same as the character would have been if Evan had collected them. So, if they would have been ordinary income to Evan if he had collected them, they will be ordinary income to the estate. (2) The interest on the tax-exempt bond is not IRD because it is not taxable for income tax purposes, no matter who collects it. See Reg. § 1.691(a)-1(d). The principal amount of the Series EE will be a return of capital, for which there is no realization of income, so that amount does not constitute IRD. The interest on the bond will generate taxable income of $2500, which will constitute IRD either to the estate or to Gayle, depending upon who collects the bond and the interest. Since the IRD on this item is interest, the character of this income will be ordinary. (3) Any amount recovered by Gayle from the lawsuit will constitute IRD if the embezzled amount would have constituted income to Evan. If, though, either Evan or his estate had paid an income tax on this amount, it would no longer be IRD when it is collected but instead would be considered a return of capital. (4) When Gayle receives the interest on their joint account, the entire amount will constitute ordinary income to her but it will constitute IRD. (5) Normally, the sale of this property would generate a § 1231 gain, but in this case, the appreciation potentially has been subject to an estate tax because this property was included in the gross estate. Because the property passes by reason of the death of Evan, it is subject to § 1014 and will get a stepped-up, date-of-death valuation basis. Thus, there is no IRD on this property. (6) Since neither the amount of the fee nor the right to receive the fee were fixed before Evan died, none of this amount was included previously in Evan's gross income. Therefore, it constitutes IRD when it is received by the estate. This income will be ordinary income as the payments are received because it would have been ordinary income to Evan if he had collected this fee.

When the estate pays the liabilities owed by Evan, the $16,000 repayment from the line of credit will not result in any further tax consequences except to reduce the gross estate because it is not a deductible expenditure for federal income tax purposes. The payment of the property tax liability, however, does give rise to a deduction for the estate under § 164 since that was not deducted while Evan was alive. See §691(b); 1.691(b)-1.

5. TOOLS FOR SELF-ASSESSMENT

[1] IRD arises when any taxable income is realized after the death of a decedent that was not included in the decedent's gross income during his lifetime or on his final income tax return.

[2] It is possible that the receivables may have been included previously in income through the doctrine of constructive receipt, but without more facts to indicate that is the case, this is not a probability. If constructive receipt had applied, the receivables would have been included during Evan's lifetime or on his final income tax return and thus, they would not constitute IRD when they are collected by the estate.

[3] The entire amount of the interest from the Series EE bond constitutes IRD, not just the amount that accrued after Evan's death. The same applies to the interest from the joint bank account.

6. VARIATIONS ON THE THEME

How, if at all, would your answer change if Evan instead had been an accrual method taxpayer?

30 GRANTOR TRUSTS

1. OPENING REMARKS

Another means of attempting to shift income tax free to family members is through the use of a trust in which the assets revert back to the grantor. In a nutshell, the grantor trust rules tax to the grantor income from an *inter vivos* trust if the grantor retains too much control over the trust assets. The purpose of these rules is to prevent taxpayers from shifting income (and thus tax liability) to other family members while continuing to retain control over the trust property. The grantor trust rules, like most issues, are best understood through a discussion of their historical development.

In 1934, George B. Clifford transferred some securities to a trust for the "exclusive benefit" of his wife. (Note: income splitting on joint returns was not permitted until 1948). Mr. Clifford was the trustee of this trust, which was to distribute the net income (in whole or in part as he, in his absolute discretion, was to determine) to his wife. The trust was to last for a term of five years (although it would terminate earlier upon the death of either Clifford or his wife), and then the assets would revert back to Clifford. During the term of the trust, Clifford had full power to exercise voting rights; "sell, exchange, mortgage, or pledge" any of the trust securities upon such terms and for such consideration as he would determine "in his absolute discretion"; invest any income or principal in the trust; collect all income; compromise, etc., any claims held by him as trustee; and hold any of the trust property in his own name or in the names of "other persons."

Clifford paid a gift tax on the transfer of these assets to the trust, and the income was not designed to relieve him of any support obligations. There also was no restriction on the wife's use of the trust income, and she paid the income taxes on the distribution.

The IRS determined, however, that Mr. Clifford had retained dominion and control over the trust assets and thus was the owner of those assets for federal income tax purposes. According to the government, there was no substantial change in Mr. Clifford's economic position. In 1940, the U.S. Supreme Court agreed with the government, but the opinion was not a model of clarity. The Court based its decision on a number of factors, without giving precise weight to any particular factor. Clearly, though, the short-term duration of the trust, combined with the broad powers of the grantor/trustee, including the power to accumulate trust income in his discretion, plus the fact that the income was distributed to the grantor's spouse, all were important elements. The problem with the decision, however, was that it gave judges discretion to determine, through a balancing process, when a transfer of property to a trust was a successful transfer for tax purposes and when it was not. This, unfortunately, led to inconsistent results.

In 1954, Congress provided clarity and consistency to this area by enacting what are presently called the "Subchapter J" rules. These are found in Code sections 671 *et seq*. In general, the rules initially provided that if property transferred to a trust would remain in the trust and would not revert to the grantor before the end of a ten-year period, the trust income would be taxed to the income beneficiary. These 10-year trusts were known as "Clifford trusts."

In 1986, Congress repealed the Clifford trust rule and substituted a more rigorous provision. Under § 673, the grantor is treated as the owner of the trust property if he or his spouse retains a reversionary interest in either the income or the corpus having a value in excess of 5 percent of the value of the trust property. Thus, a reversionary trust generally will be considered a grantor trust, unless the reversionary term extends for a very long time. Death of the beneficiary (other than a minor child) is not excepted, so a reversionary trust for the benefit of an elderly relative will always be considered a grantor trust.

2. HYPOTHETICAL

Harriet Iverson is a divorced, 50-year-old woman with an elderly parent in a nursing home. Harriet also has a son and daughter, ages 26 and 24, respectively. She is a pediatrician who has been practicing for the past 22 years. Harriet is contemplating establishing a trust for the benefit of her mother and her children. She has given this some thought and has several alternatives in mind. She seeks your guidance and advice on the income tax consequences of these alternatives:

(A) She will transfer to a trust for the benefit of her mother 250 shares of stock in a publicly traded company. The current value of these shares is $100,000, and they generate dividends of approximately $8000 annually. Harriet has held these shares for the past 10 years. The trust will pay the income to her mother for the duration of her mother's life. Any stock dividends, extraordinary dividends, or any sales of the shares will become corpus of the trust, which will revert to Harriet upon the death of her mother.

(B) Same facts as (A) except that upon the death of her mother, the trust assets will inure to the benefit of Harriet's children, who will be paid the income from the trust until the younger child reaches age 35. At that time, the corpus of the trust will be divided equally between the two children. If either child is deceased at that point, that child's share shall be divided among that child's children, *per stirpes*. Harriet has the power, as trustee, to vote the shares of stock transferred to the trust.

(C) She will transfer $100,000 in cash to a trust for the benefit of her son and daughter, with the trust corpus to be invested in high yield investments and the income to be paid to her children. On the death of either child, the income will be distributed to the other. Upon the death of both children, the trust will revert to Harriet. If Harriet predeceases the children, the trust corpus will be distributed in equal shares to the children.

(D) She will transfer $100,000 in cash to a trust for the benefit of her son and daughter, with the trust corpus to be invested in high-yield investments and the income to be paid to her children. Harriet will name herself as trustee with the power to invade the corpus or to accumulate income for either child's benefit.

(E) Same facts as (D) except that Harriet appoints an independent trustee.

(F) She will transfer $100,000 in cash to a trust for the benefit of her grandchild, who is currently two years old. The income from the trust may be used for the education of the child or accumulated in the discretion of the trustee. The trust will terminate when the grandchild reaches age 35, and the corpus and any accumulated income will be payable to Harriet's children, if alive. If either of them is dead, the trust corpus and accumulated income will be divided *per stirpes* between the living child and any children of the deceased child. If both children are deceased, the trust corpus and accumulated income will be divided equally among any grandchildren. Harriet will appoint an independent trustee.

3. LIST OF READINGS

Internal Revenue Code: §§ 673, 674, 675, 676, 677, 678
Cases: Braun v. Commissioner, 48 T.C.M. 210 (1984)

4. SAMPLE ESSAY

It is important for Harriet to realize that it is very difficult under current law to shift income successfully to family members under a trust if the grantor retains a reversionary interest. Any retained power to control or direct the trust's assets or income will result in the income of the trust being taxed to the grantor. Such trusts are referred to as "grantor trusts" under the Internal Revenue Code. A grantor trust is not a separate taxable entity. The grantor is treated as the owner of the assets, and all income is taxed to the grantor. If a trust is a "revocable trust," it usually is considered a grantor trust, although an "irrevocable trust" also can be a grantor trust if it meets the definitions under §§ 671, 673–677 of the Code.

(A) This is a "revocable trust" since the assets will revert to Harriet upon the death of her mother. Section 673 provides that a grantor of a trust is considered the owner of trust property if she retains a reversionary interest in the income or corpus having a value in excess of 5 percent of the trust property. Since Harriet's mother is elderly, any trust for her benefit that has a reversionary interest will be considered a grantor trust because the reversionary interest will always have a value greater than 5 percent. Thus, this trust will be considered a grantor trust, and Harriet will be taxed on the income generated by the trust.

(B) This trust is irrevocable, and Harriet does not stand to benefit upon the death of her mother. The fact that she retains the power to vote the shares of stock transferred to the trust probably will not cause the trust to be considered a grantor trust. Section 675(4) provides that the power to vote or direct the voting of the stock held by the trust will be sufficient to cause the grantor to be treated as the owner of that portion of the trust if "the holdings of the grantor and the trust are significant from the viewpoint of voting control." In this case, 250 shares in a publicly held company will not likely be considered significant from the viewpoint of voting control. Thus, the income from the trust will not be taxed to Harriet.

(C) This trust will be considered a grantor trust if the value of the reversionary interest is greater than 5 percent, measured from the inception of the trust. See § 673. In general, the grantor will have to make an almost complete divestiture of interest to avoid the application of the grantor trust rules. While the fact that there are two children to consider will operate in Harriet's favor, § 673(c) requires one to assume the maximum exercise of discretion in favor of the grantor. This assumption makes it harder to fall below the 5 percent reversionary interest. If the result is that Harriet's reversionary interest is greater than 5 percent, the trust income will be taxable to her. If the value of the reversionary interest is less than 5 percent, she can avoid the tax on the income of the trust.

(D) The power to invade corpus for the benefit of a current income beneficiary, if chargeable to that beneficiary's share, and the power to accumulate income for a current income beneficiary are acceptable powers under § 674(b). Thus, if the powers meet the requirements of § 674(b), the trust will not be considered a grantor trust, and Harriet will not be taxed on the income generated by the trust, even though she is the trustee. The accumulation of income, however, eventually must be payable to the beneficiary or that beneficiary's estate or appointees.

(E) Since the trust is not considered a grantor trust, it makes no difference whether Harriet is the trustee or she appoints an independent trustee. She will not be taxed on the income generated by the trust in either case. However, if there is an independent trustee, that trustee may decide which of the children will receive the income or corpus at any given time and in what proportion. This is called a "spray trust," and it is permitted under § 674(c). Thus, by appointing an independent trustee, the trust will be able to do things it could not do if Harriet is the trustee.

(F) Since Harriet appears to have relinquished control of this income, the trust will not be considered a grantor trust, provided she has no legal obligation to support her grandchild and has no further legal obligation to support her children. See *Braun*. If she does have such an obligation, the income will be taxed to her only to the extent that the income is actually used to discharge her legal obligation. See § 677(b).

5. TOOLS FOR SELF-ASSESSMENT

[1] In (C), the 5 percent reversionary interest rule replaces the prior 10-year reversionary interest rule. The determination of the 5 percent reversionary interest requires an actuarial determination of Harriet's chances of surviving both of her children in relation to the value of the trust assets. The best explanation of this interest is that if the value that an independent third party would pay for the grantor's interest at the inception of the trust is greater than 5 percent of the value of the trust, the trust income will be taxable to the grantor. Generally, the services of an actuary will be needed to determine whether there is a 5 percent or greater reversionary interest.

[2] In (D), if the trust accumulates the income, it will be taxed to the trust under § 1(e), which applies the highest marginal rates to modest amounts of income. So, in general, the trust will pay more taxes than an individual with comparable income. In that case, avoiding the grantor trust rules may not be in Harriet's best tax interest.

[3] In (E), an independent trustee includes not only corporate fiduciaries such as banks and trust companies, but also the grantor's attorney or accountant. Since Harriet is likely to have a closer working relationship and greater

rapport with her attorney or accountant than with the trust officers of her bank, this may have more appeal to her.

[4] In (F), it frequently is difficult to determine the scope of parental obligations to support children under state law. Local law may provide that a parent has no obligation to support her children if the children have adequate resources of their own. See Reg. § 1.662(a)-4.

[5] On an examination, it is important to answer only the question asked. Going "off point" usually will be a waste of your time because you often will not gain any extra points and in a worst case, you will lose points, especially if you are talking about things not covered in class. Since this hypothetical asked only about the income tax consequences, that is what your exam answer should focus on. In real life, however, Harriet will be as interested in the collateral tax consequences of the alternatives as in the grantor trust rules, and you would be remiss in not mentioning those collateral consequences.

[6] If the income from the trust is taxed to Harriet, she will have an extra tax liability for income that she otherwise has transferred to a trust for the benefit of her family members and over which she now has no control. Thus, she may not have the cash flow to pay the extra tax liability because the earnings from the trust corpus will be a part of the trust. In that case, there may be other alternatives that are more attractive to her, such as contributing to a § 529 qualified tuition program for the benefit of her grandchildren.

[7] Although Harriet probably is trying to avoid the application of the grantor trust rules, there some things she should realize about successfully avoiding these rules. First, she may have gift tax consequences in establishing the trusts. If the trust pays this obligation, it will be taxable to Harriet. See *Diedrich v. Commissioner*, 457 U.S. 191 (1982). Second, if the income is distributed for the benefit of a child under the age of 14, the "kiddie tax" may apply. Under § 1(g), the income will be taxable to the child at the parents' tax rates.

6. VARIATIONS ON THE THEME

Would any of your answers in (B), (C), or (D) change if Harriet's children were ages 16 and 14?

31 BAD DEBTS

1. OPENING REMARKS

Under certain circumstances, the tax Code permits a deduction for a debt that becomes uncollectible. A taxpayer must clear several hurdles, however, to take this deduction. First, the debt must be a valid, enforceable one. Questions about this often arise when the debt is between family members or an individual and a closely held business. Second, the context in which the bad debt arose must be determined. The greatest flexibility is accorded to business bad debts. A business bad debt may be deducted in full under § 166 as an ordinary loss, regardless of whether the debt is wholly or partially worthless. A nonbusiness bad debt may be deducted only as a short-term capital loss and only if it is wholly worthless. However, if the nonbusiness bad debt arose in a profit-seeking transaction, it may be deducted under § 165 instead of under § 166. Third, the timing of the worthlessness must be determined. Section 166(a) allows a bad debt deduction for "any debt which becomes worthless during the taxable year." Sometimes this is simple to determine, but often it may not be. Section 6511(d) allows some flexibility by providing a special seven-year statute of limitations for refund claims based on bad debt deductions. Fourth, the amount of the deduction is limited to the amount on which the taxpayer previously was taxed. Thus, as a general rule, the taxpayer is limited to deducting her basis in the debt. Otherwise, the taxpayer would be able to double dip by obtaining a double tax benefit (i.e., obtaining a deduction on an amount that has never been included in income).

2. HYPOTHETICAL

Jack Kelley is a cash method taxpayer and the majority shareholder and CEO of a closely held manufacturing company. Four years ago, the company was struggling financially, and Jack lent it $100,000 of his personal funds. While the company had a period of slight growth for a couple of years afterward, it is now evident that it will not survive. Jack decided to liquidate the company, and after the company paid its other debts and obligations, Jack received only $20,000 of his initial loan amount. He also has a claim for his unpaid salary of $100,000 in the year of the liquidation. Finally, Jack (ever the good Samaritan) loaned $3000 to his good friend, Sam, who had lost his job. Sam repaid $500 of this amount but now informs Jack that he will be unable to repay the remainder.

In addition to these misfortunes, two years ago, Jack sold a residential rental property that he had been holding as an investment for $150,000, realizing a gain of $50,000. The buyer paid $30,000 in cash and Jack took a seller financed mortgage for the remainder. Jack reported a single gain of $10,000 in the year of the sale. The buyer had been making prompt payments until six months ago, when she informed Jack that she had lost her job and would not be able to pay the remainder of the purchase price. Jack then foreclosed on the mortgage and reclaimed the property, now valued at $135,000. He has listed it for sale, but so far, no one has expressed an interest.

Discuss the tax consequences to Jack and to the company of these "bad deals."

3. LIST OF READINGS

Internal Revenue Code: §§ 165; 166; 1038; 1211
Regulations: § 1.166–1
Rulings: Rev. Rul. 77–383, 1977–2 C.B. 66
Cases: U.S. v. Generes, 405 U.S. 93 (1972); Perry v. Commissioner, 92 T.C. 470 (1989); Bugbee v. Commissioner, 34 T.C.M. 291 (1975); Hunt v. Commissioner, TCM 1989–335

4. SAMPLE ESSAY

Section 166(a) allows a deduction for "any debt which becomes worthless within the taxable year." The first threshold requirement under § 166, whether the deduction arises in the business context or the nonbusiness context, is that the debt must be bona fide. Reg. § 1.166–1(c). Even if there is evidence of a loan, such as a note, the taxpayer must establish that at the time the loan was made, there was an expectation of repayment. See *Bugbee*. Thus, if the debtor is insolvent at the time the loan was made, this is indicative of a gift, rather than a true loan. The courts also will look at how the parties treated the "indebtedness." For instance, they will look to whether any repayments were ever made and whether an interest rate was set. Loan validity issues frequently arise in the context of intrafamily transfers and transfers to closely held companies. In the latter context, the issue is whether the transfer constitutes a loan or a contribution to capital that results in an increase in the transferor's stock basis. If it is a contribution to capital, the taxpayer will recognize the loss under either § 165(c)(1) or § 165(c)(2), when the stock is sold.

If it is determined that the loan is bona fide, it then must be determined whether the debt is a business debt or a nonbusiness debt. In *U.S. v. Generes*, the U.S. Supreme Court held that advances to a corporation by a shareholder/employee were considered nonbusiness bad debts unless the taxpayer could show that the dominant motive in making the advances was to protect his job. Otherwise, the advances were considered a protection of the taxpayer's investment and not attributable to his business. In *Generes*, the Court compared the taxpayer's salary to the amounts of the advances and determined that where there is a large discrepancy between the two (more than $158,000 in advances versus about $12,000 in salary from the company), it is an indication that the taxpayer has not advanced the monies to protect his job but rather to protect his investment.

In this case, Jack advanced $100,000 to the company, the same amount as his salary from the company. Thus, it appears that his dominant motive for advancing the funds was to protect his job, and the debt should be viewed as a business bad debt. If so, he will be able to deduct the $80,000 as an ordinary loss under § 166(a). If, however, the debt is determined to be a nonbusiness bad debt, the character of the deduction is a short-term capital loss. See Rev. Rul. 77–383. In that event, Jack, as an individual taxpayer, would be able to take the loss to the extent of any capital gains plus an additional $3000 over that amount per year. See § 1211(b).

Finally, § 165(g) provides that if any security that constitutes a capital asset becomes worthless during the taxable year, it will be treated as the loss from the sale or exchange of a capital asset. A security is defined, in part, under § 165(g)(2)(C) as "a bond, debenture, note or certificate, or other evidence of indebtedness, issued by a corporation or by a government or political subdivision, with interest coupons or in registered form." Presumably, the note that Jack receives from the company does not fall into this category. If that is the case, his deduction will be ordinary in nature. If it is not the case, and the note does fall into that category, the loss will be a capital one.

The claim for unpaid salary may be the easiest of the claims to establish as due, owing, and worthless. However, Jack will not be able to deduct this amount because he is a cash method taxpayer and was never taxed on it. Thus, he has no basis to deduct.

The loan to Sam also raises issues of whether the debt is bona fide and whether Jack had a legitimate expectation of repayment. If not, the "loan" is considered a gift. If so, the debt is a nonbusiness bad debt, and Jack can take a § 166 deduction for it in the year in which it becomes worthless. Sometimes, this point may not be easily determined, and because of that problem, § 6511(d)(1) provides a seven-year statute of limitations for deductions relating to bad debts and worthless securities. There are a variety of factors that the IRS and the courts have looked to in order to determine whether a debt is worthless. These include the insolvency of the debtor, death, bankruptcy, subordination, and refusal to pay. If Jack passes these hurdles (bona fide debt, wholly worthless) then he may deduct the $2500 as a short-term capital loss under § 166(d).

Section 1038 applies to the foreclosure of the rental property. This section provides that the transaction is tax neutral: Jack will not recognize any gain or loss from the reacquisition of the property, and the remainder of the debt will not be deductible under § 166. Since Jack presumably was taxed on the $30,000 down payment when he received it, he will have no further tax liability.

5. TOOLS FOR SELF-ASSESSMENT

[1] Bad debt problems require some threshold issues to be resolved before the tax consequences can be determined. The first is whether the debt is a valid, enforceable one. This issue is likely to arise when the "loan" is between family members and in the *Bugbee* situation in which the "debtor's" ability to repay is in doubt at the time of the loan. Those situations put the lender in a vulnerable position with the IRS because the validity of the debt may be subject to challenge.

[2] The second threshold issue is whether the debt is a "bad" debt—i.e., uncollectible. It may be difficult to determine when that point arises. Because of this difficulty, there is a special statute of limitations of seven years under § 6511(d)(1) for refund claims related to bad debts and worthless securities under §§ 166 and 165(g). Also, if the lender gratuitously forgives the debt, it is not deductible as a bad debt because then it is "transformed" from a debt into a gift.

[3] Section 166 allows a deduction of any worthless debt, whether it is business, nonbusiness/profit seeking, or personal. The threshold questions are the same, regardless of the type of debt involved. The treatment of the deduction

varies, however, with the most advantageous treatment afforded business deductions. Regardless of the character of the deduction, both business and nonbusiness/profit-seeking debts are allowed above the line under § 62 while personal bad debts are deductible only below the line as itemized deductions.

[4] A nonbusiness bad debt held by an individual taxpayer is deductible only if the debt is wholly worthless, whereas a business bad debt is allowed whether wholly or partially worthless. Note, though, that the term "wholly worthless" is a bit misleading. It does not mean that a partial recovery knocks the taxpayer out of any deduction under § 166. It simply means that there is no deduction until the remainder of the debt becomes "wholly worthless." If the debt is a nonbusiness bad debt, such as the loan to Sam, a partial repayment of $500 is a nontaxable event as a recovery of capital (provided none of this amount is attributable to interest). When it is clearly established that the remainder of the loan will not be repaid, Jack will be able to obtain a § 166(d) deduction at that time.

[5] If the debt is a business debt that is partially worthless, (for instance, if there is a determination of such by a bankruptcy court), the taxpayer is able to charge off the uncollectible amount on her books and records in the year of the determination. Note further that the IRS considers the taxpayer's burden of proof under § 166(a)(2) (partially worthless debts) to be much heavier than under § 166(a)(1)(wholly worthless debts).

[6] Section 166 allows a deduction only of items for which there is a basis. Basis arises through an investment or, in this case, an advance to a debtor or through inclusion in income. Since the salary was never included in income because Jack never received it, there is no basis to deduct. It makes sense that a taxpayer will not be able to obtain a tax benefit (i.e., a deduction) for an amount that was never included in income.

6. VARIATIONS ON THE THEME

What results if two years later Sam's fortunes reverse, and he pays Jack the $2500 that he owes? What results if the company had not been liquidated, and Jack had been able to obtain the §166 deduction for the bad debt, but then the company had repaid another $20,000 of the loan amount?

32 INTEREST DEDUCTIONS

1. OPENING REMARKS

Back in the "old days," personal interest on items like credit cards was deductible. But then the tax rates were higher. In 1986, the Reagan administration was successful in passing tax legislation designed to "simplify" the tax Code by reducing the rates and the number of tax brackets. The legislation also was designed to be "revenue neutral," so it neither raised new revenue nor decreased the overall revenue. Since the rates were lowered, the tax base had to be broadened, which meant that some tax benefit provisions had to go. One of them was the deduction for personal interest. A policy rationale behind the elimination of this deduction was that the government should not subsidize and thereby encourage private debt. Instead, its efforts should be directed toward encouraging savings, although debt is viewed as acceptable under the tax Code if it is incurred for an acceptable purpose, such as home ownership.

Interest payments on business or investment debt is deductible generally, although the treatment of the deduction will vary according to the category (i.e., business or investment) in which it falls. Under some circumstances, the deduction may not be allowed at all if the taxpayer does not actively participate in the underlying activity.

2. HYPOTHETICAL

Lydia Monroe is a single, cash method taxpayer who owns a small bookstore that she acquired last year. She borrowed $100,000 to start this business, and she hired an employee, purchased inventory, and signed a commercial lease for a five-year period. Two years ago, Lydia became a limited partner in a partnership with two other partners. The partnership borrowed $200,000 through a nonrecourse loan and purchased rental real estate. A management company manages the real estate, and the partnership pays the taxes and maintenance on the property, most of which come from the rentals of the property.

Lydia owns her home, subject to a $250,000 recourse mortgage, and last year she purchased a Lexus automobile for her personal use for $60,000, trading in her six-year-old Honda on the deal. She has a five-year auto loan on this car. Also last year, she borrowed $10,000 from her bank and purchased $5000 of stock in a publicly held corporation and $5000 of tax-exempt bonds, all of which she holds for investment. She has two credit cards, both of which she uses for personal purposes, and she owes about $12,000 on these cards combined. Finally, Lydia is paying off her education loans. She estimates that these loans will be fully paid off in five years.

Discuss whether and when Lydia might be able to deduct any of the interest that she pays on these various loans.

3. LIST OF READINGS

Internal Revenue Code: §§ 62; 163; 221; 263A; 265; 469
Regulations: § 1.163–8T(a) and (c); 1.469–5T
Rulings: Rev. Proc. 72–18, 1972–1 C.B. 740

4. SAMPLE ESSAY

Section 163(a) allows a deduction of interest paid or accrued within the taxable year on certain types of indebtedness. However, what Congress giveth with one hand, it taketh away with the other. Section 163(h)(1) provides that individual taxpayers may not deduct personal interest paid or accrued during the taxable year, although there are several exceptions to this provision. Section 163(h)(2)(A) excludes "interest paid or accrued on indebtedness properly allocable to a trade or business (other than the trade or business of performing services as an employee)." Thus, interest on the $100,000 that Lydia borrows to start her business will be deductible under § 163, as long as the loan proceeds are spent entirely on her trade or business. Since not all types of interest are treated equally for tax purposes, the regulations require that the loan proceeds be traced to the specific expenditure. See Reg. §1.163–8T. If the proceeds are spent on Lydia's business, the interest will be deductible in full above the line under § 62(a)(1) in the year that she pays it since she is a cash method taxpayer. Interest on business indebtedness is deductible under the most liberal of the interest deduction rules.

Section 163(h)(2)(B) also excepts investment interest from the general rule of nondeductibility of personal interest. However, interest on indebtedness "incurred or continued to purchase or carry obligations" that are "wholly exempt" from taxation is not deductible because § 265(a)(2) disallows any deduction of interest on this type of indebtedness. Proposed interest deductions that are attributable to income that is tax exempt or tax preferred are known as a "tax arbitrage." The deductibility of other investment interest is subject to limitations, and the extent of the limitations depends on the type of investment. Under § 163(d), interest used to finance portfolio indebtedness used to purchase assets generating dividends, interest, royalties, etc., may be deducted only to the extent of net investment income, defined as total investment income less investment expenses. See §§ 163(d)(1) and (d)(4).

The problem with the $10,000 loan used to purchase the stocks and bonds is whether the interest on the loan can be bifurcated into a deductible portion and a nondeductible portion. Rev. Proc. 72–18 allows such a bifurcation if Lydia can directly trace the proceeds of this loan. To the extent that the loan was used to purchase the tax-exempt bonds, that portion of the interest incurred on the debt will be disallowed under § 265(a)(2). The portion of the interest payments traceable to the $5000 of the $10,000 of loan proceeds used to purchase the publicly held stock should be deductible against the dividend income generated by the investment. Any other portfolio income may be offset by these payments as well, and any excess investment interest may be carried forward indefinitely. See § 163(d)(2). But it will not be available for use against business income or income from a "passive activity."

Section 163(h)(2)(C) excepts "interest taken into account under § 469 in computing income or loss from a passive activity of the taxpayer." Interest incurred in connection with a passive activity is further limited in deductibility under § 469 and can be taken only against ordinary income from the activity. Lydia's investment in the limited partnership constitutes a "passive activity." Section 469(c) defines a passive activity as (1) a trade or business in which the taxpayer does not materially participate and (2) rental activities. The regulations provide that a limited partner is not considered an active participant in any activity of the limited partnership. Reg. § 1.469–5T(e)(1). Section 163(d)(3)(B)(ii) provides that investment interest does not include any interest taken into account in computing passive activity income or loss under § 469. Similarly, § 163(d)(4)(D) provides that investment income and expenses do not include "income or expenses taken into account under section 469 in computing income or loss from a passive activity." This means that interest payments in a passive activity cannot be used to offset investment income or business income. Instead, passive losses (including interest deductions) can be used only against income from the passive activity, unless the taxpayer disposes of her entire interest in the passive activity.

Section 163(h)(2)(D) exempts from the general rule of nondeductibility "any qualified residence interest." Qualified residence interest is defined under § 163(h)(3) as any interest paid or accrued during the taxable year on acquisition indebtedness or home equity indebtedness on a qualified residence. A qualified residence is the principal residence of the taxpayer (within the meaning of § 121) and one other residence selected by the taxpayer for this purpose and used as a residence. § 163(h)(4)(A). If the mortgage is an acquisition indebtedness incurred in acquiring the residence, there is a $1 million limit on the amount of indebtedness that can be considered for purposes of § 163. If it is home equity indebtedness, the cap is $100,000. Also, the deduction is subject to a phase-out for higher-income taxpayers under § 163(h)(3)(E)(ii).

Section 163(h)(2)(F) excludes "any interest allowable as a deduction under section 221 (relating to interest on education loans)." Thus, interest on an education loan must be deducted under § 221, not under § 163. In order to take this deduction, Lydia must meet several requirements. First, the loan must be a "qualified education loan" under § 221(d). Second, there is a cap on the amount of interest deduction that may be taken. For taxable years after 2001, the cap is $2500. Third, the deduction will be partially phased out if Lydia has adjusted gross income over a certain amount. For taxable years 2010 through 2012 there is an increased phaseout limit of $60,000 to $75,000 for single taxpayers and $120,000 to $150,000 for joint filers. After 2012, the phaseout limits return to the lower ranges of $50,000 to $65,000 for single filers and $100,000 to $130,000 for joint filers. Thus, if the taxable year is 2011 and Lydia has adjusted gross income greater than $75,000, she will not be able to deduct her education interest at all. But if she is able to deduct all or any of this interest, it will be deductible above the line under § 62(a)(17).

5. TOOLS FOR SELF-ASSESSMENT

[1] Generally, the best way to answer a question with multiple issues is to approach the issues chronologically, since the occurrence of one event may have an effect on another event. In this problem, however, the best approach is to separate out the various items of interest that are treated differently under the Code.

[2] The most liberal interest deduction is accorded to interest incurred on business indebtedness. Interest on an indebtedness used to operate a trade or business is deductible in full, without limitation, except in two instances. The first is when the interest is required to be capitalized under § 263A because it is attributable to an asset that is constructed or acquired by the taxpayer. Inventory held for sale to customers in the ordinary course of business is excluded, so the interest on indebtedness used to purchase the inventory is not required to be capitalized. See § 263A(a). The second is where the passive activity loss rules apply under § 469. But in the case of an active trade or business, these rules do not apply.

[3] The limitation on the deductibility of interest on indebtedness incurred to finance an investment is inconsistent with comparable deductions under § 212 for expenses incurred for the production or collection of income, although it is consistent with the limitation on such deductions under § 280A. The policy rationale behind the § 163(d) limitation is that interest is deductible against ordinary income, but when the investment property is sold, any gain is taxed at capital gains rates. Because of this mismatch, the deduction of investment interest is more complex than the deduction of business interest.

[4] Because of the additional limitation on passive activity losses, investment losses must be separated into two distinct "baskets" so that the losses from portfolio investments are not commingled with losses from passive activities.

[5] The deduction of home mortgage interest is the primary tax benefit of home ownership. The exclusion of gain on the sale of the residence also is a significant tax benefit, although there is a cap on the amount of the exclusion and a time limit on the ability to use this benefit. Moreover, qualified residence interest is not subject to the tracing rules of Reg. § 1.163–8T.

[6] Note that § 163 is the authorizing provision that allows the deduction of interest payments. Even though the interest is incurred for education that is not directly connected to a trade or business, § 163(h)(2)(F) allows its deduction, provided that it falls under § 221. Section 221 defines the qualifying loans and allows the deduction of interest on such loans. Section 62 directs the taxpayer to take the deduction above the line. Any amount of interest on an education loan that is phased out under § 221 and not allowed as a deduction may not be deducted under § 163.

6. VARIATIONS ON THE THEME

What results if Lydia obtains a home equity loan of $10,000 and purchases more tax-exempt bonds? Will this change the deductibility of any of her interest payments?

33

ADJUSTED GROSS INCOME AND SOCIAL SECURITY BENEFITS

1. OPENING REMARKS

After all items of gross income in the taxable year have been calculated, the next step is to consider whether there are any "special" deductions that may be taken under § 62. These deductions are called "above-the-line" deductions, and they are very advantageous because, unlike itemized deductions, they may be taken in full and are not subject to limitations and phase-outs. In addition, they offset gross income directly to produce adjusted gross income, which is an important concept for individual taxpayers because it is the measuring point for several other deductions. For instance, it is the measuring point for the "miscellaneous itemized deductions" for employees under § 67 and medical expenses under § 213. In this exercise, we see that adjusted gross income is also the measuring point for the taxation of social security benefits.

Social security taxes are imposed against income that also is subject to federal income tax. Thus, there is no deduction for federal income tax purposes for the amount of social security taxes paid by an employee. (In the case of a self-employed taxpayer who must pay the full amount of the social security tax, there is a deduction of half of that amount. Thus, self-employed taxpayers are on par with employees, as far as the social security tax is concerned.). Despite this double taxation, the receipt of social security benefits may trigger an income tax on those benefits, depending on the amount of the taxpayer/recipient's adjusted gross income and the amount of the social security benefits received. Currently, the maximum amount of social security benefits subject to the income tax is 85 percent.

2. HYPOTHETICAL

Nancy Osbourne is a 70-year-old retired schoolteacher. Her husband died several years ago, and Nancy lives alone. She has four sources of income: retirement from the Teachers' Retirement System of $3700 per month (all of which is taxable), investment interest income of $6500 per year (all taxable), social security benefits of $1000 per month, and $500 per month from private music lessons that she gives in her home. Three years ago, Nancy bought some stock on a tip from her broker for $5000. The stock has not done well, and this year, it began to drop even more rapidly. Her stockbroker recommended that Nancy sell the stock, so she did and received $3500 on the sale. Are Nancy's social security benefits taxable? If so, how much tax will she have to pay?

3. LIST OF READINGS

Internal Revenue Code: §§ 61, 62, 86

4. SAMPLE ESSAY

Under § 86, Nancy first must compute her modified adjusted gross income for the year. This is adjusted gross income, determined without regard to § 86, plus any tax-exempt interest. See § 86(b)(2). This amount will include the $44,400 that she receives per year from the Teachers' Retirement System, the $6500 of investment interest, and the $6000 from the music lessons. This amount equals $56,900. The deductions allowed under § 62 include losses from the sale or exchange of property under § 62(a)(3). Thus, the $1500 loss that Nancy suffers on the sale of her stock will reduce her gross income to $55,400. This is her modified adjusted gross income.

Nancy's social security benefits are taxable if her modified adjusted gross income plus one-half of the social security benefits that she receives during the year exceed her base amount of $25,000. See § 86(c)(1). Adding half of her social security benefits to her modified adjusted gross income produces $61,400. This exceeds her base amount by $36,400. Since this amount is greater than the social security benefits that she received, 85 percent of her social security benefits are included in her gross income. See § 86(a)(2)(B). Thus, $10,200 of her social security benefits are taxable.

Nancy's total gross income is $67,100 ($56,900 + 85 percent of $12,000). Her total adjusted gross income is $65,600 ($67,100 less $1500).

5. TOOLS FOR SELF-ASSESSMENT

[1] Note that while Nancy does not have any tax-exempt interest, her modified adjusted gross income is not the same as her adjusted gross income because the latter figure also will include any taxable social security benefits. Also, the character of her loss will not matter because even if it is a long-term capital loss—the most limited of the investment losses—it will be allowed against ordinary income to the extent of $3000 of loss. See § 1211(b). Since Nancy's loss is within that range, she will not have to worry about being able to take it in full in the year of the realization.

[2] Section 86(a)(1)(B) applies to taxpayers who have very little income. If the gross income plus one-half of the social security benefits do not exceed the base amount, none of the social security benefits are taxable. This is the trade-off for the choice Congress made to tax social security benefits. On the one hand, a seemingly more equitable way to tax these benefits is to tax the amount of social security benefits that exceed the amount of contributions to the social security system that the taxpayer has made. This certainly would be more equitable in Nancy's case. On the other hand, though, under the present system, individuals with very little income to support themselves in their older age will be exempt from the tax, regardless of the amount they have contributed to the system.

[3] In the case of a higher-income taxpayer, such as Nancy, the taxability of her social security benefits is determined under § 86(a)(2), instead of under § 86(a)(1)(A). Section 86(a)(2)(A) will apply if the taxpayer just misses the application § 86(a)(1)(B). This means that the excess of the modified adjusted gross income over the base amount must be equal to half of the social security benefits or slightly over that amount. In that case, less than 85 percent of the benefits will be subject to tax. If a great deal over the

amount, the lesser of amount under § 86(a)(2) is 85 percent of the social security benefits received during the taxable year, so 85 percent of the social security benefits will be subject to tax. See § 86(a)(2)(B).

6. VARIATIONS ON THE THEME

How, if at all, would your answer change if instead Nancy had received only $18,000 per year from the Teachers' Retirement System and also had $2500 in nontaxable interest from some bonds that she purchased many years ago?

34

PERSONAL EXEMPTIONS, STANDARD DEDUCTIONS, ITEMIZED DEDUCTIONS, AND TAX CREDITS

1. OPENING REMARKS

In 1944, Congress enacted a provision allowing taxpayers to simplify their returns and to alleviate the need to keep records of deductible items. This provision authorized a "standard deduction" that all individual taxpayers are entitled to take, although the amount varies according to filing status. If a taxpayer has deductible items that exceed the amount of the standard deduction, the taxpayer may elect under § 63(e) to itemize the deductions and forgo the standard deduction.

Section 63(d) defines the standard deduction as the sum of the "basic" standard deduction and the "additional" standard deduction. For the 2010 taxable year, the basic standard deduction for an unmarried taxpayer or a married taxpayer filing separately is $5700, while the basic standard deduction for married taxpayers filing jointly is $11,400. The additional standard deduction is an additional amount for taxpayers age 65 or older, plus an additional amount for taxpayers who are legally blind. See § 63(f). For tax years beginning in 2009 and 2010, the additional amount is $1100 with an increase to $1400 if the taxpayer is unmarried and is not a surviving spouse, as defined in § 2(a). Both spouses, as married taxpayers, are entitled to the additional amount if both are age 65 or over or if both are blind. Thus, if married taxpayers are both over age 65 and legally blind, they may claim four additional amounts.

In some cases, the standard deduction may either be limited or unavailable, as in the case of taxpayers who are dependents (for tax purposes) of another taxpayer and for married couples who file separately where one spouse itemizes deductions.

In addition, all individual taxpayers are entitled to an exemption, adjusted annually for inflation, for themselves, their spouses, and any dependents. For the 2010 taxable year, the exemption amount is $3650. There is a phase-out of the exemptions for high-income individuals, and no exemption is allowed if a taxpayer can be claimed as a dependent on another taxpayer's return. For most lower-income individuals, there is no requirement that a tax return be filed unless the individual's income exceeds the standard deduction plus the exemption amount, although the individual will have an interest in filing if that individual has had income tax withheld from wages or wants to claim refundable credits.

While the vast majority of Americans take the standard deduction, they also remain eligible to take deductions "above the line." These are the deductions authorized by § 62 of the Code, and they are in stark contrast to itemized deductions that only provide a tax benefit to the extent that they exceed the standard deduction. Itemized deductions, like the personal exemptions, may be phased out for higher-income taxpayers. Itemized deductions are defined under § 63(d) as all allowable deductions other than those authorized under § 62 (above-the-line deductions) and personal exemptions.

Credits offset tax liability directly and are not phased out. They generally accomplish a variety of social, economic, and conservation goals such as welfare for low-income taxpayers (earned income tax credit), encouragement of education (education credits), relief for two-earner families (dependent care credit), preservation of historic properties (rehabilitation credit), and preservation of the environment (energy credit and reforestation credit). The most prevalent credit is the credit for income tax withheld from salary or wages under § 31.

2. HYPOTHETICAL

Peter and Pamela Quinlan are a young couple who have been married for seven years. They are cash method taxpayers who file a joint income tax return. They have two children, Babs and Bobby, ages 5 and 2 respectively. Pamela is a homemaker while Peter is a family practice doctor who practices with a group of other doctors. Peter earns $280,000 per year, and the couple has investment income of $50,000 per year. In the current taxable year, the Quinlan's had the following expenses: $7000 in medical expenses, including prescription drugs; $15,000 in alimony that Peter pays his former spouse; $10,000 in charitable contributions to their church; $20,000 in mortgage interest and real estate taxes on their home; and $5500 for private school for Babs, who is a gifted child. Peter's employer (a limited liability medical company) withheld $85,000 in federal income taxes from his compensation. Assume that the current taxable year is 2010. Discuss the Quinlans' income tax consequences.

3. LIST OF READINGS

Internal Revenue Code: §§ 1(a); 25A; 31; 61; 62; 63; 68; 151; 152; 163; 164; 170; 213

4. SAMPLE ESSAY

The Quinlans have gross income of $330,000 attributable to Peter's salary and their investment income under § 61. The only above-the-line deduction that they have is the $15,000 of alimony that Peter pays to his former spouse. See § 62(a)(10). This will reduce their adjustable gross income to $315,000. Since the Quinlan's have significant allowable deductions that do not fall within §§ 62 or 151, they will obtain a tax benefit by itemizing their deductions. Their largest itemized deduction is the $20,000 in "qualified residence interest" authorized by § 163(h)(3). The $10,000 in charitable donations are authorized under § 170. The medical expenses are authorized under § 213, but like some itemized deductions, they are subject to a limitation. In this case, the limitation is a floor of 7.5 percent of adjusted gross income, which means that the Quinlans will be able to deduct medical expenses only to the extent those expenses exceed $23,625. Since their expenses are less than this amount, they are not able to take any deduction for their medical expenses. Under the facts of this problem, it does not appear that the Quinlans will be entitled to any tax benefit for Babs's tuition expense. Thus, their total itemized deductions will be $30,000, attributable to the mortgage interest and their charitable donations. This will reduce their taxable income to $285,000. Since they file a joint tax return, they are eligible to take two personal exemptions for themselves plus two dependency exemptions for their children. For the taxable year 2010, this is a total of $14,600 in personal exemptions, resulting in taxable income of $270,400. Under the tax rates at § 1(a), the Quinlans' tax liability will be $83,606.90. The amount that was withheld from Peter's compensation will be allowed under §31 as a credit against this liability. This results in a refund of $1,393.10 for the Quinlans.

5. TOOLS FOR SELF-ASSESSMENT

[1] Note that beginning in 2010 and extending through 2012, the phase-out on itemized deductions and personal exemptions for high-income taxpayers under § 68 is repealed. Thus, there will be no more phase-out of itemized deductions, so itemized deductions may be taken in full in these years, regardless of the income level of the taxpayer. Beginning in 2013, however, the full phase-out will again apply. The repeal of the phase-out represents a compromise between the Obama administration and Congress to extend the "Bush tax cuts" for a limited time.

[2] Note also that a similar phase-out applies to personal exemptions under § 151(d)(3). This phase-out also has been eliminated for taxable years 2010 through 2012 but will be revived in 2013.

[3] Under current law, the same marginal tax rates apply to all individuals, regardless of filing status, but the amounts to which the rates apply differ according to filing status. There are four filing statuses for individual taxpayers: (1) married filing jointly and surviving spouses, (2) heads of household, (3) single taxpayers, and (4) married filing separately. For taxable years 2010 through 2012, there are six tax rate brackets that apply to the income ranges within each bracket: 10 percent, 15 percent, 25 percent, 28 percent, 331 percent, and 35 percent. Beginning in 2013, the rates revert to the higher rates applicable prior to 2001: 15 percent, 18 percent, 31 percent, 36 percent, and 39.6 percent. See § 1.

6. VARIATIONS ON THE THEME

Assume instead that Peter was a teacher earning $85,000 per year and has investment income of $5000. In the current taxable year, the Quinlans have the following expenses: $7000 in medical expenses, including prescription drugs; $1500 in charitable contributions to their church; and $8000 in mortgage interest and real estate taxes on their home. Peter's employer withheld $18,000 in federal income taxes from his compensation. Discuss the Quinlans' income tax consequences.

35 TAX SHELTERS

1. OPENING REMARKS

Justice Sutherland, in *Gregory v. Helvering*, 293 U.S. 465, 469 (1935), stated "The legal right of a taxpayer to decrease the amount of what otherwise would be his taxes, or altogether avoid them, by means which the law permits, cannot be doubted." Taxpayers have been taking advantage of this right since the beginning of the tax system itself.

Technically, a tax shelter is a device or investment that results in a tax benefit, usually a reduction or deferral of taxes, and technically, tax shelters are legal. There are a variety of shelters routinely used by taxpayers that are sanctioned by the tax Code, such as the deduction of home mortgage interest, depreciation deductions from rental property, and an employer sponsored § 401(k) plan. In the bull market of the 1990s, however, some otherwise well-respected accounting and law firms marketed "abusive" tax shelter transactions to some of the country's largest corporations and wealthiest individuals. These transactions subsequently have been (and continue to be) challenged by the government and consequently, the term "tax shelter" has acquired a pejorative meaning because many of these transactions have been determined to be shams. In fact, some cases have resulted in criminal prosecutions and convictions. The extent of the tax shelter problem is staggering, with the government estimating that abusive tax shelters have cost the treasury billions of dollars in lost revenue.

The government has mounted an all-out attack on these abusive shelters, and this attack has taken several forms. One is tougher registration requirements for any investment or device that might be considered a tax shelter (other than those directly permitted under the Internal Revenue Code), and another is identifying abusive transactions that will be closely watched and perhaps challenged by the government. The latter are called "listed transactions." The IRS also has offered settlement initiatives to taxpayers to encourage those who have invested in these shelters to come forward voluntarily and pay the taxes they owe.

In general, the difference between a legitimate tax shelter and an abusive one is in the purpose of the transaction. A legitimate tax shelter has a bona fide business purpose with real economic substance. An abusive tax shelter is one that exists solely to reduce the investor's tax liability, and without this result, the transaction would not make sense.

2. HYPOTHETICAL

Russell Smith is the CEO of the Widget Corporation, a publicly held company. Both Smith and Widget Corporation are cash method taxpayers. Under the company's stock option plan, Russell holds options that upon exercise will allow him to purchase 50,000 shares of Widget Co. stock at $10 per share. Widget Co. stock currently is selling at $100 per share. Russell's long-time tax advisor, in whom he had great confidence, advised him to sell the options to a partnership specially organized for this purpose. The partners were Russell (also the managing partner) and his wife. The partnership issued an unsecured, nonnegotiable 30-year promissory note in the face amount of $4.5 million, the fair market value of the options. The note provided for a balloon payment of the $4.5 million principal amount at the end of the 30-year period. The partnership then exercised the options, received the shares, and sold them over a short period of time, realizing $5 million in the process.

According to Russell's tax advisor, no tax was due on the sale. He based this advice on the § 83 regulations, which at the time provided that a cash method taxpayer did not recognize income on the receipt of an unsecured promise to pay until the payment occurred. Since an unsecured note was considered a "mere promise to pay," there was no cash equivalency problem for Russell when he received the note from the partnership. Thus, there are no tax consequences to him. As to the partnership, it was "deemed" to have paid $5 million, which includes the exercise price of $500,000 that it actually paid plus the face amount of the note. Since the partnership sold the shares within a short period of time, the amount realized was equal to the partnership's basis in the shares and hence, no tax owed.

Although Russell eventually will have to pay a tax liability when the partnership pays off the note, that point is going to be at the end of 30 years. Under time value of money principles, Russell saves a great deal of money by deferring his tax liability for 30 years.

After engaging in this nifty little scheme and going about his merry way for a couple of years, things suddenly took a turn for the worse for Russell when the IRS announced that it would challenge transactions similar to this one on the ground that they are not at arm's length and lack a business purpose. Therefore, the exercise of the options by the partnership was considered an exercise by Russell. The IRS also identified this type of transaction as a "listed transaction."

Subsequently, the IRS offered a settlement initiative to those engaged in this type of transaction in order to resolve issues quickly and avoid protracted and costly litigation. Under this initiative, the Commissioner agreed to waive civil fraud penalties, and although those involved in the scheme would owe a negligence penalty, this amount was half of what it otherwise would have been.

Russell has decided (wisely) not to trust his former tax advisor, and he now seeks your advice about what to do. Should he consider the IRS's offer? Should he instead do nothing and take his chances in court? What are the pros and cons of this choice? What advice would you give him?

3. LIST OF READINGS

Internal Revenue Code: § 83

Rulings and Announcements: IRS Notice 2003–47, 2003-2 C.B. 132**;** IRS Announcement 2005–19, Executive Stock Option Settlement Initiative, 2005-11 I.R.B. 744; IRS News Release, Settlement Offer Extended For Executive Stock Option Scheme, IR-2005–17 (Feb. 22, 2005); IRS Fact Sheet, Executive Stock Option Settlement Initiative, FS-2005–11 (Feb. 2005)

4. SAMPLE ESSAY

Russell is not alone in this predicament. The shelter described in this hypothetical was marketed in the late 1990s and early 2000s by otherwise well-respected financial institutions and professional service firms. Russell should give serious consideration to accepting the settlement initiative because the government has had considerable success in challenging the abusive tax shelter transactions, and his chance of prevailing in court appears to be slim. If he loses in court, he will be facing a multitude of penalties that easily can end up costing him much more than he ultimately will pay if he accepts the settlement initiative. In addition to the costs of the litigation, which can be considerable, he runs the risk that if he loses the case, the government will impose the 75 percent civil fraud penalty against him.

Another reason why Russell should give serious consideration to accepting the settlement initiative is that this scheme raises serious questions about corporate governance, since these transactions were designed for the personal benefit of executives, often at the expense of shareholders. See IRS News Release, IR-2005–17. In specific, the deferral of the income inclusion upon exercise of the options and sale of the stock means that the company foregoes a tax deduction that it otherwise would have been entitled to under § 83(h). This, in turn, means that the company paid higher taxes in the year of the exercise by the partnership than it otherwise would have if the transaction had been a straight § 83 transaction. If Russell is still the CEO of Widget Co., he probably will not want to draw attention to this scheme. If not, he should take the settlement initiative because there is likely to be publicity if the case goes to trial.

In short, the settlement initiative appears to be the best option for Russell because his chance of prevailing in court is slim, and the government will forgive most of the penalties if he voluntarily comes forward and takes the settlement initiative. The IRS has stated in a fact sheet issued in conjunction with the settlement initiative that it will "aggressively pursue" any taxpayer who has invested in this scheme and does not take the settlement initiative. It further warns that such taxpayers are likely to be discovered through "disclosures from investor lists secured through promoter audits of professional firms and financial institutions," or "if necessary, [through] the use of John Doe Summonses issued to promoters and Information Document Requests issued in corporate tax examinations targeting disclosures of executives' Notice 2003-47 transactions." FS-2005–11.

5. TOOLS FOR SELF-ASSESSMENT

[1] The general rule of thumb is that if you are presented with a transaction with tax consequences that look too good to be true, it probably is. The corporate tax shelter transactions are very complex, and often were marketed under terms of confidentiality to keep the IRS from finding out about the schemes. They took a variety of different forms, of which the Executive Stock Option (ESO) scheme was only one. The IRS has offered settlement initiatives on several of the shelters, although the terms of the settlements vary. In reality, the ESO settlement offer has expired. The Initiative gave taxpayers until May 23, 2005, to come forward under the terms of the Initiative. But the problem illustrates the real dilemma facing these investors, most of whom relied on their trusted tax advisors' assurances that the transactions in which they were investing were legal. As one such investor later said: "Who can you trust anymore?"

TAX PROCEDURE

36

1. OPENING REMARKS

The tax system operates as a system of voluntary compliance, which means that each taxpayer must fill out and file her own tax return. The government does not simply present a bill at the end of the taxable year, although it may present a bill after that time if the taxpayer does not correctly complete the return or pays less than the amount owed. There are several methods through which the government may present this bill. The normal way is through an informal communication called a "30-day letter" in which the government notifies the taxpayer that there is a discrepancy between the amount of tax on the return and the government's recalculated figure. The taxpayer then will have 30 days to respond to this letter. During this 30-day period, the taxpayer may request a conference with the Appeals Division of the IRS to resolve the problem. While there is no right to an administrative appeal, the taxpayer usually is granted a conference with the Appeals Division if the taxpayer has been issued a 30-day letter and does not agree with the findings. According to the IRS Web site, the Appeals Division resolves over 100,000 cases per year.

If the taxpayer does not respond to the 30-day letter or if a satisfactory resolution has not been reached in that period of time, the government then will send the taxpayer a "90-day letter" or statutory notice of deficiency. Section 6211 defines a deficiency as the amount by which the tax imposed exceeds the excess of the amount of tax shown on the taxpayer's return, if the taxpayer filed a return showing a tax liability, plus the amounts previously assessed (or collected without assessment) as a deficiency, over the amount of any rebates. A deficiency cannot be collected until it has been assessed. An assessment is a recording of the tax liability on the summary rolls of the government. See § 6203. Under normal rules, a tax liability may be assessed in two ways. The most common is through voluntary assessment, also known as summary assessment. When the taxpayer fills out a tax return, the amount listed on the return is summarily assessed. Thus, if this amount is not paid, the government can immediately begin a collection action. The second way is through the assessment procedure, in which the government must send the taxpayer a 90-day letter, notifying the taxpayer that there is a proposed deficiency and allowing the taxpayer 90 days to contest it. At the end of that time, the deficiency will be assessed, unless the taxpayer has filed a petition in the Tax Court.

The 90-day letter is a jurisdictional requirement for Tax Court jurisdiction. The Tax Court has deficiency jurisdiction, which means that it is a sue-first-pay-later forum. The federal district court and the U.S. Court of Federal Claims both are refund fora, so the taxpayer must pay first and file a claim for refund before being eligible to bring suit in either of these courts.

2. HYPOTHETICAL

Tom and Tina Utley are married, calendar year taxpayers who timely filed their 2006 federal income tax return on March 25, 2007, and received a letter from the IRS on March 4, 2010, dated March 1, 2010, stating that they owe an additional $8500 for the 2006 taxable year attributable to some deductions that the IRS is disallowing. The letter further states that they have 90 days from the date of the letter to contest this liability, either by filing a petition in the U.S. Tax Court or by communicating directly with the IRS. The Utleys do not believe that they owe this amount, and they are perplexed as to why they received this letter. They want to know what the letter means and what alternatives are available to them. They further seek your advice as to what they should do.

3. LIST OF READINGS

Internal Revenue Code: §§ 6212; 6213; 6501; 6503; 6532(a)
Cases: Anastasato v. Commissioner, 794 F.2d 884 (1986)

4. SAMPLE ESSAY

The statutory notice of deficiency (a/k/a "90-day letter") serves several purposes: (1) it notifies the taxpayer that the IRS is proposing a deficiency; (2) it restricts the government from assessing the deficiency or initiating a collection action during the 90-day period; (3) it tolls the statute of limitations on assessment for the period during which the government is prohibited from assessing, plus an additional 60 days; (4) it is the jurisdictional basis on which the taxpayer is allowed to petition the U.S. Tax Court to be heard prior to payment of the deficiency; and (5) it forms the basis of the pleadings in the Tax Court.

The first stage in the collection process is the assessment of a deficiency. Under normal rules, the government must mail a statutory notice of deficiency before the expiration of the statute of limitations on assessment. Thus, the government does not have an unlimited period of time to assess. Section 6501(a) provides that the normal statute of limitations is the later of three years from the due date or the date the return was filed. If more than 25 percent of the gross income reported on the return has been omitted, the statute is increased to six years. See § 6501(e). If no return is filed or if the filed return is false or fraudulent, there is no statute of limitations, so the government has an unlimited amount of time to assess. See § 6501(c).

Since the Utleys filed their return early, their normal three-year statutory period runs from the due date of the return, April 15, 2007, and will expire three years later, on April 15, 2010, provided none of the exceptions to the normal rule apply. Thus, the notice of deficiency is timely mailed. Section 6213 provides that the taxpayer shall have 90 days to file a petition in the Tax Court and that no levy or collection may be begun within this period. Although there is a short period of time remaining on the original statute of limitations (e.g., from March 1 to April 15, a total of 45 days), the mailing of the notice of deficiency stops the running of the statute for the 90 days that the IRS is prohibited from assessing the deficiency, plus an additional 60 days, for a total of 150 days. See §§ 6503(a); 6212.

If the Utleys believe the notice was issued in error, they can submit evidence to the IRS that there is no deficiency or the deficiency is less than the amount proposed in the notice, and perhaps the IRS will rescind the notice. Such a rescission is authorized under § 6212(d) and is done through the Appeals office. If granted, the notice of deficiency will be treated as though it were never issued. Thus, there is no restriction on further notices, and the taxpayer may not file a petition in the Tax Court. Since there is very little time remaining on the statute of limitations, the IRS probably will ask the Utleys to sign a Form 872, agreeing to extend their statute of limitations on assessment. See § 6501(c)(4).

If the Utleys ignore the notice, they will be assessed at the end of the 90-day period and will have lost their chance to be heard in the Tax Court. At that point, they will have no other choice but to pay the deficiency, plus interest and penalties, and file a claim for a refund. If the claim is denied or not acted upon within six months, the Utleys then may bring suit in the federal district court for a refund. See § 6532(a)(1).

If the Utleys are unsuccessful in resolving the issue with the IRS, their best bet is to file a petition in the Tax Court. If they decide to file the petition, the statute of limitations will be tolled until the Tax Court decision is final, which includes the period of appeals, which can run for several years. Filing a Tax Court petition raises two issues for the Utleys. First is the issue of interest and any time-sensitive penalties, which will be running until the tax is paid, if the court should decide against the Utleys. They have two choices to avoid this problem. They can pay the tax as a deposit once the Tax Court petition has been filed, or they can post a bond to stop the running of interest. The second issue is whether the Tax Court is the best forum for them. Since the Tax Court is a prepayment forum with deficiency jurisdiction, it generally will be more cost effective for the taxpayer to be heard in the Tax Court than in any other court. There is no jury in the Tax Court, though. The case will be heard by a judge, who generally has greater experience and expertise in the tax area.

If the Utleys think the notice is totally baseless, they might be well-advised to take their case to the Appeals Division of the IRS and request a rescission of the notice. Failing that, their only other feasible alternative will be to file a petition in the Tax Court. Otherwise, they will have to pay the tax liability, including interest and penalties in full, request a refund, and bring suit in the federal district court if the refund request is denied.

5. TOOLS FOR SELF-ASSESSMENT

[1] From an ethical perspective, it is important to bear in mind that clients frequently try to dictate the result that will produce the lowest tax liability. This is why many tax professionals are now facing stiff civil and criminal fines for their work with tax shelters. Avoid the temptation to throw caution to the wind because of the amount of money or the particular client involved. There is an ability to structure transactions to reduce the client's tax liability, but this must be done legitimately.

[2] Normally, the first thing an attorney (or an accountant) will consider is the statute of limitations. If it has expired, the IRS may not collect the tax liability, even though the amount, otherwise, is owed.

[3] A request to extend the statute of limitations is routine under these circumstances, and the IRS probably will not consider the taxpayer's request without such an agreement. The standard agreement is for a six-month extension, which can be restricted to the issues in question.

Generally, the taxpayer has more to gain than to lose in signing an extension of the statute of limitations.

6. VARIATIONS ON THE THEME

Would it make any difference if the Utleys instead had received a 30-day notice instead of the 90-day letter? Discuss.

TABLE OF ARTICLES

TABLE OF CASES

TABLE OF CODE AND REGULATION SECTIONS

Code Sections

Regulations

TABLE OF RULINGS